Cascading Style Sheets:
The Designer's Edge

Cascading Style Sheets:

The Designer's Edge™

Molly E. Holzschlag

SYBEX®

San Francisco • London

Associate Publisher: Dan Brodnitz

Acquisitions and Developmental Editor: Willem Knibbe

Production Editor: Liz Burke

Technical Editor: Eric A. Meyer

Copyeditor: Sally Engelfried

Compositor: Owen Wolfson

Graphic Illustrator: Eric Houts

Proofreaders: Nancy Riddiough, Emily Hsuan, Amey Garber

Indexer: Ted Laux

Book Designer: Mark Ong, Side By Side Studios

Cover Designer: John Nedwidek, Emdesign

Cover Illustrator/Photographer: John Nedwidek, Emdesign

Letter from the Publisher

Dear Reader,

Thank you for choosing *Cascading Style Sheets: The Designer's Edge*. This book is part of a new wave of Sybex graphics books, all written by outstanding authors—artists and professional teachers who really know their stuff, and have a clear vision of the audience they're writing for.

At Sybex, we're committed to producing a full line of quality web and graphics books. With each title, we're working hard to set a new standard for the industry. From the paper we print on, to the designers we work with, to the visual examples our authors provide, our goal is to bring you the best graphics and digital video books available.

I hope you see all that reflected in these pages. I'd be very interested in hearing your feedback on how we're doing. To let us know what you think about this, or any other Sybex book, please visit us at www.sybex.com. Once there, go to the product page, click on Submit a Review, and fill out the questionnaire. Your input is greatly appreciated.

Best regards,

Daniel A. Brodnitz
Associate Publisher
Sybex Inc.

For Mary Inman with all my love

Acknowledgments

Writing *CSS: The Designer's Edge* has been a particularly good experience because of the people involved. I'd like to take a moment to praise them heartily here.

From Sybex, Willem Knibbe is an extremely flexible and insightful developmental editor, and there is no doubt that his guidance helped me greatly. Liz Burke kept all the details on track and made sure everything came together effectively. Special thanks to Dan Brodnitz for his assistance and support. Jordan Gold is truly golden, and for his years of ongoing interest in my work, I'm very grateful. Finally, a personal thanks to Sybex's main man, Dr. Rodnay Zaks who, along with Sybex in general, has helped provide me with some of the best projects and working relationships I've experienced.

From Waterside Productions, my literary agent David Fugate has been one of the true white knights, charging in to fix what needs fixing and talking me through the darker days.

From the markup and CSS community: Many thanks to all of my colleagues and peers within the community for being around to answer questions and solve problems: Porter Glendinning, Christopher Schmitt, Eric Costello, Owen Briggs, Rob Chandanais, Douglas Bowman, and all the denizens of the XHTML-L and CSS-Discuss lists. Thank you one and all for your ongoing passion for these important topics. Also, a note of thanks to Bryan Hillebrandt for stepping in and helping with some editorial issues.

Perhaps the most important acknowledgment here goes to my friend and colleague Eric A. Meyer, who technically edited this book and wrote the forward. Eric is considered the world's foremost authority on CSS. I am thrilled to have worked closely with him on a topic that he knows so deeply! Eric is by far one of the kindest technical editors I've worked with, too, never condescending when correcting foolish errors, always helpful at providing suggestions or additional resources to help me improve my own skills.

Continued love and appreciation to my mom, stepfather, and two brothers. This core family group, while being geographically separate from me, is the binding force of my life. Add to that my closest friends, Michael, Mary, Patty, and Claire, and I just realize how blessed I am.

Finally, to the readers of my books, visitors to my websites, and attendees at conference events, my most sincere love and appreciation. You are the constant inspiration. I only hope that through my work I will continue to serve you well.

About the Author

Coined "one of the greatest digerati" and deemed one of the Top 25 Most Influential Women on the Web, there is little doubt that in the world of web design and development, Molly E. Holzschlag is one of the most vibrant and influential people around.

Currently serving as Education Director for the World Organization of Webmasters (WOW), she is working tirelessly to promote standards-based education and certification for webmasters worldwide.

With over 20 web development book titles to her credit, Molly is also a popular columnist and feature writer for such diverse publications as *Macworld*, *PCMagazine*, IBM developerWorks, and Builder.com. She is an engaging speaker and teacher, appearing regularly at a range of conferences including Comdex and Internet World.

As a steering committee member for the Web Standards Project (WaSP), Molly works along with a group of other dedicated web developers and designers to promote W3C recommendations. In more academic arenas, Molly teaches webmaster courses for the University of Arizona, University of Phoenix, and Pima Community College. She wrote the very popular column, "Integrated Design," for *Web Techniques Magazine* for the last three years of its life and spent a year as Executive Editor of WebReview.com.

For more information about Molly's books, articles, classes, and for a range of reference materials, visit www.molly.com/.

Foreword

Six years. That's how long it's been since CSS was first unleashed upon the Web, with the publication of the CSS1 Specification and the release of Internet Explorer 3 for Windows. When Netscape 4 came along the next year, we had a case of two browsers supporting CSS, which seemed like a dream come true. Unfortunately, the dream turned out to be something of a nightmare, since the two browsers barely agreed on anything when it came to CSS, and they had more bugs than they did correct behaviors. And so we entered a dark period of time where the promise of CSS kept luring cutting-edge designers to their doom, dashed against the jagged edges of really bad browser implementations.

Of course, every dark age has its end and is often followed by a frenetic blossoming of ideas, techniques, and advances that would have been previously unthinkable. The most famous of these times, at least in the West, is the Renaissance, the products of which affect us even today. In a way, CSS is experiencing the beginning of its Renaissance, and it's an incredibly exciting time to be working in web design. It's almost like the first explosion of web design techniques that followed the advent of the table-and-spacer revolution. That was an exciting time as well, although most of us weren't aware how much damage we were doing to the structure of the Web. It's only been in the last couple of years that we've had a chance to clean up our mess, and CSS is the fulcrum on which the reclamation of the Web pivots.

So how do I know we're in a Renaissance? Two reasons, really. The first is that browsers have finally cleaned up their acts and started doing basic things in a consistent way. By this, I'm referring to the very, very good standards support that modern browsers embody. The ability to create pages that display consistently between browsers is the key, and that ability has never been greater. Of course, there are still some problem areas, but that's part of what keeps the job interesting, right? We can no more expect perfection of our browsers than we can of ourselves—even though we keep pushing for it anyway. In many ways, the calls for improved standards support these days are a plea for some icing on the standards cake, instead of that bleak, bygone era when we begged desperately for any cake at all.

The second thing that tells me we're entering a Renaissance is the appearance of a book like this one: a good introduction to CSS aimed at designers. For a long time, the leading CSS books (including my own) were targeted at the kinds of people who already understood the HTML specification backward and forward and wrote web pages by hand in Notepad or emacs. That's to be expected, since most technologies get adopted first by code jockeys.

But CSS is a visual language, one that was meant to be used by designers from the beginning. Books aimed at that particular audience are long overdue, frankly, and I'm thrilled to see them emerging at long last. I'm even more thrilled that we're getting one from Molly Holzschlag.

I'll never forget the first time I came into contact with Molly. I was writing CSS articles for *Web Review*, and she had just taken over as Executive Editor. We swapped a few e-mails back and forth and got along smashingly from the word go. Molly's one of those people who's hard not to get along with, really. Eventually, in response to a comment from me, Molly pointed me to a page on her website that had some portraits of her. I fired up a web browser and took a look.

"Wow," said my wife Kat, leaning over my shoulder to peer at the monitor, "she's really beautiful."

At the time, we had no idea how right Kat was. We've since discovered that Molly truly is a beautiful person in so many ways, it would get sort of embarrassing to list them all here, so I'll settle for the one thing that stands out most when I think of Molly: her terrific sense of humor. This made me really happy when Molly was my editor at *Web Review*. I always like to work with an editor with a sense of humor. It keeps them from getting too worked up over my stunningly casual attitude toward writing schedules.

There have been many conferences where the best time of the whole week was just hanging out with Molly (and optionally other web folks) in some hotel bar, chatting randomly and cracking jokes, like a sitcom writers' summit gone deeply geeky. It's always a pleasure to make Molly laugh, because she has a great laugh. A very distinctive one, I might add. It makes it a lot easier to find her at crowded receptions; just wait for someone to amuse her. Failing that, just look for the biggest, noisiest, cheeriest knot of people. The odds are that Molly is somewhere very near the center of that knot.

Spend any time around her, you get to pretty much one unavoidable conclusion: Molly is a character. That's good. The industry needs more characters, because they make things interesting, and more fun, on a personal level.

You might think from all this that Molly is less than serious about her work. Nothing could be further from the truth. I've seen Molly teach classes, and I've been privileged to co-teach a day-long seminar on XHTML and CSS with her. Molly is one of those rare people who is bright enough to understand the technology, eloquent enough to explain it, and empathetic enough to instinctively know where students are likely to run into trouble—and to lead them around the pitfalls before anyone falls in. If somebody does stumble, Molly is right there to help them up with a more detailed explanation, an illuminating example, or simply an encouraging word. She is deeply committed not only to teaching, but to teaching well.

Molly truly wants to share as much of her knowledge and skills with as many people as she can possibly manage, and you can see it in every word. I commend you to her capable hands and hope you will find CSS as fascinating as I do, six years later and still counting.

Eric A. Meyer
www.meyerweb.com
December 2002
Cleveland, Ohio

Contents

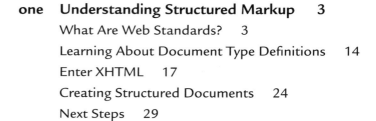

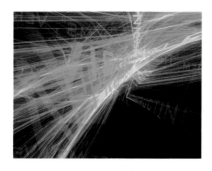

Introduction

We have not learned to design the Web.

This is not to say that we haven't done some profound work when it comes to web design, usability, technological progress, and innovation. But to get to this point in the web's history, we've had to borrow guidelines from other media, hack and workaround our way through browser inconsistencies, and bend markup so far out of its normal shape that we've nearly broken it.

CSS has been around for a long time, but the main problem has not been with CSS, rather, it's been browser support problems for CSS. But with the release of Netscape 6.*x* browsers and the prevalence of IE browsers, along with somewhat less common but CSS-savvy browsers such as Opera, we can now begin to turn to CSS for at least some of our design concerns.

As a result of the growing proliferation of browsers on the Web that can support CSS, web designers and developers will be seriously challenged to begin looking at web design in new ways. The bad news is that those with little experience in CSS will have to learn how to write a whole new language!

The good news, however, is that it's not that difficult a language to learn if you've been working with HTML for some time. And there's more good news, because once you've learned to employ CSS in your site designs, you'll find that you are left with a lot less work and a lot less document overhead, such as numerous font tags and graphic image spacers. Your documents will be cleaner, much easier to manage, and load and render much more quickly as a result.

Philosopher Bertrand Russell said, "War does not determine who is right—only who is left." For web designers and developers, it's browser wars that have made our lives very difficult. Those difficulties have sent some less committed web workers running into the night. Those of us who are left must find our way to steadier ground.

If we seek innovation in design, we must look first to the web browser, for it is within the web browser that our visual designs are rendered. We must also look at our practices with HTML and XHTML. The heart of the information regarding how web browsers and web authors should ideally be practicing lies under the auspices of the World Wide Web Consortium (W3C), www.w3.org/. Known as recommendations or specifications and sometimes referred to as standards, HTML, XHTML, CSS, and many other languages and methodologies are being developed by the W3C with very clear guidelines as to how to use them.

Fortunately, there's been enough discussion over the past years of the importance of using W3C recommendations and specifications as de facto web standards. Many browser manufacturers, web authors, and tools manufacturers are starting to pay detailed attention to getting on with creating a consistent means for web authors to achieve consistent results across browsers.

For those web authors working in today's transitional time, several ideas that exist in markup are coming to the forefront as a concern. The primary issue in terms of CSS is first described in HTML 4, which asks for a separation of presentation and document formatting ideally, and demands it in its most strict interpretation. This means reserving CSS for design and reserving the document for the more straightforward structuring of content.

But web documents have not been historically developed that way. Instead, we have developed and learned to rely on presentational elements and attributes for alignment, color, size, and so on. This is the most common practice in use on the Web today, but that will ideally change as the rationale and implementation for CSS grows.

We have not yet learned to design the Web. It's going to be the people using CSS in the next few years who will come up with the innovative design ideas we need to help drive the potential of the Web in general. It is my hope that this book will help you to become one of those innovators, and I wait with enthusiasm to hear about the successes from those readers who use the techniques described here to design their sites.

About the Book

CSS: The Designer's Edge effectively teaches web designers and developers to properly structure documents and use CSS as an empowering design technology. The topic is taught in a linear way, covering main concepts in markup and CSS in depth, with plenty of visual images to aid in the visualization of how CSS works.

The ideal reader for this book:

- Has a working knowledge of HTML
- Wants to work with CSS for presentation
- May already work with CSS but needs a stronger foundation to work effectively
- Is committed to understanding the languages of the Web in order to use them properly
- Is interested in strengthening skills to be more innovative with CSS design

Where *CSS: The Designer's Edge* differs from other books on CSS is that it is a clearly written book that instructs the reader carefully regarding the detailed technical, creative, and inspirational needs of today's working web professional.

How the Book Is Structured

CSS: The Designer's Edge has three parts, each containing three chapters. Part I, "Technology," teaches structured markup and CSS in detail as languages. This provides the foundation for the designer who seeks to use CSS in complex and important ways. Part II, "Design," digs deep into the primary uses of CSS: typography, color, and page layout. Part III, "Vision," provides insights from working websites developed with structured markup and CSS, helping readers gain a deep perspective of how the markup and CSS are interacting to provide refreshing designs that also adhere to contemporary specifications.

WWW. Along the way, you'll find notes, tips, and sidebars that add insight, perspective, and provide additional resources to help you go beyond the scope of the material contained within the book itself. When you see a symbol like this one in the margin, you'll know you can go and download the code from www.sybex.com. (Navigate to the book's page, click the Download link, and follow the directions that appear.)

Technology

CSS is emerging as the true language of web design. Being a great web designer means being fluent in the language, especially as we embark on a time where web browsers can more effectively bring to life the power and elegance of CSS. With CSS, we can bridge the gap between science and art. To create a sophisticated web page means to understand the visual and also to understand how the visual is created through the technology.

To learn and use CSS effectively, you must have an understanding of the underlying technical structure of both web markup and CSS itself. To that end, the following chapters focus on demonstrating structured markup, how CSS integrates with markup, and how CSS works *as a language* to enable you to express innovative and progressive ideas through your work.

*One cannot help but be in awe
when he contemplates the mysteries
of eternity, of life, of the marvelous
structure of reality.*

—Albert Einstein

one

Understanding
Structured Markup

Just as a schooled artist must study anatomy, so must a web designer study the structures that are the infrastructure of a design. It is imperative for web designers who want to write great CSS to understand how web markup has evolved, grown, and changed. It's also critical to have a detailed understanding of how markup works if you want to achieve excellence when writing CSS.

To prepare for that excellence, you'll learn about the historical emergence of markup and the current need to return to a structure temporarily lost in the frenzy of web design and development in the late '90s. The web design profession has matured, so best practices and standard methods are emerging to help us create very clean, very powerful means of delivering great sites for use today and well into the future.

In this chapter you will learn:

- The significance of standards
- The meaning of structure
- Ideas central to markup
- In-depth information about HTML and XHTML
- How HTML and XHTML relate to CSS
- How to create structured HTML and XHTML documents

What Are Web Standards?

Chances are you fit into one of several categories when it comes to authoring documents. You might be a person who uses a visual editor such as Microsoft FrontPage, Dreamweaver MX, or Adobe GoLive exclusively, letting the visual environment guide the markup. Or, you might be specifically a markup author, pounding out your tags and attributes in a text editor such as Emacs, vi, Notepad, or SimpleText. Maybe you like to write your own documents but prefer working with an HTML-style editor such as HomeSite or BBEdit.

As with more and more web professionals, a hybrid methodology may exist for you: you might work using a visual editor and do some hand-authoring, too.

No matter your method, you probably know something about HTML, even if you've learned it by viewing source or reading books and have never studied it formally. And, while you might have heard the term *web standards*, it's not a very clear term and may have confused you as to what it means and why it's important.

The term *web standard* is a confusing one not just because it's inaccurate, but because it also suggests conformity. I use the term to refer to what is actually *a series of specifications and recommendations created by the World Wide Web Consortium* (W3C). The W3C is not an authoritative standards body per se. They're not going to drop by your office and give you a ticket for noncompliance. The primary functions of the W3C are to research, develop, and publish information on technologies and activities related to the Web (see Table 1.1).

Table 1.1: A Sample of Technologies and Activities of the W3C

Technology or Activity	Purpose
Accessibility	To ensure documents are accessible to all people
Cascading Style Sheets (CSS)	To provide a style language for presentation of documents
Document Object Model (DOM)	To provide consistent object models within browsers
Hypertext Markup Language (HTML)	To author web documents
Internationalization	To facilitate proper encoding and display of multilingual and international documents
Synchronized Multimedia Integration Language (SMIL)	An XML-based language to facilitate multimedia synchronization: video, audio, text
Scalable Vector Graphics (SVG)	An XML-based language to facilitate scalable vector-based graphics and animation
Extensible Hypertext Markup Language (XHTML)	To author documents for the web and alternative devices
Extensible Markup Language (XML)	To provide a universal format for structured documents and data

For more specific information related to these technologies, as well as descriptions of the many other issues the W3C concerns itself with, visit www.w3.org/.

When you design your website, no matter which method you use, you are working in part with W3C technologies. And, while the W3C is not an authoritative organization that you *must* follow, it certainly provides a base from which designers can learn consistent and intelligent practices.

Following a W3C specification—a *web standard*—does *not* mean that design options are limited. I suggest the opposite. Innovation requires intermittent periods of stability and chaos. Currently, we are in a transitional time as web professionals. We're trying to make sense out of the chaos of the past years and achieve some stability in our designs, tools, and methods. It makes sense: we're looking to find some conventions to make our jobs easier.

Building the next level of the Web's infrastructure as cleanly as possible provides the matrix for new levels of innovation. I think people are sensing this, and this is why many people are starting to get interested in standards. Web professionals are starting to realize it's a cool—and necessary—thing to pay attention to in order to keep the technology moving forward in a mature way.

A standards-based site also does not suggest that the site will be unattractive, use text-only, or have few visual elements. In fact, this book exists in part to prove that standards-based sites can not only be attractive, but also downright innovative.

Back to the Future

Most readers are aware of HTML, and many are also aware of its successor in web markup, XHTML.

But where did these languages come from, and how come we're going through such a radical shift in the way we as designers and developers work?

Let's begin with the Standardized General Markup Language (SGML). It is what is known as a *meta-language*. SGML is essentially a massive *document type definition* (DTD) used to create other markup languages.

 DTDs are plain-text documents that describe the elements, attributes, and other allowed components of a given markup language such as HTML or XHTML, along with its version and type, such as HTML 4.01 Strict. You'll read more about these distinctions and how they influence your design options later in this chapter.

HTML is derived from SGML. The early use of HTML led to some great and innovative approaches, bending the language to allow for increasingly more complex visual sites. The best—and most problematic—example of this is HTML tables, which were originally added to HTML to manage data tables more effectively than the preformatted text element pre. By turning off table borders, suddenly a de facto grid system for laying out even the most popular site content was born, as you can see in Figure 1.1. As the example shows, the primary site design method became tables.

As the examples show, the primary site design method became tables. But tables were problematic for several reasons, including:

- Tables, especially when particularly complex or deeply nested, create overhead in terms of size and speed.
- Complex tables can be difficult to manage, especially across web teams.
- Tables of this nature are often inaccessible to those with visual or mobility-related impairments.

Other problems came to the forefront as various browsers introduced proprietary markup not related to work being done at the W3C. The so-called "browser wars" began in the early 1990s and still exist to a large degree. Browser manufacturers sometimes let corporate agendas get in the way of the greater good. The irony is

Figure 1.1: eBay's Home Page with all table borders turned on

that the browser manufacturers were (and are now still) members of working groups for standards and yet continue to only slowly implement W3C recommendations while aggressively trying out new technologies in an effort to dominate the browser space.

Not all aspects of the browser wars was bad. In fact, early on, this competition allowed for a time of great innovation. Everyone broke rules: designers, developers, browser and tools vendors. It was an important exercise. However, now the time has come to clean up our practices if we want to move forward in the expanding potential of the web and create a strong, next-level infrastructure.

While these difficult issues in HTML and browser support were being examined, Extensible Markup Language (XML) was coming to light. XML, also derived from SGML, is a more streamlined meta-language that is especially useful for sharing documents and information on the Internet and related networks.

HTML was re-evaluated in the context of XML—with its emphasis on rigor, conformance, and extensibility. This evaluation resulted in the publication of a new markup language, XHTML 1. Introduced in January 2000, XHTML 1 officially replaced HTML 4.01 as the most contemporary available specification. XHTML is now in its 1.1 version, with version 2 on the horizon.

 Just because a specification is currently recommended does not necessarily mean it is the specification with which you must work. In other words, it's perfectly acceptable to be writing HTML 4.01 instead of XHTML 1.1. The goal is to know the specifications well enough to be able to make decisions about which method will work best for your circumstances.

XHTML is considered by the W3C as a *reformulation of HTML as an XML application*. XHTML at its most basic is HTML vocabulary in a well-structured XML document. At its most complex, XHTML is extensible and customizable. You'll read more about this and see examples as you read further in the chapter.

But Why Standards?

So why should you follow standards? A lot of people say, "Hey, I can use nonstandard markup that works just fine."

There are several reasons why understanding and following standards makes sense. Here are a few:

- You will save time. If your documents follow standards, you achieve a level of efficient work practices. Troubleshooting becomes easier because of document consistency. Team members will work more efficiently in an environment where documents follow structure and logic.
- Saving time means saving money. If you are able to save time by ensuring that your documents are standards compliant, stable, and use CSS for style, you will be able to both profit from the process *and* pass the resulting savings on to your clients.
- You'll reduce complicated pages so browsers will interpret and display a page quickly and accessibility concerns will be addressed. This means a happier end user.
- You'll have better job opportunities. If you are still creating web pages in a visual editor without understanding the underlying markup and have not spent any time studying standards, you are restricting yourself in terms of advancement within the profession.

- You will become part of the solution, not the problem, as the infrastructure of the web becomes increasingly more complex.
- Standards set the stage for extending content beyond the limits of the Web to wireless devices such as smart phones, pagers, and PDAs; alternative devices such as MSNTV (formerly WebTV); and a range of devices yet to come.

To sum up, early case studies suggest that compliance probably saves money for everyone in the website food chain—from site owner to developer to ISP. Those are the immediate advantages. Longer term, working with standards addresses many technical, creative, and even social concerns. Technically, websites will be more easily maintained and also readily available for many platforms beyond the Web. Creatively, you can apply style sheets that will easily make a site look good on a computer screen, on a PDA screen, even in print. Socially, you remove barriers to access by cleaning up your hacked markup and paying attention to accessibility concerns.

Making a Case for Standards: The Web Standards Project

One of the difficulties of becoming familiar with standards is that the W3C tends to focus on the development and creation of technologies rather than the dissemination of educational material related to their work.

The documents at the W3C are often prohibitive for busy people who don't want to read through the minutia—much less translate clumsy academic writing into useful guidance. The need for more interesting documentation is currently being addressed by the W3C, which has several committees that are working to make their findings more readily understandable and available to the public at large.

In a desire to see the long-term benefits of standards be implemented by browsers, software developers, and designers and developers themselves, a grassroots, volunteer-driven organization called The Web Standards Project emerged. Members of The WaSP (as most people refer to it) work to evangelize standards and educate others about them. The group has recently expanded to include educational initiatives, and its website is an example of an attractive, usable site that adheres to W3C standards and professionally acquired best practices.

The WaSP, however, is a truly independent organization. While understanding the long-term benefits that W3C work does, WaSP members have (and will continue if necessary) to openly criticized certain activities of the W3C. Part of The WaSP mission is to encourage the W3C to live up to its potential.

For more information about The WaSP and its activities, see www.webstandards.org/.

Exploring HTML Concepts

By the time HTML 4 emerged in 1998 as the recommended specification for web markup, a rigorous evaluation had been given to the state of affairs occurring with browsers and language. With HTML 4 came several directives that have shaped the languages that have since evolved and the practices related to those languages. The most critical concerns voiced when HTML 4 was introduced include the following:

- The need to separate document structure and style in order to return documents to a more accessible, cross-platform state. As CSS Level 1 had been completed in 1996, this was a means of encouraging designers and developers to use CSS.
- A desire to improve document rendering.
- A highly motivated need to encourage the authoring of accessible documents.
- The need to encourage web professionals, web development tools manufacturers, and browser developers to adhere to a common base of guidelines.

These critical concepts have followed through to the final version of HTML—HTML 4.01—and beyond, into XHTML.

 NOTE HTML 4.01 contains only minor editorial changes from HTML 4. It is canonically important, however, because the HTML 4.01 DTDs were used as the basis for XHTML 1. As this discussion progresses, you'll see examples of HTML 4.01. Most people authoring to standards (and using HTML) use an HTML 4.01 DTD.

The following sections will provide deeper insight into the concerns that HTML 4 raised; this will help you gain a more profound appreciation for how these ideas have influenced the growing interest in using CSS.

Separation of Document Structure and Style

One of HTML 4's prime directives is to separate document formatting from the presentation of that document. This is a critical issue, because most of the HTML in use today is misused—it's filled with errors that provide endless problems and make accessibility, document rendering speed, and cross-browser consistency nightmarish to achieve.

What Is Document Structure?

For the purposes of this book, document structure for the purposes of this book is the skeletal structure of a Web document. This skeletal structure includes:

- A DOCTYPE declaration
- An html element
- A head with title
- A document body
- Structural elements only, used in a logical manner for managing content. In this category you'll find such things as headings (h1, h2, h3, h4, h5, h6), paragraphs and breaks (p, br), and lists (ul, ol, dl).

 NOTE A DOCTYPE declaration defines the document type and DTD version. DOCTYPE declarations appear at the top of a structured document. These declarations are described in detail in the "Learning About Document Type Definitions" section later in this chapter.

A structured document results in a tree. Listing 1.1 shows a valid HTML 4 document with the required structural components and some content marked up with basic elements.

Listing 1.1: An HTML 4 Document with Basic Structure

```
<!DOCTYPE HTML PUBLIC "-//W3C//DTD HTML 4.0//EN"
        "http://www.w3.org/TR/REC-html40/strict.dtd">

<html>
<head>

<title>Working with Structure</title>
```

```
</head>

<body>

<h1>Welcome</h1>

<p>Welcome to the site where structure matters!</p>

<h2>Getting Into Structure</h2>

<p>In order to begin working with structure, you need to be aware of:</p>

<ul>
<li>DOCTYPE declarations</li>
<li>Properly structured head and body components</li>
<li>Logical structures for content markup</li>
</ul>

</body>
</html>
```

Figure 1.2 demonstrates the document tree that results from Listing 1.1. Document trees become especially important when working with CSS because of the concept of inheritance—which means style features defined for an element will pass to its children—and how elements are related to one another, influencing the way your style sheets will be interpreted.

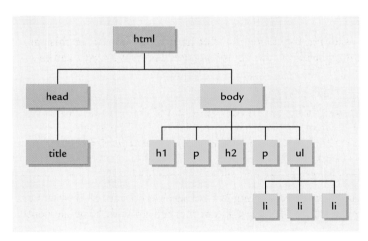

Figure 1.2: Document tree with parent, child, and leaf nodes

Documents are broken down into a document root (typically the html element) and any child relationships (the head and body are children to the root, and the body has four children, h1, h2, p, and ul). Finally, there are the leaf nodes: the three bullet items denoted by the li element. Each li element is, of course, a child to the ul element.

NOTE The concept of inheritance is explored in depth in Chapter 2, "Learning CSS Theory."

Document Presentation

Presentation mostly refers to anything that involves visual details. Examples of presentation include the following:

- Color (see Figure 1.3)
- Text formatting and typographic design (see Figure 1.4)
- Background graphics (see Figure 1.5)
- Borders, padding, spacing (see Figure 1.6)
- Layout of pages (see Figure 1.7)

Figure 1.3: The colors in this page are all generated using HTML color attributes.

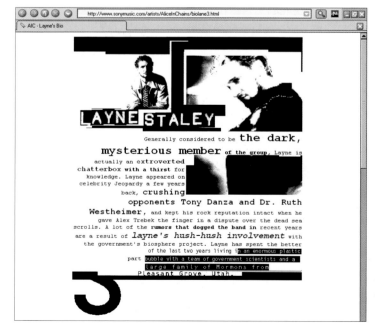

Figure 1.4: The range of fonts, colors, and sizes in this image are generated by HTML.

Figure 1.5: This early web page still looks great because of its background.

Figure 1.6: HTML defines the borders, padding, and spacing of page elements.

Figure 1.7: This site uses tables rather than CSS for layout, a common current practice.

HTML 4 was the first HTML version to formally recommend that in its most idealistic expression, authors should leave the HTML document empty of presentational detail and address presentational concerns using—you guessed it—Cascading Style Sheets (CSS).

> **NOTE** One of the greatest features of CSS is that their presentation methods go beyond the screen. You can prepare style sheets so documents can be styled for many types of media, including print, aural devices, PDAs, and cell phones.

Improving Accessibility and Document Rendering

Originally, HTML was designed to be a language that could be easily and readily distributed across various platforms and read by anyone, regardless of their software. But innovation and competition within the browser sector quickly changed that reality. With Microsoft and Netscape Communications Corp. rushing hither and yon to create the coolest technology on the block, the consistency of HTML's semantic structure was disrupted when new, browser-based tags and attributes emerged—many unsupported by competing browsers. Most of these tags and attributes had to do with presentation or visual design, including Netscape's renowned blink tag and the dreaded Microsoft IE marquee tag (Figure 1.8).

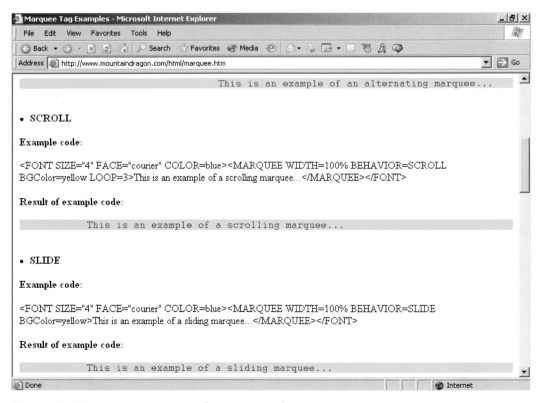

Figure 1.8: IE's marquee *tag—not only proprietary, but annoying, too.*

One of HTML 4's goals was to bring organization back to HTML. A related goal was to improve accessibility of documents. By using some new element and attribute options within HTML 4, document authors and page designers could now help individuals understand and negotiate pages no matter what their platform—or physical abilities.

Many people with impaired or no vision have tremendous difficulty accessing today's World Wide Web. This is largely because electronic screen readers that browse the screen and read the content aloud are significantly more challenged by complex graphical pages. However, with a little forethought, authors can make this process much easier. Individuals with other physical limitations are also assisted by devices—and whether it's a screen reader or special keyboard, the methodologies that HTML 4 proposed to aid access have begun to play a growing role in accessibility and improved rendering of documents.

Accessibility is becoming a hot topic due to recent legislation worldwide that certain kinds of sites must be made accessible to all people, including those with disabilities. In the United States, accessibility has become especially important for federal agency websites as well as those sites created by anyone receiving federal contracts to fund their sites. This is due to legislation regarding accessibility in the U.S.; specifically, it relates to a portion of legislation known as Section 508.

 NOTE To learn more about Section 508 and what it details, see `www.section508.gov/`.

The rendering of documents in a web browser can be improved by adhering to common practices. At its most strict, HTML 4 suggests that the author leave tables behind as a means of presenting layout and instead use Cascading Style Sheets for the positioning of objects on a page. The use of CSS in this way not only improves the rendering of documents within supporting browsers, but it also helps you address accessibility concerns by ensuring that it is the structured document and its content, not the presentation of that content, that gets distributed to those accessing the pages using assistive methods.

The Web Accessibility Initiative (WAI)

The Web Accessibility Initiative (WAI) of the W3C is dedicated to promoting awareness worldwide about accessibility. The WAI provides the following:

- Accessibility guidelines and tips
- Accessibility tests
- Accessibility validation options
- News on accessibility activities

To learn more about the WAI, see `www.w3.org/WAI/`.

Going Global

Just as access is important to those with disabilities, it is equally important to ensure that multilingual, international, and localized sites can be developed.

To accommodate access for international users, the W3C makes a concerted effort in HTML 4 and beyond to address international issues for authors, user agents, and development tools.

Current areas of activity include the following:

- Increasing awareness among web and browser developers regarding international access issues
- Stressing the importance of Unicode as a mechanism for character encoding
- Creating study groups within the W3C to look at details of international concerns

The importance of internationalization is easily seen with a visit to any multi-lingual website. If you'd like to see a variety of international sites, check out the BBC's international websites, each written and displayed in a different language, www.bbc.co.uk/.

 For more information on internationalization concerns, visit www.w3.org/International/.

Learning About Document Type Definitions

Another piece of the puzzle that HTML 4 provided was a means by which web designers could move away from the haphazard practices of yesterday and embrace the longer-term ideals of standards. This came about with the creation of three distinct DTDs within HTML 4. Each of these definitions contains specific information about which elements and attributes are available in HTML and how they could be used, depending upon the goals of the designer.

A DTD is a plain-text document that contains rules about the way a given language works. In the case of HTML, the DTDs are publicly available at the W3C. Figure 1.9 shows a portion of a W3C DTD viewed within a web browser.

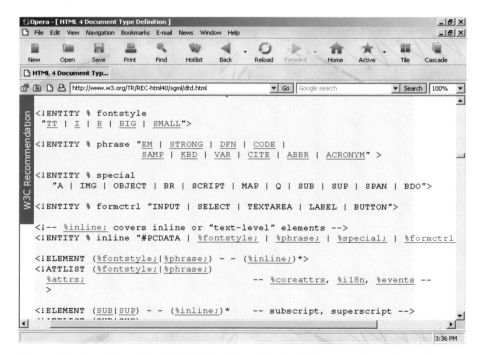

Figure 1.9: A portion of the HTML 4.01 Transitional DTD as seen in the Opera browser

The Three Flavors of DTDs in HTML 4.0/4.01

Three types of DTDs, referred to as *interpretations*, were first defined in HTML 4 and later influenced HTML 4.01 and XHTML 1. These DTD interpretations are as follows:

Strict The Strict DTD is the most optimistic of the three, with almost all presentational elements and attributes completely unavailable to use if you want a valid document. (See the next section, "Compliance and Validation.") The recommended means of addressing presentation at this level is, of course, CSS.

Transitional Also referred to as "loose," this DTD was developed with the understanding that CSS was not then (and is still not now) completely available in all cases. The Transitional DTD allows for simple presentational elements and attributes, including even those that had been deprecated in favor of a better technology, such as the font element (note that this is even true in the XHTML 1 Transitional DTD). Ideally, document authors choosing a Transitional DTD understand that they are working toward the goals the Strict DTD embodies. To that end, while you *can* use deprecated elements in a Transitional DTD, you are not particularly *encouraged* to do so.

Frameset The Frameset DTD is specific to the creation of framesets, which as most readers are aware, is a different type of document from a conventional HTML page. Framesets can be considered the control documents that restructure a browser's interface and give the designer control over how to do that. The Frameset DTD only includes information for frameset documents, so the only time you will use a Frameset DTD is when you are creating a frameset. Conventional pages within your frames can be marked up using any HTML language, version, and DTD.

No doubt you're wondering how DTDs influence the way a document is read by browsers. The truth is that only recently did the inclusion of a DOCTYPE citing a specific DTD influence the way a given browser interpreted a document. (See the "DOCTYPE Switching" sidebar later in this chapter.) For the most part, if you include something nonstandard in a document, the browser's going to display it if it knows the markup you're using. Following a DTD means following the language's rules, and this relates mostly to the creation of *compliant* and *valid* documents.

Compliance and Validation

Two key concepts when working with web standards include *compliance* and *validation*:

* A compliant document is one that conforms to the DTD that is referenced by its DOCTYPE.
* A valid document is one that is tested for compliance using a validator such as that provided by the W3C, http://validator.w3.org/.

 With any application, bugs exist. So it is with validators, too. For a helpful guide on commonly encountered validation problems, see "Liberty! Equality! Validity!" at http://devedge.netscape.com/viewsource/2001/validate/.

There have been some arguments about the usefulness of validation. I consider validation to be an important process when working seriously with HTML, XHTML, and CSS. Validation aids in education by providing warnings and errors regarding document compliance.

The only consideration is that validation errors can be as confusing as grammar rules in a Microsoft Word document! You have to learn a bit of process when it comes to troubleshooting.

 NOTE You'll step through the validation process with HTML and XHTML in this chapter, and you will learn to validate CSS later in the book. Interestingly, the W3C validator is the most used service of the W3C.

Comparing DTDs in HTML 4

A good way to learn a bit about the way DTDs work is to compare portions of them with each other. In this case, first examine the DTD portion in Listing 1.2.

Listing 1.2: Excerpt from HTML 4.01 Strict DTD—Paragraphs

```
<!--========= Paragraphs ==========-->

<!ELEMENT P - O (%inline;)* -- paragraph -->
<!ATTLIST P
%attrs;                     -- %coreattrs, %i18n, %events --
>
```

Notice how this DTD portion shows how paragraphs are handled in HTML 4.01 Strict. The only attributes allowed are *core* attributes (%coreattrs) needed for style, scripting, and accessibility (id, class, style, title); *internationalization* attributes (%i18n) required for internationalization (lang, dir); and *event* attributes (%events), used for scripting as well (onclick, onmouseup, etc.).

Now examine Listing 1.3, which describes how paragraphs are handled in HTML 4.01 Transitional.

Listing 1.3: Excerpt from HTML 4.01 Transitional DTD—Paragraphs

```
<!--========= Paragraphs ==========-->

<!ELEMENT P - O (%inline;)* -- paragraph -->
<!ATTLIST P
%attrs;                     -- %coreattrs, %i18n, events --
%align;                     -- align, text alignment --
>
```

The attributes in this DTD are a bit different. You'll notice that the align category of attributes is included as well (align=x where x is left, right, center or justify). Alignment isn't allowed in the Strict DTD because of the idea that presentation should be separated from the document structure and its content.

 NOTE The HTML 4.01 Strict DTD can be found at www.w3.org/TR/html401/sgml/ dtd.html. The HTML 4.01 Transitional DTD is available at www.w3.org/TR/ html401/sgml/loosedtd.html. All of the DTDs in this chapter are public and online at the W3C website, www.w3.org/.

Enter XHTML

XHTML 1 is, again, the rewrite of HTML as an XML application. The primary concepts in HTML 4—especially the separation of document structure from presentation and issues concerning accessibility and internationalization—remain intact in XHTML 1. What's more, the three DTD offerings (Strict, Transitional, and Frameset), originally from HTML 4 and later refined by HTML 4.01, are essentially the same DTDs in XHTML 1.

Despite these similarities, there are quite a few differences of great importance from both theoretic and semantic standpoints.

XHTML in Theory

XML brings several important ideas and incentives to web designers and developers through XHTML:

Reintroduce structure back into the language Picking up on the SGML and XML idea that documents should be written in conformance with the rules set out within the languages, XHTML makes it clear to authors that structural and semantic rules should be adhered to and *must* be adhered to in order to create compliant pages.

Provide designers with incentives to validate documents Validation carries with it some controversy, but it's a powerful learning tool that helps you find your mistakes, fix them, and in the process, understand the way a specific DTD works. Validation, therefore, is an encouraged practice.

Accommodating new devices Part of the drive to accommodate XML in the web development environment has to do with the interest of delivering web-based content to other devices such as PDAs, cell phones, pagers, set-top boxes, WebTV (now known as MSNTV), and even television.

With XHTML 1.1, the concept of separation of structure and presentation is complete. XHTML 1.1 has only one public DTD, based on the Strict DTD in XHTML 1. Web authors also have the option to work with *modularization*.

Modularization breaks HTML down into discrete modules such as text, images, tables, frames, forms, and so forth. The author can choose which modules they want to use and then write a DTD combining those modules into a unique application.

This is the first time you really see the extensibility introduced by XML at work: instead of having only the public DTDs to choose from, authors can create their own applications.

 An overview of XHTML modularization can be found at www.w3.org/MarkUp/ modularization. The actual XHTML 1.1 recommendation is at www.w3.org/ TR/xhtml11/. Modularization is a fascinating and rather dramatic change to the way we approach pages, but it is beyond the scope of this book to cover it in detail.

Semantic Changes from HTML

In practice, XHTML works a bit differently from HTML. XHTML is much more rigorous than HTML and demands close attention to details.

- It is recommended but not required that an XHTML 1 document be declared as an XML document using an XML declaration.
- It is required that an XHTML 1 document contain a DOCTYPE that denotes that it is an XHTML 1 document and also denotes the DTD being used by that document.
- An XHTML 1 document has a root element of html. The opening tag of the html element should contain the XML namespace xmlns and the appropriate value for the namespace.
- The syntax and structure of the document must follow the syntactical rules of XHTML.

XML Prolog, *DOCTYPE* Declaration, and Namespace

An XHTML document may contain several structural elements to be considered correct.

The XML Prolog

The XML Prolog is a declaration that can appear above your DOCTYPE declaration. The prolog is recommended but not required. Part of the reason it is not required is that some browsers (including IE 4.5 for Mac, IE 6 for Windows, and Netscape 4 for Windows) will display XHTML pages inappropriately if it is used.

So, most XHTML 1 authors interested in the best interoperability leave it out. However, because the encoding information is important in many instances—particularly when working with international documents—if you don't use the XML declaration, you are encouraged to be sure encoding is set on your server or in a meta tag. Here's an example of the XML prolog, which states the XML version of the document as well as the document's encoding:

```
<?xml version="1.0" encoding="UTF-8"?>
```

The DOCTYPE Declaration

There are only three DTDs available in XHTML 1: Strict, Transitional, and Frameset, all carrying over with some minor differences from HTML 4.01. The DOCTYPE declaration declares the language version, interpretation, and location of the related DTD.

The way a DOCTYPE declaration is written is important for the reasons described in this DOCTYPE Switching sidebar. The following shows the available DOCTYPE declarations for HTML 4.01, XHTML 1.0, and XHTML 1.1, as they should be written.

HTML 4.01 Strict

```
<!DOCTYPE HTML PUBLIC "-//W3C//DTD HTML 4.01//EN"
    "http://www.w3.org/TR/html4/strict.dtd">
```

HTML 4.01 Transitional

```
<!DOCTYPE HTML PUBLIC "-//W3C//DTD HTML 4.01 Transitional//EN"
    "http://www.w3.org/TR/html4/loose.dtd">
```

HTML 4.01 Frameset

```
<!DOCTYPE HTML PUBLIC "-//W3C//DTD HTML 4.01 Frameset//EN"
    "http://www.w3.org/TR/html4/frameset.dtd">
```

XHTML 1.0 Strict

```
<!DOCTYPE html PUBLIC "-//W3C//DTD XHTML 1.0 Strict//EN"
    "http://www.w3.org/TR/xhtml1/DTD/xhtml1-strict.dtd">
```

XHTML 1.0 Transitional

```
<!DOCTYPE html PUBLIC "-//W3C//DTD XHTML 1.0 Transitional//EN"
    "http://www.w3.org/TR/xhtml1/DTD/xhtml1-transitional.dtd">
```

XHTML 1.0 Frameset

```
<!DOCTYPE html PUBLIC "-//W3C//DTD XHTML 1.0 Frameset//EN"
    "http://www.w3.org/TR/xhtml1/DTD/xhtml1-frameset.dtd">
```

XHTML 1.1

```
<!DOCTYPE html PUBLIC "-//W3C//DTD XHTML 1.1//EN"
    "http://www.w3.org/TR/xhtml11/DTD/xhtml11.dtd">
```

DOCTYPE Switching

In many recent browsers, an implementation for managing standard versus nonstandard markup has emerged. Browsers with this feature, referred to as **DOCTYPE** Switching, will behave in different ways *depending upon the DTD* that is declared in your document, or if in fact the DTD is declared at all.

This behavior involves switching *modes* to best represent standard versus nonstandard markup. The two modes are *quirks mode*, which behaves just as any legacy browser would, and *strict rendering mode*, which follows the standard.

Those pages containing older or transitional HTML **DOCTYPE**s or no **DOCTYPE** at all are displayed using quirks mode. Documents with correct Strict or XHTML **DOCTYPE**s use strict rendering mode.

This switching becomes more important as you delve into CSS, because certain rendering modes create different results. I'll point these concerns out as you move through the CSS chapters in the next part of the book.

A switching table created by Eric A. Meyer (technical editor of this book) can be found at `www.meyerweb.com/eric/dom/dtype/dtype-grid.html`. Another table, by Matthias Gutfeldt, is available at `http://gutfeldt.ch/matthias/articles/doctypeswitch/table.html`. This table shows how various browsers will relate to given **DOCTYPE** declarations.

The XML Namespace for XHTML

An XML namespace is a collection of unique element and attribute names. In XHTML, the namespace points to the related document at the W3C. The namespace is placed in the root element of the document tree, `html`:

```
<html xmlns="http://www.w3.org/1999/xhtml">
```

XHTML Syntax

Once an XHTML document contains the necessary declarations and basic structural information, you can examine the syntax changes resulting from XML's influences on web markup, including:

- Heavy focus on logical markup
- Case sensitivity
- Well-formed syntax
- Specific management of empty and non-empty elements
- Quotation requirements
- Escaping of script characters
- Management of minimized attributes

Each of these changes brings a marked amount of rigor to your authoring practices. Whether you end up using HTML or XHTML to mark up the documents you'll be styling with CSS, the knowledge of these practices will greatly influence your ability to write your style sheets with equal logic and organization.

Logical Markup

It can't be expressed enough that anyone wishing to learn CSS must understand the value of logical markup. When you work with content, the proper use of headers, paragraphs, breaks, lists, and so on should follow a sensible tree.

If you've ever wondered why an h1 is bigger than an h6 instead of the other way around, consider that headers in a document are meant to be organized by level of topic importance, like in an outline.

Let's say you've got three important places to go today: Bank, Post Office, Grocery Store. If you were creating a document tree out of those three topics, they would all be level 1 headers. The main activities you want to do at each stop would comprise your level 2 headers, and so on.

Paragraphs of content should be structured properly, too. Other items, such as lists, can easily organize information in a logical way. As you build your page, keep the tree concept in mind because you can work off of the elements in your tree when creating your style sheets—as you will see in many examples throughout the course of this book.

Using the Bank, Post Office, Grocery Store example, Listing 1.4 shows how this structure might pan out within a document.

Listing 1.4: Exploring the Logical Structure of Level 1 and 2 Headers

```
<h1>Bank</h1>
<p>Today I need to go to the bank.</p>
<h2>Cash Check</h2>
<p>My first order of the day is to cash my check.</p>
<h2>Transfer Funds</h2>
<p>I also need to transfer funds from one account to another. Once I'm done
with that, I can go to the post office.</p>

<h1>Post Office</h1>
<p>After the bank, I need to stop at the post office.</p>
<h2>Mail Packages</h2>
<p>I have three packages to mail.</p>
<h2>Buy Stamps</h2>
<p>I need to buy stamps, I'm always forgetting! Once done with the bank and
post office, I'm off to the grocery store.</p>

<h1>Grocery Store</h1>
<p>I have a few things to get at the grocery store.</p>
<h2> Salad Fixings</h2>
<p>Since it's summer, all I want to eat are lots of fresh veggies.</p>
<h2>Wine</h2>
<p>I'm having company Friday night and need a few bottles of a decent
wine.</p>
```

Of course, you can go on to develop your markup to use additional headers. The important lesson is tapping into using headers the way they were intended. The problem prior to style sheets was that designers were limited to what the default display was of their header (unless they also used a font tag and attributes to modify it). With CSS, the logic can be restored to the page while the separate presentation rules can leave the customized look of these components in your hands.

Figure 1.10 shows this sample page, unstyled. In Figure 1.11, I added a few simple CSS styles for the headers.

Figure 1.10: Studying logical structure, unstyled   *Figure 1.11: The same document, styled*

Case Sensitivity

HTML is not case sensitive. This means that HTML elements and attributes names can be in upper-, lower-, or mixed-case:

```
<body background="my.gif">
or
<BODY BACKGROUND="my.gif">
or even
<BoDy background="my.gif">
```

All of these examples mean the same thing in HTML.

On the other hand, XML *is* case sensitive. This means that XHTML is also case sensitive. In XHTML 1, all elements and attribute names *must* be written in lowercase:

```
<body background="my.gif">
```

 Attribute values, such as "my.gif", can be in mixed case. This is especially important in instances where the files are on servers with case-sensitive file systems.

Well-Formed Syntax

Many HTML browsers are quite forgiving of HTML errors and many HTML tools don't conform to standards. As such, some web designers have either inadvertently created poorly formed markup or learned bad habits.

The following example will work in many browsers:

```
<b><i>Welcome to MySite.Com</b></i>
```

It will display as both bold and italic in a forgiving browser. But, if you take a pencil and draw an arc from the opening bold tag to its closing companion, and then from the opening italic tag to its closing companion, you'll see that the lines of the arcs intersect. This demonstrates improper nesting of tags and is considered poorly formed.

 In a conforming browser, assuming the content displayed at all, it would be italic but not boldface.

In XHTML 1, such poorly formed markup is unacceptable because the potential problems resulting from nonstandard methods are unacceptable. The concept of *well-formedness* must be adhered to in that every element must nest appropriately. The XHTML 1 equivalent of the prior sample is as follows:

```
<b><i>Welcome to MySite.Com</i></b>
```

Draw the arcs now, and you'll see that they do not intersect. These tags are placed in the proper sequence and are considered to be well-formed.

Management of Non-Empty and Empty Elements

A *non-empty element* is one that contains an element and some content:

```
<p>This is the content within a non-empty element.</p>
```

An *empty element* is one that has no content, just the element and any allowed attributes, such as hr, br, and img. XML says that empty and non-empty elements must be properly terminated. In HTML, non-empty elements often have optional closing tags.

In HTML, I could write the paragraph above as follows:

```
<p>This is the content within a non-empty element.
```

This is considered correct. XHTML 1 demands that non-empty elements be properly terminated with a closing tag, as in the first example.

Another example is the list item, li, element.

In HTML, you could have a list like this:

```
<ul>
<li>Bank
<li>Post Office
<li>Grocery Store
</ul>
```

or like this:

```
<ul>
<li>Bank</li>
```

```
<li>Post Office</li>
<li>Grocery Store</li>
</ul>
```

In XHTML 1, *only* the latter method is allowed.

Empty elements work a bit differently. They are terminated in XML with what is known as a *trailing slash:*

```
<br>
```

becomes:

```
<br/>
```

Due to problems some browsers accustomed to interpreting HTML have with this method, a workaround was introduced, adding a space before the slash: br /. You should always use the space prior to the trailing slash in XHTML documents.

Here's an XHTML example of the image element, which is an empty element:

```
<img src="my.gif" height="55" width="25" border="0" alt="picture of me" />
```

Other empty elements of note are hr, meta, and link.

Quotation Rules

Quotation marks in HTML are arbitrary in that you can use or not use them around attribute values without running into too much trouble. There's no rule that says that leaving values unquoted is illegal. The following is perfectly acceptable in HTML:

```
<table border=0 width="90%" cellpadding=10 cellspacing="10">
```

Despite the fact that some attribute values are quoted and others are not, browsers will render this markup just fine. However, if you want to conform to XHTML 1, you'll have to quote all of your attribute values:

```
<table border="0" width="90%" cellpadding="10" cellspacing="10">
```

 You can never go wrong when you quote your attribute values in HTML, so get in the practice of always quoting values!

Other Markup and Code Concerns in XHTML

There are two other important concerns of which to be aware when working with XHTML:

Escaping certain characters in any inline script Let's say you have a JavaScript within your document. Any ampersand (&) must be *escaped* properly (that is, coded as an entity, not input using the keyboard symbol) as & for that document to be valid.

No attribute minimization is allowed *Attribute minimization* is a phenomenon that occurs in HTML, where an attribute is minimized to only the attribute name. An example of this is the nowrap attribute. In HTML, the attribute name can stand alone, with no value. However, in XHTML, minimization is not allowed—the attribute name is its value. Therefore, to be valid in XHTML, the HTML nowrap attribute must become nowrap="nowrap".

As you can see, none of these changes are monumental. A bit different, yes, but if you begin to use XHTML, you'll find that your markup is a lot more consistent. That consistency is part of what makes XHTML so attractive—it provides a strong foundation upon which to build future constructs as well as to help you and your team members manage documents within a site more efficiently.

Creating Structured Documents

No doubt you're itching to get your hands into the work and actually create a structured document. You will now learn to create a structured HTML 4.01 document as well as an XHTML 1 document.

Authoring a Structured HTML Document

Open your favorite web design tool. You can use anything you like as long as it allows you to work by hand and, when you save your changes, your changes remain intact. You can also use any plain text editor such as Notepad or SimpleText.

1. Begin with the DOCTYPE declaration. In this case, I've chosen HTML 4.01 Strict because I don't intend to have any presentational elements or attributes within the document, just the structure and content:

   ```
   <!DOCTYPE HTML PUBLIC "-//W3C//DTD HTML 4.01//EN"
       "http://www.w3.org/TR/html4/strict.dtd">
   ```

2. Add the root element. In this case, it will be html. Note that I've added both the open and closing tags:

   ```
   <html>

   </html>
   ```

3. Within the html tags, add the head element, along with the title:

   ```
   <head>
   <title>Structured HTML Document</title>
   </head>
   ```

4. Add the body element below the closing </head> tag:

   ```
   <body>

   </body>
   ```

Listing 1.5 shows a complete HTML 4.01 Strict Document that contains all the necessary components to begin working with HTML 4.01.

Listing 1.5: A Conforming HTML 4.01 Strict Document Template

```
<!DOCTYPE HTML PUBLIC "-//W3C//DTD HTML 4.01//EN"
    "http://www.w3.org/TR/html4/strict.dtd">

<html>
<head>
```

```
<title>Structured HTML Document</title>
</head>

<body>

</body>

</html>
```

Now that the necessary structural components are complete, you can add some content and structure according to the logical ideas described earlier in this chapter. Listing 1.6 shows my HTML 4.01 document with content. You can follow my lead, or be creative and add your own content.

 Be sure to use only structural markup when managing your content. Do not use visual presentation such as color, alignment, text styles, and so on. If you aren't sure about something, you can either try to look it up within the DTD, or better yet, wait till the end of this section, where you'll walk through validation. If you've got an error, the validator will let you know.

Listing 1.6: A Conforming HTML 4.01 Strict Document with Logical Styles

```
<!DOCTYPE HTML PUBLIC "-//W3C//DTD HTML 4.01//EN"
    "http://www.w3.org/TR/html4/strict.dtd">

<html>
<head>
<title>Structured HTML Document</title>
</head>

<body>

<h1>weblog</h1>

<p><em>left turn</em>
<h2>August 17, 2002</h2>

<p>Sitting at the light at Fort Lowell.  I'm facing East waiting to take a
left turn onto Campbell. Boys in a car next to me, shirtless in the summer
heat. The driver is tall, built. I can smell their beer sweat from here,
hear hardcore music pound.

<p>Not meaning to, I find myself staring at the young boy in the passenger
seat. He looks like someone I once knew.

<p>He sees me looking.  Suddenly, he comes up out of his seat in a leap of
ferocity. Or maybe, insanity. He throws himself across his friend, he's
reaching out the window for me, screaming.

<p>The light turns green so his friend takes off and I turn left.
```

```
<hr>

</body>

</html>
```

Save the document, as you'll be validating it in just a bit. Figure 1.12 shows the unstyled page. In Figure 1.13, you can see my content here as viewed from within my website.

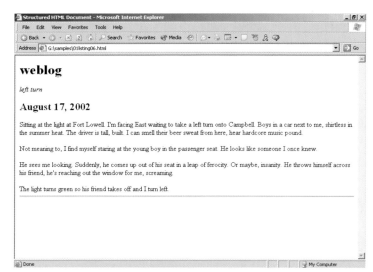

Figure 1.12: Unstyled markup

Figure 1.13: The styled entry at Molly.Com

Creating a Structured XHTML Document

The process here is essentially the same, although there are specific differences as noted earlier in terms of the XML Prolog and the XHTML syntax in use.

As with the prior exercise, open your favorite editor and begin a new document.

1. This time, you'll begin by adding the XML Prolog. Remember, this is recommended but not required, and in most cases it's best to leave it out of a document to avoid browser rendering problems. However, here you'll learn to include it.

   ```
   <?xml version="1.0" encoding="UTF-8"?>
   ```

2. Now add the DOCTYPE declaration. In this case, I've chosen XHTML 1.1, which is based on the XHTML 1 Strict DTD:

   ```
   <!DOCTYPE html PUBLIC "-//W3C//DTD XHTML 1.1//EN"
       "http://www.w3.org/TR/xhtml11/DTD/xhtml11.dtd">
   ```

3. Now, add the root element. Note that I've added both the open and closing tags:

   ```
   <html>

   </html>
   ```

4. Within the opening html tag, add the XML namespace for XHTML:

   ```
   <html xmlns="http://www.w3.org/1999/xhtml">
   ```

5. Within the html tags, add the head element, along with the title:

   ```
   <head>
   <title>Structured XHTML Document</title>
   </head>
   ```

6. Add the body element below the closing /head tag:

   ```
   <body>

   </body>
   ```

Save the document for validation. Listing 1.7 shows a complete XHTML 1.1 Strict Document that contains all the necessary components to begin working with XHTML 1.1.

Listing 1.7: A Conforming XHTML 1.1 Document Template (with XML Prolog)

```
<?xml version="1.0" encoding="UTF-8"?>

<!DOCTYPE html PUBLIC "-//W3C//DTD XHTML 1.1//EN"
    "http://www.w3.org/TR/xhtml11/DTD/xhtml11.dtd">

<html xmlns="http://www.w3.org/1999/xhtml">
<head>
<title>Structured XHTML 1.1 Document</title>
</head>

<body>

</body>

</html>
```

Now I'm going to add the same content to this document that I did to the HTML 4.01 document, but I will modify the document to be in conformance with XHTML. In this case, that means closing the non-empty paragraph elements and properly terminating the horizontal rule in accordance with XHTML.

Listing 1.8 shows the results.

Listing 1.8: XHTML 1.1 Document with Content

```
<?xml version="1.0" encoding="UTF-8"?>

<!DOCTYPE html PUBLIC "-//W3C//DTD XHTML 1.1//EN"
    "http://www.w3.org/TR/xhtml11/DTD/xhtml11.dtd">

<html xmlns="http://www.w3.org/1999/xhtml">
<head>
<title>Structured XHTML 1.1 Document</title>
</head>

<body>

<h1>weblog</h1>

<p><em>left turn</em></p>
<h2>August 17, 2002</h2>

<p>Sitting at the light at Fort Lowell.  I'm facing East waiting to take a
left turn onto Campbell. Boys in a car next to me, shirtless in the summer
heat. The driver is tall, built. I can smell their beer sweat from here,
hear hardcore music pound.</p>

<p>Not meaning to, I find myself staring at the young boy in the passenger
seat. He looks like someone I once knew.</p>

<p>He sees me looking.  Suddenly, he comes up out of his seat in a leap of
ferocity. Or maybe, insanity. He throws himself across his friend, he's
reaching out the window for me, screaming.</p>

<p>The light turns green so his friend takes off and I turn left.</p>

<hr />


</body>

</html>
```

Validating Your Documents

In this section, you'll use the W3C validator to test your documents. First, you'll test the HTML document, then the XHTML document. Then, you'll do some validation tests on your own.

Validating the Document

The W3C validator can validate a document online or by upload. To validate your document online, you'll first need to place it on a web server. To validate your document by upload, be sure you know the name and location of the document.

Then, follow these steps:

1. Point your web browser to `http://validator.w3.org/`.
2. If you are validating an online document, enter the address of your document in the Validate by URI address field. If you are uploading your file, click the Upload Files link and add the file from your hard drive. Leave all the other options as they are.
3. Select the Validate This Page or Validate This Document button. The validator will now compare your document to the DTD you described in the document.

First validate your HTML document, then repeat this step with your XHTML document. You may find that the validator returns errors as well as warnings. An error is a problem with the markup that must be fixed for the document to be valid. A warning provides you with information that might assist you in improving your document. Warnings will not affect your document's validity.

If any errors are reported, examine what they are, troubleshoot your document, make any necessary changes, and revalidate until your document passes the validation test.

Encoding Warnings

If you are uploading files, you will generate a warning with the HTML example here regarding proper encoding.

Encoding is ideally set on the server, so this error should not appear when you are validating from an online source, assuming your server is properly configured.

Note that a warning of this nature does not interfere with your document's validity; it's simply a means of alerting you to a potential problem.

Another means of adding encoding is to place the proper encoding information into a `meta` tag. The document using the XML prolog should not generate this warning on upload or online test because the prolog contains the encoding information. In this case, the encoding is the ISO character set for Latin-1 characters.

```
<meta http-equiv="Content-Type" content="text/html; charset=iso-8859-1" />
```

Setting your encoding in a `meta` tag will ensure that you do not receive this warning.

Validating Other Documents

At this point it will serve you well to begin validating other documents that you have been working on recently. Find a document that you know might be problematic (has font tags, uses nested tables, uses proprietary browser tags—anything like that will do). Then, try validating the document with a range of DTDs.

Next Steps

Now that you have a clear idea of the way markup works in a contemporary, standard fashion, it's time to dig into the real topic at hand: CSS.

In the next chapter, you will explore CSS principles, structure and syntax, and visual models.

In theory, there is no difference
between theory and practice;
In practice, there is.

—Chuck Reid

CHAPTER

Learning CSS Theory

You are by now well aware of the importance of separating document presentation from document structure. This process helps streamline your web documents and moves us into a future where document management, portability, and accessibility all co-exist with innovative visual design. You've had a look at HTML and XHTML, and you've seen how important it is to create documents that are logical and structured. It's time to focus our study on presentational design for web and web-related documents. This means learning the language of CSS.

In this chapter, you will learn:

- What CSS is and does
- How to integrate CSS with markup
- Important CSS concepts such as cascade, inheritance, and specificity
- Browser rendering models for CSS

What Is CSS, Really?

CSS is simply a *style language* that allows you to describe how to define presentational aspects of a document. It is not a difficult language per se. But it is complex.

 The term *style language* refers broadly to any language that influences the presentational properties of documents. Think of style as any design characteristic: typeface, background, text, link colors, margin controls, and placement of objects on a page.

Now that you have learned a little about the history and rationale of markup in Chapter 1, "Understanding Structured Markup," it's time to discover what the concepts of CSS embrace in theory, and how that theory in turn becomes practice.

Status of CSS

CSS Level 1 (CSS1) first became a W3C recommendation in 1996. The CSS Level 2 (CSS2) specification, which is the one most authors and browsers are currently interested in using and supporting, became a World Wide Web Consortium (W3C) recommendation in 1998. It's fascinating to think that CSS has been around in some form for quite a long time in web terms. But how frustrating to imagine that CSS, which has so much power and elegance, had to wait until the first part of this decade to even be considered for regular use.

CSS Level 3 (CSS3) is being developed. In its current draft form, CSS3 has been modularized in the sense that XHTML, too, has been modularized—that is, it's broken up into grouped sections such as text, lists, tables, and so on. The CSS3 specification describes aspects of CSS by its natural modules: fonts, backgrounds, color, and so on.

 The original specification for CSS1 is at www.w3.org/TR/REC-CSS1-961217. That spec was revised in 1999; the revision is at www.w3.org/TR/REC-CSS1. If you'd like to read the current CSS 2 spec, you can do so at www.w3.org/TR/REC-CSS2/. The CSS3 working draft is available at www.w3.org/TR/css3-roadmap/.

CSS can be used for HTML, XHTML, and XML documents. It's also important to note that CSS is not the only style language available. The Extensible Style Language (XSL), and the Extensible Style Language with Transformations (XSLT), can both be used with XHTML and XML documents, but these languages work significantly differently from CSS and are beyond the scope of this book.

 XSLT is an extremely powerful tool that allows designers and developers to manipulate the structure of a document. This allows authors to transform XML (including XHTML) into other document formats, including HTML, XHTML, and even PDF. If you're interested in XSLT, check out the XSLT working draft, www.w3.org/TR/xslt11/.

Principles of CSS

Just as with HTML and XHTML, CSS has a number of important principles. These principles were largely defined in CSS1, and CSS2 picks up on them as follows:

Compatibility The W3C created CSS to be both backward and forward compatible. Any browsers with CSS2 support should contain support for CSS1, and any browser with CSS1 support should read what it can of CSS2 style sheets and ignore what the browser doesn't recognize.

Structured CSS should be based on the structure of the documents to which they are attached. This is why it was so critical to study and understand the structure of documents as you did in Chapter 1 *prior to* creating CSS documents. Changing a style sheet should have no actual impact on the markup and content structure, but of course it will impact the presentation of that document.

Vendor, device, and platform independence Both CSS as a language and the documents to which CSS extends are ideally independent of any vendor, device, or platform. This independence was an original reason that the Web and HTML were developed in the first place. Part of the challenge at this point is to regain this independence, because it frees us of the heavy multibrowser, multiplatform testing responsibilities we've endured these past years.

Improvement of document maintenance Web designers and developers can manage the presentation of their documents much more efficiently with CSS. One style sheet can style countless documents, so managing style within a site means editing that style sheet and not the numerous, individual documents with which it is integrated.

Simplicity The language of CSS is simplistic and human readable—it's easy to understand just by looking at the code. CSS2 has turned out to be more complex than CSS1, and CSS3 will be even more complex than both, but there is a general goal to ensure that the properties within CSS are streamlined.

Performance Usually, the use of CSS will decrease the amount of overhead. Where previously you might have used complex tables and images to achieve layout, CSS will streamline your presentation as well as the number of requests sent to the server during an active session. Streamlining results in not only improved browser rendering of documents, but also better network performance.

Flexibility There are numerous ways to apply CSS, as you'll see later in the "Integrating Style" section later this chapter. This flexibility in application gives you much more choice in terms of how you use style in a given environment.

Richness As all designers reading this book are aware, the need for rich visual alternatives when designing sites is imperative. CSS addresses many of these concerns by providing designers with a variety of means to express visual ideas in the most efficient and accurate way.

Binding to other technologies CSS can be used along with other technologies, such as JavaScript, and its meaning can be altered by such scripts. This provides even deeper control for authors and designers, and it offers a means of using CSS as part of dynamic content development.

Accessibility By successfully separating structure from presentation with style sheets, you automatically end up with a more accessible document because the remaining document is logical and free of complicated tables. Beyond that, CSS features help make web documents more accessible by controlling fonts, reducing confusing and problematic table layouts and single-pixel GIF images, and providing access to multiple media outputs such as aural and Braille (see the next section, "Applications of CSS").

Certainly, realizing and furthering these goals depends on browser support. As with the goals of HTML and XHTML, these are ideals that, unfortunately, cannot always be reached due to the problems inherent to CSS support. As CSS support becomes more and more stable, the principles of CSS can be more readily achieved.

Important CSS Terms In order to follow the technical discussions in this book, it's important to get a feel for the language used to describe aspects of CSS. These terms are laid out in the CSS specifications and have precise meanings, and it's important to understand them before delving more deeply into the actual language.

Some of the terms most critical to this book include:

Style sheet A set of statements that describes the presentation of a given document. A *valid* style sheet must be written according to the grammar and rules of CSS; for example, a valid CSS2 sheet follows all the rules of the CSS2 specification. You'll look at the validation process for style in Chapter 3, "Writing CSS."

Source document, document The document or related documents to which a style sheet is applied. The *document language* refers to the language the document is written in, such as HTML, XHTML, or XML.

Element I discussed elements in detail in Chapter 1. An element is a tag or tagset and any of its related content. Elements in markup are critically important in CSS because they are the primary syntactical structure of the document language. As a result, you'll build many of your style rules based on elements.

Attribute A value that is associated with an element and consists of an attribute name and value, such as `align="right"`. Many attributes in markup are presentational and therefore ideally replaced with style sheets.

Content Any content that is associated with an element.

Document tree The tree of elements that evolves from the source document(s). An example of a simple document tree is in Chapter 1.

Canvas The area of the browser where the document is displayed.

Child A sub-element of a parent element.

Sibling An element that shares the same parent as another element.

User agent This is any program that interprets the document language and style sheet. A web browser, for example, is a user agent.

For more important CSS-related terminology, see `www.w3.org/TR/REC-CSS2/conform.html#q1` and `www.w3.org/TR/REC-CSS1#terminology`.

Applications of CSS

What's especially interesting is that CSS is not reserved for use only in the web browser; it's also used for a variety of media types. What's more, you can define multiple style sheets so your page can be differently rendered depending upon the media in question.

Style sheets can in fact describe the presentation of a document for the following types of delivery:

Aural Aural CSS is built primarily for speech synthesizers used by those with blindness. Aural style sheets allow you to define various aspects of how the document will be read, such as the volume and voice characteristics to use.

Braille and embossed Braille These media types allows you to use CSS to define the presentation of a document for output to Braille devices and printers.

Handheld This media type is used when styling a document's presentation in small devices such as PDAs, pagers, and cell phones.

Print Want your pages to look good in print as well as screen? Well, you can define print styles using the print media type to do just that.

Projection Styling documents for this media type allows authors to use their documents for projected presentations.

Screen The screen media type is for styling documents to appear onscreen.

TTY This media type is for use with devices having limited display features, such as teletype machines.

TV This media type is for television and related devices.

As with all aspects of CSS, if the browser doesn't have support for a given media type, that feature can't be used.

Now that you have an understanding of CSS's principles and application and an awareness of important terms, it's time to explore the various types of style sheets.

Integrating Style

Style can be delivered to a document by a variety of methods. The method with which style is connected with a document is referred to as *integration*. There are a variety of ways to integrate style, and how you decide to integrate style will depend largely upon what you are trying to accomplish with a specific document or number of documents.

Essentially, there are three main types of style sheets:

Author These are style sheets you create for your users. There are several ways of doing this, and you may find yourself using more than one method at a time.

User These are style sheets a user can create to view sites and even to override any author styles. These are rarely used, but they are interesting and have at least one important application, which I'll discuss in a bit.

User Agent This can be considered as the default browser style; it is the agent's own set of rendering behaviors. While this book isn't concerned with the User Agent styles, it's important to be aware of them.

In the following sections, you'll explore the primary methods of authoring style sheets for users, with a short discussion on user-defined styles.

Inline Style Sheets

The inline integration method allows you to take any tag and add a style to it. Using inline style gives you maximum control over a precise element of a web document, even just one character. Say you want to control the look and feel of a specific paragraph. You could simply add a `style="x"` attribute to the paragraph tag, and the browser would display that paragraph using the style values you added to the code.

Listing 2.1 shows an XHTML document with a simple inline style rule (in bold) that defines the header font as Arial. You'll read more about style rules in the "Exploring CSS Grammar" section later this chapter.

Listing 2.1: Inline Style   WWW.

```
<!DOCTYPE html PUBLIC "-//W3C//DTD XHTML 1.0 Transitional//EN"
    "http://www.w3.org/TR/xhtml1/DTD/xhtml1-transitional.dtd">

<html xmlns="http://www.w3.org/1999/xhtml">

<head>
```

```
<title>Inline Style Sample</title>

</head>

<body>

<h1 style="font-family: Arial">Welcome!</h1>

</body>

</html>
```

Figure 2.1 shows the results.

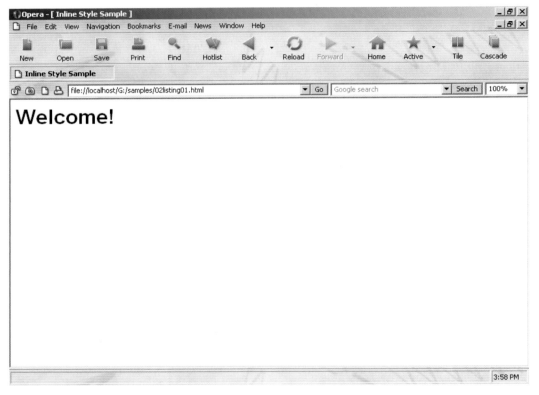

Figure 2.1: Using inline style

Inline style is useful for getting precise control over something in a single document, but because it only applies to the element in question, you most likely won't be using inline style as frequently as other integration methods.

Embedded Style Sheets

Embedding allows for control of a full document. Using the `style` element, which you place within the head section of a document, you can insert detailed style attributes to be applied to the entire page.

Embedding is an extremely useful way of styling individual pages that may also have other style methods influencing them. You can also style a single page or use multiple embedded sheets. The latter is especially useful if you'd like your document to have different styles for different media types.

In Listing 2.2, you'll see the same simple style rule I used in Listing 2.1, but this time within an embedded style sheet using the style element. I've also added the `type` attribute to define the MIME type of the sheet, and the `media` attribute to define this particular sheet to be used for presenting the document onscreen.

Listing 2.2: Embedded Style Sheet

WWW.

```
<!DOCTYPE html PUBLIC "-//W3C//DTD XHTML 1.0 Transitional//EN"
    "http://www.w3.org/TR/xhtml1/DTD/xhtml1-transitional.dtd">

<html xmlns="http://www.w3.org/1999/xhtml">

<head>

<title>Embedded Style Sample</title>

<style type="text/css" media="screen">

h1  {
    font: Arial;
}

</style>

</head>

<body>

<h1>Welcome!</h1>

</body>

</html>
```

As you can see, the style rule looks essentially the same as it did in the inline example, but it's now applied via the `style` element as opposed to the `style` attribute. Unlike the inline example, which applied only to that specific `h1`, this rule will apply to all the `h1` elements within the document, unless a class or inline style is applied.

Notice the inclusion of the type attribute in the style element shown in Listing 2.2. The type attribute is *required* in HTML 4 and XHTML documents. The attribute value, text/css, defines the MIME type of the style document. Be sure to use this attribute *every* time you define an embedded style sheet.

If you'd like to have a different style for a different media type, you can add another style sheet. In Listing 2.3, I show two embedded style sheets, the second one styled for print rather than screen.

Listing 2.3: Embedding Multiple Style Sheets

```
<!DOCTYPE html PUBLIC "-//W3C//DTD XHTML 1.0 Transitional//EN"
    "http://www.w3.org/TR/xhtml1/DTD/xhtml1-transitional.dtd">

<html xmlns="http://www.w3.org/1999/xhtml">

<head>

<title>Embedded Style Sample</title>

<style type="text/css" media="screen">

h1  {
    font: Arial;
}

</style>

<style type="text/css" media="print">

h1  {
    font: Times;
}

</style>


</head>

<body>

<h1>Welcome!</h1>

</body>

</html>
```

When the site visitor seeks to print preview (Figure 2.2) or print the document from a compliant browser, the print version will appear in the Times font rather than the Arial font.

Figure 2.2: Previewing the print style

Linked Style

Also referred to as an "external" style sheet, a linked style sheet contains as many style rules as you like and helps to provide a most powerful means for you to create master styles that you can apply to one page or one billion pages.

An external style sheet is exactly that—all of the style is placed in an external file. You can link to the style sheet from any document you wish, using the link element in the head portion of those documents with which you'd like to integrate the style.

The external style document is a text document that you can write in any editor or tool that allows you to save a document as text. To create a linked style sheet, follow these steps:

1. Open your text or HTML editor of choice.
2. Enter the style rule or rules you'd like. For the h1 rule in Listings 2.1 and 2.2, you'd type in the following:

```
h1  {
    font: Arial;
}
```

3. Select File ➢ Save and save your file with the name of h1style and a .css extension (style.css).

You'll notice that the CSS file contains no additional information and tags. This is because an external style sheet is simply a list of style rules. You may also use style sheet commenting (discussed later in the "Exploring CSS Grammar" section), but no declarations, elements, attributes, scripting, or other constructs should be in this document.

The next step is to link the document or documents you want to integrate with this style sheet:

1. In your document, place a link element within the head section. I'm using XHTML, so my link element, which is an empty element, uses the trailing slash, unlike HTML:

    ```
    <link />
    ```

2. Add the rel attribute, which describes the integration relationship type, in this case, a style sheet:

    ```
    <link rel="stylesheet" />
    ```

3. Add the type attribute and appropriate type, just as you would for an embedded sheet:

    ```
    <link rel="stylesheet" type="text/css" />
    ```

4. Include the media for which the sheet is intended. This can be any of the media types described earlier: print, screen, Braille, aural, and so on. In this instance, I'll use the screen value.

    ```
    <link rel="stylesheet" type="text/css" media="screen" />
    ```

5. Reference the source file using the href attribute and the location of the source file. In this case, both documents are residing in the same directory, so I'll reference it relatively:

    ```
    <link rel="stylesheet" type="text/css" media="all" href="style.css" />
    ```

6. Save your document as h1styletest.html.

Listing 2.4 shows the complete XHTML document with the link element included.

WWW. **Listing 2.4: The XHTML Document and External Style Sheet Are Now Integrated**

```
<!DOCTYPE html PUBLIC "-//W3C//DTD XHTML 1.0 Transitional//EN"
    "http://www.w3.org/TR/xhtml1/DTD/xhtml1-transitional.dtd">

<html xmlns="http://www.w3.org/1999/xhtml">

<head>

<title>Linked Style Sample</title>

<link rel="stylesheet" type="text/css" media="screen" href="style.css" />

</head>

<body>
```

```
<h1>Welcome!</h1>

</body>

</html>
```

Simply load your document into a style sheet compliant browser, and you'll see that the h1 will render using the Arial font.

As with embedded sheets, you can link to as many style sheets as required to achieve your goals. If you wanted to have a different print sheet, you'd create the external style sheet containing whatever rules you wanted for print display, save it with an appropriate name and the .css extension, and integrate that sheet using the link element within the document.

Listing 2.5 shows the document, now integrated with two external style sheets.

Listing 2.5: Multiple Linked Style Sheets Described in an XHTML Document

```
<!DOCTYPE html PUBLIC "-//W3C//DTD XHTML 1.0 Transitional//EN"
    "http://www.w3.org/TR/xhtml1/DTD/xhtml1-transitional.dtd">

<html xmlns="http://www.w3.org/1999/xhtml">

<head>

<title>Linked Style Sample</title>

<link rel="stylesheet" type="text/css" media="screen" href="style.css" />

<link rel="stylesheet" type="text/css" media="print" href="print.css" />

</head>

<body>

<h1>Welcome!</h1>

</body>

</html>
```

Using multiple linked sheets is a common practice, especially now that designers are working with CSS for layout but still dealing with legacy browsers. A CSS author might put all of the style rules for fonts and colors into one sheet and all the rules related to layout into another. And, as you can see here, the use of multiple sheets to address multiple device presentation is a particularly exciting and incredibly powerful aspect of CSS.

 The order in which you list your linked style is important because it will influence the order and manner in which the sheets are read and interpreted. For more information on this issue, see "About the Cascade" later this chapter.

Imported Styles

Imported styles work similarly to the linked style except that it uses the `@import` rule, a specialty rule that allows you to import a style sheet rather than link to it directly. Imported styles have inconsistent support so using linked style is typically recommended.

However, it's become a convention among designers and developers using CSS to exploit the *lack* of support for `@import` rules in certain browsers. This way, if a style isn't supported by a browser that doesn't support the `@import` rule, using `@import` means you can completely mask your imported styles from those browsers. This has become especially useful when using CSS for layout and attempting backward compatibility with certain problematic browsers. A more detailed example of this use is in Chapter 6, "Working with CSS Layouts."

Using the `@import` method involves creating an external sheet just as you would for linking purposes, and importing it into the document using the `@import` rule. Listing 2.6 shows how the external document created earlier, `style.css`, can be imported into an XHTML document.

Listing 2.6: Importing Style

```
<!DOCTYPE html PUBLIC "-//W3C//DTD XHTML 1.0 Transitional//EN"
    "http://www.w3.org/TR/xhtml1/DTD/xhtml1-transitional.dtd">

<html xmlns="http://www.w3.org/1999/xhtml">

<head>

<title>Linked Style Sample</title>

<style type="text/css" media="screen">@import "style.css";</style>

</head>

<body>

<h1>Welcome!</h1>

</body>

</html>
```

A compliant browser will now properly render the imported style, whereas a noncompliant browser will ignore the rule (Figure 2.3).

NOTE While you can use other embedded and linked sheets along with imported sheets, always place your imported sheets first within the head portion of your document to avoid potential rendering conflicts.

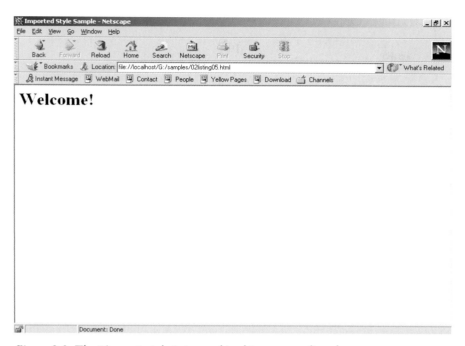

Figure 2.3: The @import *style is ignored in this noncompliant browser.*

User-Defined Style Sheets

While it's something you are rarely likely to use, a user-defined style sheet is any style sheet that the user can use to override other CSS and HTML or XHTML styles included in a document.

Most site visitors don't know how to do this, of course, so it's not something that's talked about a great deal. However, a user-defined style sheet can be helpful to anyone who requires special rendering of documents. If you have a certain type of color blindness or require your fonts to be quite large to read a document, the creation and implementation of such a sheet could be invaluable. For example, if you were colorblind you could create a sheet that would force all pages viewed to render with specific background and text colors that you can see. Similarly, you could use a user-defined sheet to ensure that all fonts appeared at a size that was readable to you.

Cascade, Inheritance, and Specificity

One of the powers of style sheets is that there is a hierarchy of relationships. These relationships are defined by the concepts of cascade, inheritance, and specificity within the language of CSS.

About the Cascade

Cascade refers to the method by which conflicts between style rules are resolved. As you've seen, multiple sheets and types of sheets can be used, each applied one after another. This creates a hierarchy of application. What's more, multiple rules can be applied, and which order these types of sheets and rules are interpreted by the browser relies on the concept of the cascade.

In terms of types of style sheets, you can combine inline, embedded, and linked styles, or any number of individual types of style sheets, for maximum control. Say you have a large site that you're controlling with a single style sheet. Now say you have a page on which you want to alter some of the styles. No problem. You can place the modified style as an embedded sheet within the individual page. The browser will first look for the embedded style and apply that information.

You also can override both styles by adding an inline style. When all three forms are in place, the CSS-compliant browser looks for inline style first, then the embedded style, and then the linked sheet; it reads the information in that order. But what happens if you have conflicting rules? The cascade exists to deal with that problem as follows:

1.   User agent styles (base styles defined within the web browser) are default.
2.   External style sheets will override user agent styles.
3.   Embedded style sheets will override external style sheets and user agent styles.
4.   Inline style sheets will override all.

NOTE   An exception is if the author marks a given rule as `!important`. In CSS2, any rule containing this demarcation overrides any other rule anywhere in the cascade.

To show how conflicts are resolved by the cascade, I created a document with an embedded sheet and inline styles in Listing 2.7.

In this case, one concept of cascade can be seen in action: the inline h1 style takes precedence over the embedded h1 style (see Figure 2.4).

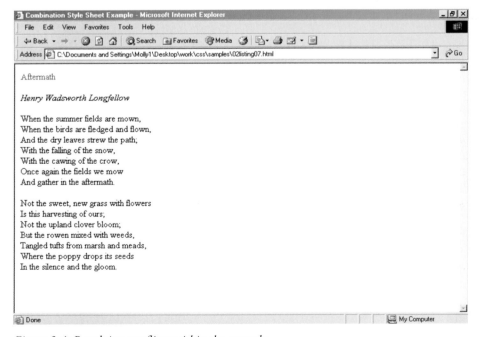

Figure 2.4: Resolving conflicts within the cascade

Listing 2.7: Conflicts between Style Sheets

```
<!DOCTYPE html PUBLIC "-//W3C//DTD XHTML 1.0 Transitional//EN"
    "http://www.w3.org/TR/xhtml1/DTD/xhtml1-transitional.dtd">

<html xmlns="http://www.w3.org/1999/xhtml">

<head>

<title>Combination Style Sheet Example</title>


<style type="text/css" media="all">

h1  {
    font: .85em Verdana;
    color: blue;
}

p  {
    font: .95em Verdana;
}

</style>
</head>

<body>
<h1 style="font-family: Times; font-size: .95em;">
Aftermath</h1>

<p><em>Henry Wadsworth Longfellow </em></p>

<p>When the summer fields are mown,<br />
When the birds are fledged and flown, <br />
And the dry leaves strew the path;<br />
With the falling of the snow,<br />
With the cawing of the crow,<br />
Once again the fields we mow<br />
And gather in the aftermath.  </p>

<p> Not the sweet, new grass with flowers<br />
Is this harvesting of ours;<br />
Not the upland clover bloom;<br />
But the rowen mixed with weeds,<br />
Tangled tufts from marsh and meads,<br />
Where the poppy drops its seeds<br />
In the silence and the gloom.</p>

</body>
</html>
```

Another example of a cascade concept within CSS is the use of multiple external sheets in the same document:

```
<head>
<link rel="stylesheet" type="text/css" href="molly1.css" />
<link rel="stylesheet" type="text/css" href="molly2.css" />
<link rel="stylesheet" type="text/css" href="molly3.css" />
</head>
```

If there are conflicts between rules (as shown in Listing 2.6), the *last* style sheet in this list will first apply any styles that aren't in the middle one, and the middle one will then apply any styles that aren't in the first one. And, as mentioned earlier, any imported style sheets *must* come first in the hierarchy to be properly interpreted.

Inheritance

Other factors influence the way CSS rules apply. One predominant concept is *inheritance*. Inheritance relies on the document tree, which defines specific elements as ancestral and descendant, depending on where in the structure they exist.

The body element contains other markup that describes the way the content of the page is displayed: headers, paragraphs, lists, images, and so on. All elements within the body are considered descendants of the body element.

This concept continues down the tree hierarchy. Think of it as a family tree, in fact. If you have a paragraph, the elements directly descended from that paragraph are the children of that parent, and so on. This system is referred to as *containment hierarchy*.

Inheritance claims that unless you specify differently, a style will be inherited by the child of a parent. For example, if you write a style asking that a specific text color be applied to a paragraph, all tags within that paragraph will inherit that color unless you state otherwise. So, if you write:

```
<p style="color: blue">Speaking of style, I bought the <em>best</em> pair
of shoes in Las Vegas.</p>
```

The entire paragraph will appear in blue (see Figure 2.5), even the content within the em element because, in this case, that element is a child of the parent element, p.

There are two exceptions to inheritance. The first is any technical exception within the specification, and the second is, of course, any failure on a web browser's part to properly interpret inheritance.

Technical exceptions include such CSS properties as related to the box model (where every element can generate a box; see the "Understanding Visual Models" section later this chapter): margins, padding, backgrounds, and borders. This is not an oversight of the specification, it's an intentional exception. In the parent-child example above if a margin property had been set for the paragraph, the emphasis element would conceivably inherit that margin, adding unwanted visuals to your pages and forcing you to write more rules to undo what inheritance would do in that context. Thus CSS prevents some properties, like those that set margins, from inheriting.

Browser exceptions are naturally the most frustrating inheritance exceptions. Writing your CSS based upon the proper structure of documents can help you avoid problems with inheritance because you will have a clear idea of which elements exist within the tree and what their relationships are.

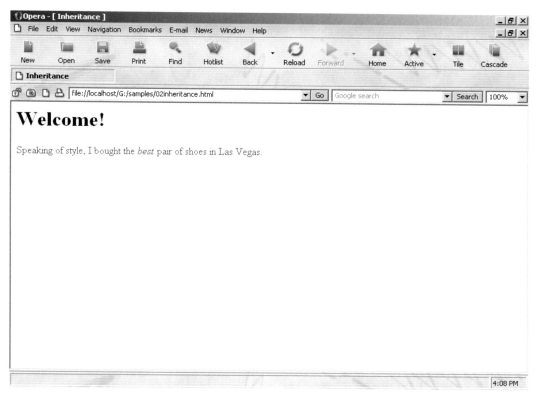

Figure 2.5: The child element inherits from the parent.

Specificity

Yet another component of CSS that works to resolve conflicts within rules is *specificity*. Specificity explains the importance (also referred to as *weight*) of a given rule within a style sheet.

    Specificity is broken down by selector types. Selectors are described in greater detail in the "Exploring CSS Grammar" section later this chapter. Different kinds of selectors are given different kinds of weight within CSS. An id, for example, carries more weight than a simple selector such as p. That means that any rule relating to the id will have higher specificity than the rule pertaining to the p, and if there are any conflicts between the style rules for id and p, the rule related to id, having greater weight, will be the style that is applied.

 Inherited values have no specificity at all, not even a specificity of zero. This automatically means that any rule you write for an inherited value has more weight than the inheritance. If I wrote a rule for the child element em in the example in this section, that rule would override the inherited styles from the parent element p.

Exploring CSS Grammar

CSS is a language and has clearly defined grammar. In this section, you'll learn the components of a style rule. Style rules can be compared to a sentence: they have individual pieces, just like nouns and verbs that must exist in a specific order. In this section, you'll learn about selectors (complex but primary building blocks within a rule), style properties, and how selectors and style properties combine to create rules. You'll also learn to create classes—a custom means of applying style—understand the role of IDs, and how to use grouping, which is a form of CSS shorthand, to more easily write your rules.

Selectors

Selectors are CSS constructs that identify the elements within your markup that will receive the properties and values you assign. In CSS2, there are 14 kinds of selectors: the original seven from the CSS1 specifications with some modifications and an additional seven.

 NOTE: Not all selector types are supported in all browsers. This section will provide you with the general information, and as you work through the book using different kinds of selectors, you'll learn how to use them more explicitly.

Element Selectors

An element selector refers directly to an HTML (or XHTML) element. So, the CSS selector h2 corresponds to any h2 element in the documents with which it is integrated.

Style sheets will typically begin with element selectors, because you are taking the document tree structure and denoting each element for which you'd like a style. You'll create rules made up of other CSS components to go along with these selectors, and these rules will be placed in a declaration block. Here's a selector and an empty declaration block:

```
h1  {
}
```

If I have a simple document containing all the required elements and then some content style with h1, h2, h3 headers, paragraphs, and an unordered list, I could prepare a list of related CSS selectors along with declaration blocks, as follows:

```
body  {
}

h1  {
}

h2  {
}

h3  {
}
```

```
p  {
}

ul  {
}

li  {
}
```

As you can see, these element selectors look exactly like their corresponding HTML or XHTML elements, except they do not have the angle brackets surrounding them. Any rules written for these selectors will apply to all instances of the element *unless* another rule is in place for a particular selector.

 Declaration blocks in CSS always begin and end with a curly brace. Individual rules within a block are completed with a semicolon. The way blocks are authored will vary depending upon the preference of the author. Some authors prefer to write the selector and keep the declaration block all on one line (for example, h1 {   }), whereas other authors fashion their style sheets to look similar to the method in this book.

Class Selectors

In CSS you can create class selectors, which provide you with infinitely more design options than an element selector. Class selectors are integrated into your documents using the `class` attribute within any opening tag of the element to which you'd like to apply the class. There are two variants of class selectors: general and specific.

A general class selector is any class you create denoted by a dot and then the class name. To create a class called "small" that will provide a smaller size text alternative for any element, I'd write the class:

```
.small
```

Later, once the associated rule is written (for example, .blue {font-size: 10px;}), I would then add the `class` attribute to the element I would like to influence:

```
<a class="small">What's new</a>
```

This paragraph will now appear with the rule associated with the class, `.small`. I can use this class anywhere that makes sense.

To apply the same presentational aspects of this class to a paragraph on my page, I'd write:

```
<p class="small">This month finds us working on several important home
projects. We're ripping up the carpet on the stairs and replacing it with
wood. It's a lot of work, but the results are looking great!</p>
```

My paragraph will now appear in the smaller style I created, but any other paragraphs or elements on the page will not, unless I use this class, or another style rule that defines the same font and size, with a given element.

A more specific way of writing class selectors is to relate them to an element selector. This means you can only apply the class to that particular element. You write these selectors by first denoting the element, then the class:

```
p.small
```

You can write as many specific classes for an element as you like; for example:

```
p.small  {
     font-size: 10px;
}

p.medium  {
     font-size: 12px;
}

p.large  {
     font-size: 14px;
}
```

And so forth. The main advantage to using a more specific class attribute is that it prevents any overlap. Specific rules can't apply to an element for which they are not written. On the other hand, the flexibility of a general class can be a particularly powerful and streamlined approach to creating broad styles that can be applied to any element.

ID Selectors

ID selectors are quite similar to class selectors, but there are some differences—both semantic and behaviorally.

From a semantic perspective, ID selectors are written differently from class selectors. Instead of the dot (.) followed by the class name, you use a hash mark (#) followed by the ID name:

```
#section1
```

And, instead of using the class attribute, you use the id attribute when integrating the style into your HTML or XHTML document:

```
<div id="section1">This is the first division on my page.</div>
```

Behaviorally, the importance of IDs is that they relate to one element and one element only. While classes can be broadly or specifically applied, they can by nature refer to numerous elements. An ID is only allowed to be used once, as in the preceding example. What you should *not* do is the following:

```
<h1 id="section1">Welcome!</h1>
<div id="section1">This is the first division on my page.</div>
```

Interestingly, many browsers will forgive you and still interpret your style rules if you do this. However, it's bad form—not just because it goes against the syntax, but also because IDs are a critical piece of many dynamic events. If you inadvertently use multiple IDs with the same value, you can interfere with the proper interpretation of any dynamic content.

Contextual (Descendant) Selectors

You probably won't be using this type of selector too much, but descendant selectors do provide a fine level of control if you're looking to combine aspects of inherited style.

If you look at the earlier example of the parent-child relationship between a paragraph with an emphasis element within it, you'll see how descendant selectors can work. In that example, the em element and its contents inherited the rule features from the parent element, p.

If you want to assign a different style rule to the descendant element, you can use the syntax provided by the descendant selector to do so. Place the parent element first, then the descendant element, with only a space between them:

```
p em
```

Then, whatever you write in the ensuing declaration block will apply to the descendant selector. Keep in mind that the rule specified for this selector won't apply to any other em elements on the page, *only* those em elements that are descendants of paragraphs.

Pseudo Class Selectors

Used most frequently to style links, pseudo class selectors can also be used for other purposes, such as adding a hover effect to any element, whether it's a link or not.

What's especially powerful about pseudo class selectors when used with links is that you can combine these selectors with class selectors to create multiple link styles that can be applied to a single page—something you could never do with HTML or XHTML alone.

Link pseudo class selectors begin with the anchor selector, followed by a colon and the pseudo class name. The available conventional link pseudo class selectors are as follows:

```
a:link
a:visited
a:hover
a:active
```

You can then write rules for each of these class selectors and they will apply globally to all normal links.

 The pseudo class selectors :active and :hover are also classified as "dynamic" pseudo classes, which are discussed in the "Dynamic Pseudo Class Selectors" section later in this chapter.

As mentioned, you can combine these selectors with a class, which enables you to create multiple link styles. To do this, you begin with the anchor, followed by a dot, then the class name, followed by the colon and pseudo class. Some examples include:

```
a.main:link
a.subnav:link
a.footer:link
```

In these examples, the links with the classes of main, subnav, and footer can each have different style rules created for them.

If you have problems using link pseudo classes and find that aspects of your style aren't applying properly, it's possible that you are having trouble with specificity. Pseudo classes have an equal specificity between them and with HTML element selectors. This means that the selector occurring *last* will win out over the others. You must follow the link/visited/hover/active order of these selectors within your style sheet, or you may have unpredictable results.

Pseudo Element Selectors

Taking its cue from the print world, which has many conventions when it comes to displaying various typographic elements, CSS provides its authors with some means of grabbing on to these conventions.

As of CSS2, there are a total of four pseudo element selectors to assist you in achieving your typographic goals. Table 2.1 shows the four pseudo element selectors and describes their purpose.

Table 2.1: Pseudo Element Selectors in CSS2

Selector	Purpose
:first-line	To select and apply style to the first line in a given element
:first-letter	To select and apply style to the first letter in an element
:before	Allows content specified in the style sheet to be inserted before a given element
:after	Allows content specified in the style sheet to be inserted after a given element

To apply a different style to the first line in a paragraph, use the syntax for the pseudo element:

```
p:first-line
```

If you want to add content before or after an element, you need to define that content within the style sheet. This is an unusual quirk of CSS in that you're actually placing content in the sheet, which goes against the main concept of separating presentation from the document and its structure and content! This process is referred to as *generated content* and the practice is not generally recommended because of this conflict.

 To learn more about generated content, please see www.w3.org/TR/REC-CSS2/generate.html.

To generate content using the before and after pseudo selectors, you define the element to which the rule should be applied, the before or after pseudo element, the content property, and the content in quotes:

```
h1:after {
    content: "header note"
}
```

In supporting browsers (which at this writing include only Opera and Gecko-based browsers), you'll see the words "header note" appear after every h1 in the document.

 NOTE You cannot use any HTML or XHTML elements within the content value.

Selector Groups

Selector groups allow you to group selectors together that will all receive the same style. This provides a shorthand method for you, cutting down on authoring time, and ensures that these styles are applied consistently.

To make all headers have the same font, instead of writing individual rules for all the header levels in a document, you can group those elements by placing them all on one line, separated by commas:

```
h1, h2, h3 {font-family: Arial, sans-serif;}
```

Now the rule you apply to this group will correspond to all of those elements within the document.

Dynamic Pseudo Class Selectors

This rather cool selector type allows you to add pseudo selector intelligence to anything other than links, which of course have their own pseudo classes.

Table 2.2 shows the three available dynamic pseudo class selectors and their purpose.

Table 2.2: Dynamic Pseudo Class Selectors

Selector	Purpose
:hover	Applies the style rule only when the mouse hovers over the selected element
:active	Applies style when the element is clicked
:focus	Applies style when the element has the keyboard focus (such as when the cursor is placed in a form's text box)

You can do some creative things with dynamic pseudo class selectors, especially with elements that are by nature interactive, such as forms. Using CSS this way instead of scripting is a very efficient way to achieve dynamic visual effects.

 NOTE As with pseudo class selectors, you can add a class selector to dynamic pseudo class selector for even richer options.

Language Pseudo Class Selectors

This fascinating selector helps to address language concerns, which is especially interesting in light of the work being done with internationalization, as discussed in Chapter 1.

Unfortunately, the support for this feature is currently limited, but with growing focus on internationalization-related topics, browser support should improve.

> For current browser tests with Language Pseudo Class Selectors, please see www.meyerweb.com/eric/css/tests/css2/.

In HTML and XHTML, you can denote an element as a specific language by using the `lang` attribute:

```
<p lang="es">Bienvenidos a todo!</p>
```

With language pseudo class selectors, you can now select an element based on its language encoding. You denote the selector, the `:lang` pseudo class selector, and the language value in parentheses:

```
p:lang(es)
```

Now you can provide styles for the language in question, which will be especially helpful for multilingual document presentation.

> You can find a list of language codes at www.oasis-open.org/cover/iso639a.html.

Child Selectors

Descendant (contextual) selectors allow you to style a child element separately from its parent. But what happens if you have deeply nested elements? For example, you can have numerous em elements in a division element, `div`, and paragraphs within that division can also have strong elements.

If you wrote the following descendant selector:

```
div strong
```

all of the strong elements within the `div`—even those within paragraph elements (the grand-children)—would be affected due to inheritance.

Child selectors allow you to choose *only* the child. That means you can be sure that only the em elements within the `div`, and *not* those within other structures nested in the `div`, will be affected. To achieve this, you begin by using the element, a right angle bracket, and the child element in question:

```
div>em
```

You can get even more complex. If you want to choose only the em elements within the paragraph elements within the `div`, write the selector as follows:

```
div>p>em
```

All the children within a p element, but not outside of one, will be styled with the ensuing rule.

First Child Selectors

A first child selector allows even greater precision. This type of selector applies only to the first child of a given element. To apply a style to a first child only, supply the parent element plus the first child selector syntax:

```
p:first-child
```

Any rule you write for this selector will be applied to the first child of every paragraph only.

 Support for first child selectors is still very limited in browsers.

Adjacent Selectors

Adjacent selectors help you style sibling elements. Sibling elements are those elements that reside on the same level of a document tree and share a common parent. Consider the following:

```
<p>I find books by <a http://www.marthagrimes.com/">Martha Grimes</a>
to be the quintessential escapist experience. A good mystery and a
<a href="http://www.adagioteas.com/">cup of tea</a> on a rainy day is
true relaxation.</p>
```

In this example, both anchor elements are siblings to one another because they share the parent element of the paragraph.

Styling an adjacent selector means being less concerned with the containment hierarchy, however, and more interested in the order of siblings within a parent element. An adjacent selector allows you to style one sibling that follows another. The syntax is to define the elements that are adjacent by using a plus sign (+):

```
th+td
```

With this example, you can create rules for your table headers and then describe a rule that uses the adjacent sibling selector to ensure that a table cell appearing right after a table header in the same row takes the defined style. And yes, there's very poor browser support for adjacent selectors, too.

Attribute Selectors

This fascinating type of selector also has pretty weak support, but attribute selectors are powerful because they enable you to select elements based on the attributes they have. For example, if you have a link with a particular URL, you can style by that instead of by the anchor element itself. Every instance of that URL is then styled according to the rule associated with that attribute selector.

There are four matching patterns available for attribute selectors, as described in Table 2.3.

The level of control that can be gained by using this type of selector is quite amazing when you think about it. By providing a means of selecting based on an element's attributes—and even going beyond to describe the selector based on attribute values—you can make complex decisions about how to efficiently style multiple element types within a document.

Table 2.3: Attribute Matching

Syntax	Purpose
[att]	Apply the style to a given attribute, no matter the value
[att=val]	Apply the style to a given attribute with a specific value
[att~=val]	Apply the style to any attributes with space-separated specified values
[att|=val]	Apply the style to any attributes with hyphen-separated values

Properties, Declarations, Rules

So far, you've examined a style sheet's most basic relationship: selector to element or attribute. The connecting of a selector to an element or attribute is where CSS and markup become integrated, and there's no doubt that selector types are a particularly complex aspect of CSS.

Fortunately, some relief comes with the way rules for selectors are created. It's a pretty straightforward relationship at this point. Once you describe a selector, you add CSS properties. As a selector relates primarily to a given element, a property relates to the aspects you'd like that element to have. If you have a paragraph as a selector, properties you include within a rule help to describe the paragraph's features.

Properties in CSS are numerous and fall into the following three general categories, based on their associated media group:

Visual Any properties influencing the visual representation of a document such as fonts, backgrounds, and colors.

Aural Properties relating to aural style, such as voice features.

Paged Properties relating to paged media such as print and screen.

As with literal attributes within markup, a property requires a name and a value. Here are two examples of CSS properties and a corresponding value:

```
font-family: Arial, sans-serif
color: blue
```

A property and a value combine to create a *declaration*, as in the previous examples. A selector plus a declaration form a *rule*:

```
body  {
      font-family: Arial, sans-serif;
}
```

Notice the syntax here: curly brackets to contain the declaration block (or multiple declarations) for the rule; semicolons ending each declaration. So, if you have multiple declarations within a rule, you separate them by semicolons:

```
body  {
      font-family: Arial, sans-serif;
      color: blue;
}
```

Note that my indentations are my personal style—as long as you follow the convention of placing the selector first, followed by declarations within brackets and each separated by a semicolon, you can find your own style of creating style! The previous CSS rule could just as easily be written like the following and still be perfectly correct:

```
body   {font-family: Arial; color: blue;}
```

To summarize:

- A declaration is made up of a property and a value.
- A rule is comprised of a selector and a declaration block.
- A style sheet contains at least one rule and can contain as many rules as you require.

You can find a listing of all the properties, their related values, and their media groups at www.w3.org/TR/REC-CSS2/propidx.html.

Shorthand Properties

Shorthand properties (also referred to as *grouping*) are a way to write a shorthand version of style rules. There are really only a few shorthand properties when compared to the full list of properties. Shorthand properties, the properties they can represent, and the media group(s) to which they belong are described in Table 2.4.

Table 2.4: Shorthand Properties in CSS2

Shorthand	Included Properties	Media Group
background	background-attachment background-color	visual
	background-image background-position background-repeat	
border	border-color border-style border-width	visual
border-bottom	border-bottom-color border-bottom-style border-bottom-width	visual
border-left	border-left-color border-left-style border-left-width	visual
border-right	border-right-color border-right-style border-right-width	visual
border-top	border-top-color border-top-style border-top-width	visual
cue	cue-before cue-after	aural

Table continues on next page

Table 2.4: Shorthand Properties in CSS2 *continued*

font	font-family font-size font-style font-weight font-variant line-height	visual
list-style	list-style-image list-style-position list-style-type	visual
margin	margin-top margin-right margin-bottom margin-left	visual
outline	outline-color outline-style outline-width	visual, interactive
padding	padding-top padding-right padding-bottom padding-left	visual
pause	pause-after pause-before	aural

You've already seen an example of shorthand when looking at grouped element selectors:

```
h1 h2 h3
```

You've also seen them with declarations:

```
p  {
    font-family: Arial, sans-serif;
    font-size: 16px;
    font-weight: bold;
    font-style: normal;
    line-height: 15px;
    color: black;
}
```

Fortunately, you can choose to use the font property, which is a shorthand property, and stack the values within the declaration. As a result, you can make the previous rule a lot more streamlined:

```
p  {
    font: bold normal 16px/15px Arial, sans-serif;
}
```

The major concern when grouping is the order of values. A good example of this is when working with the margin property: you must follow the property with top, right, bottom, and left margin values *in that order*. You can use the acronym TRBL or mnemonic Trouble to help remember this margin order.

```
body  {
    margin: .10in .75in. .75in. .10in;
}
```

No commas appear between individual values when values are grouped. The declaration should end with a semicolon.

Commenting CSS

There's a specific technique for creating comments in CSS, as well as a means of hiding embedded CSS from older browsers.

Comments in CSS begin with a slash (/) and an asterisk (*) and end with an asterisk and a slash:

```
/* add your comment here. The comment can be as long as you need it to be */
```

As with comments in HTML and XHTML, you can place these anywhere in the document and browsers will not seek to interpret what's within them. However, do not use HTML and XHTML comments (<!-- -->) within the style sheet itself.

You can, however, use them within HTML and XHTML documents to "hide" embedded style from browsers with no CSS support. This is a widely used practice. Without the comments, browsers that don't support the style element might try to render the style information even though the style information sits within the head portion of the document:

```
<head>
<style type="text/css">
<!--
body  {
      font-family: Arial;
      color: blue;
}
-->
</style>
</head>
```

Many designers and developers are not worried about those few browsers out there that have this kind of issue and have dropped the practice of commenting out style sheets. In fact, there are a few early browsers that don't deal well with comments, and those browsers may have rendering problems due to the comments and not the style.

 One limited but remaining concern is that some search engine technologies will index CSS as regular content unless it's commented out. Because embedded sheets sit in the head of the document, the actual CSS could end up on the search results page rather than meta-information, or along with it.

Understanding Visual Models

CSS works on a visual formatting model provided in the CSS specifications. This model helps define how web browsers process a document tree.

The visual model provides a means for every element in the tree to generate a box (or not). This is referred to as the *box model*. The means by which boxes are laid out within a page rely on this model (see Figure 2.6).

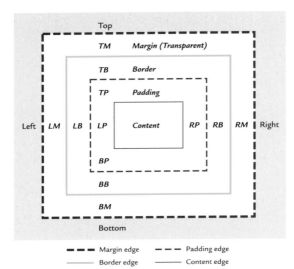

Figure 2.6:
The box model

The box model in turn relies on a number of governing rules in order to display properly. Implementations of the box model have been different in major browsers, causing problems with consistency and forcing several workarounds for layout, which you'll be reading about in Chapter 6.

 You can read the visual formatting model specifications for CSS2 here: www.w3.org/TR/REC-CSS2/visuren.html.

Box generation relies in part on the type of element the box will be generated for. There are two primary types of elements of note:

Block-Level Elements A block-level element is one that is visually formatted as a box. Block-level elements can contain both inline elements and other block-level elements. Typically, these elements start on a new line. Examples include: h1-h6, p, form, table, ol, ul.

Inline Elements An inline element is one that appears within the content, and may contain text or other inline elements. Usually there is no break after an inline element. Examples include: a, em, strong, img, input.

 A third type of element, known as a *list-item* element, is considered unique because it uses the li element, which maintains order by generating presentational markers such as bullets or numbers. The list-item element normally behaves like an inline element, which, unlike a block-level element, has no break.

A block-level element generates a *principal box*. This is a primary box that has the capacity to contain other boxes, or other block-level elements. I like to think of this as being like the old Chinese lacquered boxes that come nested inside one another. The largest box is the principal box, and the smaller boxes contained within it relate to other block-level children of the main parent element's box.

With inline elements, boxes are laid out on the horizontal with what is referred to as a *line box*.

Every box is broken down into the following areas:

Content area (text, objects) A content area has a *content edge* that surrounds the elements actual contents.

Padding Padding edges surround a box's padding.

Borders The border edge denotes a box's border.

Margins The margin edge surrounds the box margin and is further defined by its specific edges: left, right, top, bottom.

   If a margin has a width of 0, it becomes the same as the border edge. If the border edge has a width of 0, it becomes the same as the padding edge. If a padding edge has a width of 0, it becomes the same as the content edge.

Common ways to position CSS elements include:

Static A static box has normal flow based on its block or inline features.

Float A floating box shifts to the left or right.

Absolute position An absolute box is positioned specifically using demarcations along the *x-y* axis.

Relative position A relative box is positioned relative to where that box is expected to be within the flow of the document.

 As mentioned, problems with the box model exist because of different implementations in browsers. Owen Briggs writes a clear overview of this problem in his article "Content Placement Blues," which includes additional resources: www.thenoodleincident.com/tutorials/box_lesson/content_placement/text.html.

You'll get a deeper dose of what all this means to design in Chapter 6. For now, it's important to understand the basics of the model so you can begin envisioning the way CSS really works.

Next Steps

Well, you've got a lot of theory under your belt now. You not only understand the value of structured markup as studied in Chapter 1, but you've got a thorough view of the fundamental issues in CSS.

   The time has come to start practicing! In Chapter 3, you'll go through numerous exercises that are mapped to the theory in this chapter. This way, the theory doesn't remain amorphous. You'll study how to prepare a CSS document, write, classify, and group rules effectively, and use a range of selectors and properties so as to see the way they really work. You'll also learn about CSS validation, which can be very helpful to you when learning CSS.

> *It is not what you put on the canvas that the reader sees.*
>
> —Elie Wiesel

three

Writing CSS

So far, you've read a lot of theory and semantics—all important, but not very gratifying in terms of results! In this chapter, you'll have a chance to apply your newfound knowledge hands-on. While the focus here is primarily to get you used to authoring organized markup and CSS, you will get a chance to explore some CSS properties and apply style with more depth.

In this chapter you will learn:

- How to prepare your markup for CSS
- Writing rules
- How to validate your CSS

Preparing Your Documents

Last chapter we discussed that there were several means of integrating style sheets. You also had a chance to read about the cascade, inheritance, and specificity—all important concepts when it comes to constructing a style sheet.

While inline style and user style can be important, the detail work when using CSS is in linked and embedded sheets. Imported sheets are also important, particularly when trying to separate text styles from layout styles in working around problems in Netscape 4.*x*.

For this chapter, the focus will be on creating styles suitable for use in embedded, linked, and imported sheets. First, you'll prepare a markup example for external CSS, then you'll begin applying rules.

 To create embedded rules, use the style element in the head portion of the document. For details, see Chapter 2, "Learning CSS Theory."

As mentioned, your markup documents should be well structured. This is where you'll find the initial information for preparing your style sheets, because your markup provides the framework of the document tree. Consider Listing 3.1, which is a fairly long but realistic listing containing the kind of elements and content you'd find on a web page, in this case, a personal web log, or "Blog."

WWW.

Listing 3.1: Examining a Document to Be Styled

```
<!DOCTYPE html PUBLIC "-//W3C//DTD XHTML 1.0 Strict//EN"
    "http://www.w3.org/TR/xhtml1/DTD/xhtml1-strict.dtd">

<html xmlns="http://www.w3.org/1999/xhtml" xml:lang="en">

<head>
    <title>Adventures in England</title>
</head>

<body>

<h1>Wednesday June 6, 2002</h1>

<p>Heathrow airport has to be one of the ugliest airports I've ever seen,
and I've seen a lot of them. It looks like some kind of post-modern
industrial nightmare, is horribly lighted, has no circulating air to speak
of, and I thought I would grow old and gray waiting for my luggage.</p>

<p>But then things started getting fun. At the taxi stand I got my first
"alo, luv!" and a lot of good-natured, flirtatious joking from the cabbies.
My brother <a title="email linus" href="mailto:kafka@desert.net">Linus</a>
swore to me that all drivers in the UK know where they're going. As it
turns out, my driver wasn't precisely sure where my hotel was located so he
checked with his pals. This turned into quite a drama among the boys, but I
was comforted by the taxi stand manager. He had one of those great faces
that makes you want to immortalize it in paint, ink, or photo. About my
driver, the stand manager said: "Not to worry, luv, he knows where he's
going. If he makes any mistakes, just smack him on the head." Works for me.
Actually, my driver turned out to be positively wonderful, full of helpful
information and details about this and that.</p>

<p>Once out of the airport came the first glimpse of everything I'd
imagined England to be: Pleasantly humid, overcast, and  with gently
swelling green hills, swaying grasses, horses in a pasture, a thatched-roof
cottage.</p>

<p>If it weren't for the Burger King, the Holiday Inn, and the massive
Glaxo/Smith Klein complex, I really might have confused it all for New
Jersey.</p>

<h2>Enter, London</h2>

<p>Along the drive from Heathrow to my hotel, I got to see, well, gee,
almost everything one is supposed to see in London: The Tower of London,
the London Eye, the Tower Bridge, the Queen's digs. I arrived the day after
her Majesty's Jubilee, looks like it was one <em>hell</em> of a party from
the mess left behind.</p>
```

```
<p>The most striking thing to me so far is the mixing of old and new in
everything here. Architecture, fashion, you name it. The other intriguing
thing is how truly contemporary many things about London are.  As a media
person, I find the advertising especially fascinating, fun, hip, really
more sophisticated than anything I've ever seen in the US.</p>

<p><img src="blog-images/docklands1.jpg" width="200" height="100"
alt="photo: docklands wharf building" />   <img src="blog-
images/docklands2.jpg" width="200" height="100" alt="photo: view of
buildings across the thames" /></p>

<p>I'm staying in the <a title="learn more about the history of the
docklands" href="http://www.lddc-history.org.uk/">Docklands</a>, for those
unfamiliar this is the old dock areas right along the Thames. Tons of wharf
buildings and old council houses have been gentrified into new flats and
office space, as well as new buildings, shops, and what-not being built.
Very reminiscent of San Francisco's South of Market, but the architecture
is better. I took a long walk along the river front this morning, it is
quite beautiful in its way.</p>

<p>Everyone always talks about the bad English food.  My first English meal
was <em>wonderful</em>.  I had to do it: Fish and Chips and a pint of ale.
I ate that meal in a pub complete with high-backed leather chairs and
pictures of old sea captains on the wall. It was a truly great meal and
I'll remember it always.</p>

<h2>News of the Day</h2>

<p>Along with Jubilee, there's the World Cup, and with yesterday's
spectacular game between the Irish and Germans, well, I got instantly
caught up in the vibe. I think all of London was yelling hurrah at the tie
goal. There was a band of Germans in the pub watching the post-game
commentary. They appeared to be more silent and morose than usual, if
that's possible. I have no sympathy.</p>

<p>And then, there was breakfast this morning.  Goodness, here I found all
the reasons people make fun of English food.  You can have yer back bacon
and black pudding, thank you very much.  The mushrooms were fine, though,
as was the hot tea, of course. I drank so much of it I'm buzzing around
like a fly.</p>

<p><img src="blog-images/docklands3.jpg" width="200" height="100"
alt="photo: nelson pier" />   <img src="blog-
images/docklands4.jpg" width="200" height="100" alt="photo: walkway over
old dry dock" /></p>

<h2>Random observations:</h2>
```

```
<ul>
<li>Interesting pub name seen along the way: "The Hung Drawn and Quartered"
(note lack of punctuation)</li>
<li>Sign says: "Please watch the step" as opposed to "Please watch
<em>your</em> step"</li>
<li>The lift in my hotel claims to fit five people. Yeah, right. It's the
size of a teacup and rattles like bad china too. Oddly, there's a great
jazz soundtrack playing to keep those claustrophobics among us calm.</li>
<li>Sign says: "Way out reception" and I'm still wondering if that's just a
cool way to say they've got cool people on staff or it's some kind of
direction I've yet to comprehend the meaning of . . . </li>
</ul>

<p>I find the people here to be very helpful and friendly in a reserved
way, coming out of their shells once you get to talking. But one thing
puzzles me greatly.  On the phone, the English seem to get very excited
when they say goodbye. I've noticed this before, but it became very
apparent to me while making phone calls earlier today.</p>

<p>Aside from the grander horrors of the arguing world, and the weird,
unfolding tale of <a title="read more about this sad tale"
href="http://news.bbc.co.uk/1/hi/uk/england/2044874.stm">
Richard Markham and Tristian Lovelock</a>,  I am really very happy right
now. I'm cool, it's raining, the favorite drinks are tea, coffee, and beer,
and that pretty much sums up my happiness, too.</p>

<p><a href="archive-may2002.php" title="go to blog archive">view more
entries</a></p>

</body>
</html>
```

Copy this listing from the website and save it as chapter3.html. View it in your browser to get a feel for how it looks unstyled (Figure 3.1).

Some of the items of note within this document include:

- It is an XHTML 1 strict document type, encouraging strict authoring practices.
- The document contains the proper DOCTYPE and namespace.
- The document is simply but well structured, using headers, paragraphs, and lists to organize the content.
- The document contains no elements or attributes that are considered to be purely presentational, such as font styles and paragraph or image alignment attributes.

To create a thorough means of styling this document, first examine the document structure and map out the document tree. Figure 3.2 shows the condensed results of the tree, using only two paragraph examples (there are obviously more paragraphs!). Compare the figure to the markup, and you should quickly see the relationships within the tree.

`file:///G:/samples/chapter3.html`

Wednesday June 6, 2002

Heathrow airport has to be one of the ugliest airports I've ever seen, and I've seen a lot of them. It looks like some kind of post-modern industrial nightmare, is horribly lighted, has no circulating air to speak of, and I thought I would grow old and gray waiting for my luggage.

But then things started getting fun. At the taxi stand I got my first "alo, luv!" and a lot of good-natured, flirtatious joking from the cabbies. My brother Linus swore to me that all drivers in the UK know where they're going. As it turns out, my driver wasn't precisely sure where my hotel was located so he checked with his pals. This turned into quite a drama among the boys, but I was comforted by the taxi stand manager. He had one of those great faces that makes you want to immortalize it in paint, ink, or photo. About my driver, the stand manager said: "Not to worry, luv, he knows where he's going. If he makes any mistakes, just smack him on the head." Works for me. Actually, my driver turned out to be positively wonderful, full of helpful information and details about this and that.

Once out of the airport came the first glimpse of everything I'd imagined England to be: Pleasantly humid, overcast, and with gently swelling green hills, swaying grasses, horses in a pasture, a thatched-roof cottage.

If it weren't for the Burger King, the Holiday Inn, and the massive Glaxo/Smith Klein complex, I really might have confused it all for New Jersey.

Enter, London

Along the drive from Heathrow to my hotel, I got to see, well, gee, almost everything one is supposed to se in London: The Tower of London, the London Eye, the Tower Bridge, the Queen's digs. I arrived the day after her Majesty's Jubilee, looks like it was one *hell* of a party from the mess left behind.

The most striking thing to me so far is the mixing of old and new in everything here. Architecture, fashion, you name it. The other intriguing thing is how truly contemporary many things about London are. As a media person, I find the advertising especially fascinating, fun, hip, really more sophisticated than anything I've ever seen in the US.

photo: docklands wharf building   photo: view of buildings across the thames

I'm staying in the Docklands, for those unfamiliar this is the old dock areas right along the Thames. Tons of wharf buildings and old council houses have been gentrified into new flats and office space, as well as new buildings, shops, and what-not being built. Very reminiscent of San Francisco's South of Market, but the architecture is better. I took a long walk along the river front this morning, it is quite beautiful in its way.

Everyone always talks about the bad English food. My first English meal was *wonderful*. I had to do it: Fish and Chips and a pint of ale. I ate that meal in a pub complete with high-backed leather chairs and pictures of old sea captains on the wall. It was a truly great meal and I'll remember it always.

News of the Day

Along with Jubilee, there's the World Cup, and with yesterday's spectacular game between the Irish and Germans, well, I got instantly caught up in the vibe. I think all of London was yelling hurrah at the tie goal. There was a band of Germans in the pub watching the post-game commentary. They appeared to be more silent and morose than usual, if that's possible. I have no sympathy.

And then, there was breakfast this morning. Goodness, here I found all the reasons people make fun of English food. You can have yer back bacon and black pudding, thank you very much. The mushrooms were fine, though, as was the hot tea, of course. I drank so much of it I'm buzzing around like a fly.

photo: nelson pier   photo: walkway over old dry dock

Random observations:

- Interesting pub name seen along the way: "The Hung Drawn and Quartered" (note lack of punctuation)
- Sign says: "Please watch the step" as opposed to "Please watch *your* step"
- The lift in my hotel claims to fit five people. Yeah, right. It's the size of a teacup and rattles like bad china too. Oddly, there's a great jazz soundtrack playing to keep those claustrophobics among us calm
- Sign says: "Way out reception" and I'm still wondering if that's just a cool way to say they've got cool people on staff or it's some kind of direction I've yet to comprehend the meaning of . . .

I find the people here to be very helpful and friendly in a reserved way, coming out of their shells once you get to talking. But one thing puzzles me greatly. On the phone, the English seem to get very excited when they say goodbye. I've noticed this before, but it became very apparent to me while making phone calls earlier today.

Aside from the grander horrors of the arguing world, and the weird, unfolding tale of Richard Markham and Tristian Lovelock, I am really very happy right now. I'm cool, it's raining, the favorite drinks are tea, coffee, and beer, and that pretty much sums up my happiness, too.

view more entries

Figure 3.1: The unstyled content

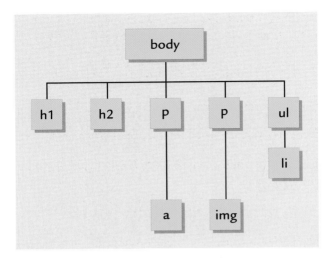

Figure 3.2:
Examining a portion
of the document tree

With map in hand, you can confidently begin to prepare your style sheet by listing out the obvious elements that are to be styled, as follows:

```
body
h1
h2
p
img
a
ul
li
```

And so begins the basis of a great style sheet. Of course, if you're creating style across many documents, you can't create as tight a tree. However, you can stay aware of the primary elements in use across a site. What's more, if you're properly structuring your documents from the get-go, you'll likely have a limited set of elements site-wide.

Presentation or Structure? Understanding *em* and *strong*

An oft-asked question is why em and strong are considered structural when they in fact do influence the presentation of their content. The em element typically produces italics, thought to be a weaker emphasis than the strong element, which typically renders its content visually as bold. The argument can and certainly has been made that these are presentational elements and not structural ones. However, in terms of the W3C specifications, they are considered structural because it is felt that their use carries meaning, whereas the b and i elements are not considered to have semantic meaning within a document.

Authoring Style Rules

In this section, you're going to create a structured style sheet built of a number of rules. You'll take the markup example provided earlier, as well as the document tree, and begin adding rules in a logical order to most of the elements within the tree using element selectors.

Then, to accommodate links, special styles, and other features to enhance the content, you'll write rules to style a range of page elements. To set up the workflow for this chapter, follow these steps:

1. Open the `Chapter3.html` document and insert the following code into the head por- tion of the document:
   ```
   <link rel="stylesheet" type="text/css" media="screen"
   href="chapter3_style.css" />
   ```
2. Open your text editor and create a document called `chapter3_style.css`.
3. Save both files to a local folder.
   Keep the CSS document open because that's where you'll be adding the rules within this chapter.

Using Element Selectors

As you learned in Chapter 2, element selectors are those selectors that relate to the actual elements within the markup. There are a number of elements in the document tree. Let's begin by walking through those and creating a style for each.

Styling the *body* Element

Because the first element that you'll want to provide style for is the body element, you'll start by creating rules for it. Typically, body element styles should contain information about the general display of the complete body of the design, such as margins, default font face and color, and any background color and images you might like.

 For more information about measurement values and their use, please see Appendix A.

Here, you'll style the margins, padding, default body text font, font color, and background color. You'll also learn how to employ grouping as you go.

To begin your first rule, write the element name:

body

and follow it with the margin rules:

```
body   {
      margin-top: 100px;
      margin-right: 20px;
      margin-bottom: 20px;
      margin-left: 100px;
}
```

 Margin properties are not inherited.

While this set of rules for the body margins is absolutely correct, you can also use grouping as a means to shorthand your rule and streamline your workflow. Using grouping in this case could result in the following rule:

```
body   {
       margin: 100px 20px 20px 100px;
}
```

 If all margin values are equal, you can group them more efficiently by writing body { margin: 20px; } (see the "Grouping Margin Properties" sidebar in this section). If they are not equal (as in this example), or use more than one value system (such as a combination of pixels and ems), either use the longhand form or this method of grouping.

Figures 3.3 and 3.4 compare a portion of the document with the unstyled and styled margins.

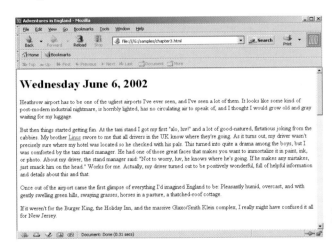

Figure 3.3: A portion of the unstyled content within a browser window

Instead of a random default, this margin is now set to 20 pixels.

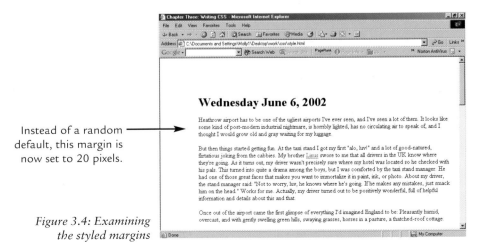

Figure 3.4: Examining the styled margins

Grouping Margin Properties

When working with margins, it's important to be aware of certain issues with grouping. First, the order of the group must be accurate. The first instance of the margin group is the top margin, the second the right, the third the bottom, and the fourth the left margin. If you specify only one measurement, such as "0", that measurement is applied to *all* of the margins. If you specify a top margin as 10 pixels but don't specify a bottom margin, the proper browser behavior would be to apply the same value to the bottom margin, and vice-versa. The same is true for left and right margins. If you specify a right margin as 100 pixels and do not specify a left margin, the browser should also display the left margin as 100 pixels.

The next step is to create a rule for your default font face. Note that this font will often be overridden by other rules within your style sheet, but it's still a good idea to put your body text font and related styles here. As you are probably aware from working with HTML, you can "stack" font family names. The first name in the stack will display if that font is available on your machine; if not, each one will be considered in turn. Using a default at the end, such as `serif` or `sans-serif`, means that if no prior font in the stack is located, the browser will display the closest font available.

```
body  {
     margin: 20px;
     font-family: "Trebuchet MS" Verdana, Arial, sans-
     serif;
     font-size: 0.95em;
     line-height: 1.3em;
     font-style: normal;
}
```

 If you're using a font name that contains any spaces, such as Trebuchet MS, you must put the name in quotations for it to be interpreted properly.

As with grouping margins, the family, size, line height, and style can similarly be grouped as follows:

```
font: normal 0.95em/1.3em "Trebuchet MS", Arial, Verdana,
     sans-serif;
```

As with margins, font grouping order is critical. The `font-weight` and `font-style` properties *must* come before size measurement and family names. If you are using both `font-size` and `line-height`, the `line-height` value comes after the size, and their difference is denoted with a slash (`/`).

 For more details about using fonts in CSS, please see Chapter 4, "CSS Typography."

Next, add a color for the text:

```
color: #333333;
```

and a color for the background:

```
background-color: #FFFFFF;
```

Listing 3.2 shows the now complete rule for the body style.

Listing 3.2: Styling the *body* Using an Element Selector

```
body    {
        margin: 20px;
        font: normal 0.95em/1.3em "Trebuchet MS", Arial,
        Verdana, sans-serif;
        color: #333333;
        background-color: #FFFFFF;
}
```

You can now save your file and view the changes. Figure 3.5 shows a portion of the content style, which you can compare to the unstyled original.

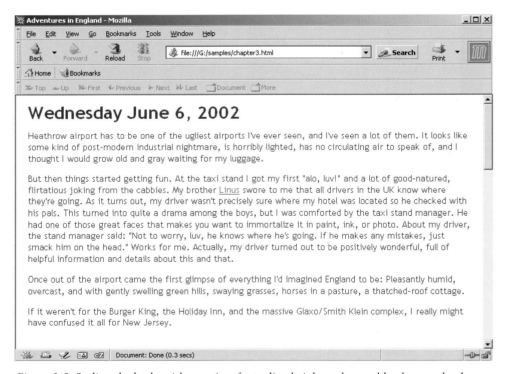

Figure 3.5: Styling the body with margins, fonts, line height, color, and background color

Adding Style to Headers

In this instance, there are only two headers within the document tree. Typically, it's wise to style at least levels 1–3. Here, you'll work with the two levels in the document, because they are going to be distinctly different in their styling, and then add a third for later use.

For the h1, you'll create a style that contains its own margin style, padding, and styled bottom border, as well as font styles. Remember that each element relates to a "box" within the browser space. The style for h1 in this example demonstrates how to use that box to style aspects of the element.

To style the header level 1, follow these steps:

1. Begin with the selector and brackets for the declarations:

```
h1  {


}
```

2. Add the margin styles. Here, I'm using negative values to pull the respective top, bottom, and left margins in closer than the default margin. That creates a tight effect but still leaves the right margin at 15 pixels:

```
h1  {
    margin: -10px -10px 15px -10px;
}
```

3. Set the padding:

```
h1  {
    margin: -10px -10px 15px -10px;
    padding: 0px 10px 5px 10px;
}
```

4. Now, add the font styles:

```
h1  {
    margin: -10px -10px 15px -10px;
    padding: 0px 10px 5px 10px;
    font: 900 2em/1.1em Verdana, Arial, sans-serif;
}
```

5. Add the text color:

```
h1  {
    margin: -10px -10px 15px -10px;
    padding: 0px 10px 5px 10px;
    font: 900 2em/1.1em Verdana, Arial, sans-serif;
    color: #aaaaaa;
}
```

6. Add the background color for the header block:

```
h1  {
    margin: -10px -10px 15px -10px;
    padding: 0px 10px 5px 10px;
    font: 900 2em/1.1em Verdana, Arial, sans-serif;
    color: #aaaaaa;
    background-color: #eeeeee;
}
```

7. And finally, add the border style for the bottom border, which will be one pixel thick and of a "dashed" style:

```
h1  {
        margin: -10px -10px 15px -10px;
        padding: 0px 10px 5px 10px;
        font: 900 2em/1.1em Verdana, Arial, sans-serif;
        color: #aaaaaa;
        background-color: #eeeeee;
        border-bottom: #bbbbbb 1px dashed;
}
```

8. Save your style sheet and preview the main document, chapter3.html, in your browser. Figure 3.6 shows the styling of the h1 header.

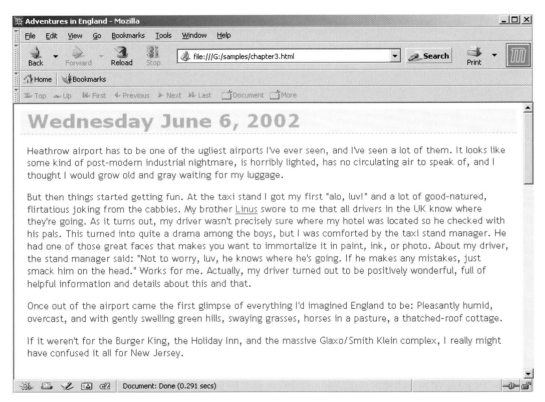

Figure 3.6: Using the element box to assign interesting style to a header

Listing 3.3 shows the entire sheet thus far.

Listing 3.3: The Style Sheet with *body* and *header* Level 1 Styles

```
body   {
        margin: 20px;
        font: normal 0.95em/1.3em "Trebuchet MS", Arial,
```

```
        Verdana, sans-serif;
        color: #333333;
        background-color: #FFFFFF;
}


h1  {
        margin: -10px -10px 15px -10px;
        padding: 0px 10px 5px 10px;
        font: 900 2em/1.1em Verdana, Arial, sans-serif;
        color: #aaaaaa;
        background-color: #eeeeee;
        border-bottom: #bbbbbb 1px dashed;
}
```

To style the h2 header, follow these steps:

1. Underneath the rules for h1, use the element selector for h2:

   ```
   h2  {


   }
   ```

2. Now, add the margins you'd like:

   ```
   h2 {
           margin: 0px 0px 5px 0px;
   }
   ```

3. And add the padding:

   ```
   h2  {
           margin: 0px 0px 5px 0px;
           padding: 0px 0px 0px 0px;
   }
   ```

4. Set the font properties:

   ```
   h2  {
           margin: 0px 0px 5px 0px;
           padding: 0px 0px 0px 0px;
           font: bold 1.2em Verdana, Arial, sans-serif;
   }
   ```

5. Add the text color:

   ```
   h2  {
           margin: 0px 0px 5px 0px;
           padding: 0px 0px 0px 0px;
           font: bold 1.2em Verdana, Arial, sans-serif;
           color: #666699;
   }
   ```

Once you're finished, save the changes. Figure 3.7 shows a comparison between the two header styles with the paragraph text temporarily removed.

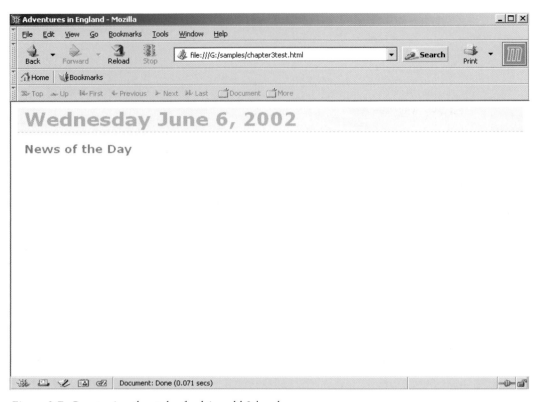

Figure 3.7: Comparing the styles for h1 and h2 headers

At this point, you'd create additional styles for headers level 3, 4, 5, and 6 should you need them. Each rule should be written consecutively so as to continue following the document tree.

Listing 3.4 shows the style sheet as it should look now.

Listing 3.4: The Style Sheet with *body* and *header* Levels Required for Your Content

```
body   {
     margin: 20px;
     font: normal 0.95em/1.3em "Trebuchet MS", Arial,
     Verdana, sans-serif;
     color: #333333;
     background-color: #FFFFFF;
}

h1   {
     margin: -10px -10px 15px -10px;
     padding: 0px 10px 5px 10px;
     font: 900 2em/1.1em Verdana, Arial, sans-serif;
     color: #aaaaaa;
     background-color: #eeeeee;
     border-bottom: #bbbbbb 1px dashed;
```

```
}

h2  {
      margin: 0px 0px 5px 0px;
      padding: 0px 0px 0px 0px;
      font: bold 1.2em Verdana, Arial, sans-serif;
      color: #666699;
}
```

Figure 3.8 shows a portion of the page that contains all of the styles you've written so far.

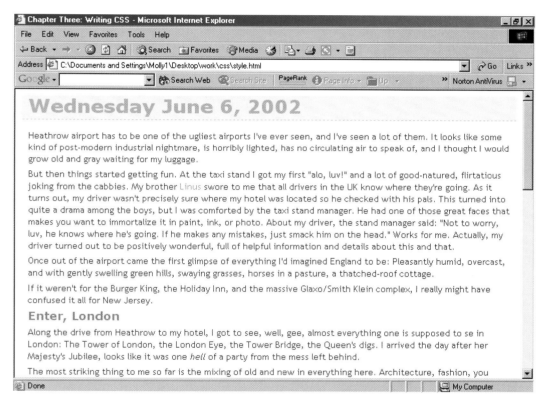

Figure 3.8: A portion of the document as it looks with the current style sheet in place

Creating the Paragraph Style

Creating styles for the paragraph is as straightforward as creating them for the body and headers. In this case, you're going to add a margin and font styles, as follows:

```
p  {
     margin: 0px 0px 5px 0px;
     font: normal 0.95em/1.3em "Trebuchet MS", Verdana,
     Arial, sans-serif;
}
```

Styling the Images

Images are unique in that they can be positioned on a page in a variety of ways. In this chapter, the concern is mostly to ensure that there is no border around the images. To do this, add the following rule:

```
img   {
    border: none;
}
```

Styling the Link

To style the link, first, you'll create a style for the main link, and then you'll move on to the next section, where you will create link rules using pseudo class selectors.

Add the following CSS rule to your style sheet:

```
a:link   {
    color: #0099CC;
    background-color: transparent;
    text-decoration: none;
}
```

This styles any standard link as blue in color, with a transparent background and no text decoration.

Listing 3.5 shows the progress of the style sheet.

WWW.   **Listing 3.5: Style with Rules for the Image and Primary Link Selectors**

```
body   {
    margin: 20px;
    font: normal 0.95em/1.3em "Trebuchet MS", Arial,
    Verdana, sans-serif;
    color: #333333;
    background-color: #FFFFFF;
}

h1   {
    margin: -10px -10px 15px -10px;
    padding: 0px 10px 5px 10px;
    font: 900 2em/1.1em Verdana, Arial, sans-serif;
    color: #aaaaaa;
    background-color: #eeeeee;
    border-bottom: #bbbbbb 1px dashed;
}

h2   {
    margin: 0px 0px 5px 0px;
    padding: 0px 0px 0px 0px;
    font: bold 1.2em Verdana, Arial, sans-serif;
    color: #666699;
    background-color: transparent;
}
```

```
p   {
        margin: 0px 0px 5px 0px;
        font: normal 0.95em/1.3em "Trebuchet MS", Verdana,
        Arial, sans-serif;
}
img   {
        border: none;
}

a:link   {
        color: #0099CC;
        background-color: transparent;
        text-decoration: none;
}
```

Finally, you'll create styles for the unordered list and list items, as follows:

```
ul   {
        font: normal 0.95em/1.3em "Trebuchet MS", Verdana,
        Arial, sans-serif;
}

li   {
        font: normal 0.95em/1.3em "Trebuchet MS", Verdana,
        Arial, sans-serif;
}
```

NOTE Setting styles only for the list item and not the ul (or ol) will sometimes cause the list items not to be rendered in the style you've created. Therefore, it's wise to set styles for both the list type and list item, as shown in Listing 3.5.

Creating Link Rules with Pseudo Class Selectors

No doubt you've seen links styled using hover effects created with CSS. In this section, you'll add styles for visited and active links, as well as creating a hover effect. Link styles, other than the element selector, require you to use pseudo class selectors.

Enter the visited link rules after the anchor element within your style sheet. Then, follow these steps:

1. Begin with the visited link pseudo class selector:

   ```
   a:visited   {

   }
   ```

2. Add the first rule, which in this case is the link color:

   ```
   a:visited   {
        color: #0077aa;
   }
   ```

3.   Add the second rule, which styles the background as transparent:

```
a:visited  {
        color: #0077aa;
        background-color: transparent;
}
```

4.   Finish up with the text-decoration property, in this case set to none. This ensures that no underlines will appear beneath the link:

```
a:visited  {
        color: #0077aa;
        background-color: transparent;
        text-decoration: none;
}
```

5.   Save your changes before continuing to add the styles for the active link. Begin with the active link pseudo selector:

```
a:active  {

}
```

6.   Add the color:

```
a:active  {
        color: #0099cc;
}
```

7.   Add the background color, which in this case is also set to transparent:

```
a:active  {
        color: #0099cc;
        background-color: transparent;
}
```

8.   Finish up by adding the text decoration property and style:

```
a:active  {
        color: #09c;
        background-color: transparent;
        text-decoration: none;
}
```

Your style sheet now contains all the common link styles: normal, visited, and active. The next step is to create a hover style, so that as a site visitor's mouse passes over the link, the link will change. The style created here causes a gray box to appear as the mouse passes the link. The box is created because all the other link examples have their background set to transparent rather than defining a color. In the case of this hover rule, the background color is defined:

```
a:hover  {
        color: #0077cc;
        background-color: #eeeeee;
        text-decoration: none;
}
```

Figure 3.9 shows a plain link, and then the hover style.

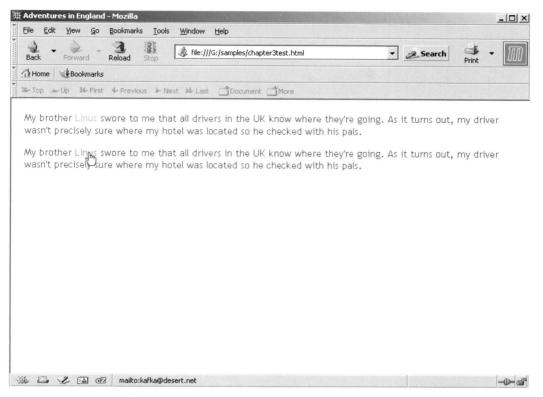

Figure 3.9: Using pseudo classes to apply a hover style to a link

Listing 3.6 shows the progress of the style sheet. Note the location and order of the pseudo elements. This is important for inheritance and proper functioning of the link styles.

Listing 3.6: Style Sheet with Element Selectors and Pseudo Class Selectors in Use

```
body  {
    margin: 20px;
    font: normal 0.95em/1.3em "Trebuchet MS", Arial,
    Verdana, sans-serif;
    color: #333333;
    background-color: #FFFFFF;
}

h1  {
    margin: -10px -10px 15px -10px;
    padding: 0px 10px 5px 10px;
    font: 900 2em/1.1em Verdana, Arial, sans-serif;
    color: #aaaaaa;
    background-color: #eeeeee;
    border-bottom: #bbbbbb 1px dashed;
}
```

```css
h2  {
    margin: 0px 0px 5px 0px;
    padding: 0px 0px 0px 0px;
    font: bold 1.2em Verdana, Arial, sans-serif;
    color: #666699;
    background-color: transparent;
}

p  {
    margin: 0px 0px 5px 0px;
    font: normal 0.95em/1.3em "Trebuchet MS", Verdana,
    Arial, sans-serif;
}

img  {
    border: none;
}

a:link  {
    color: #0099CC;
    background-color: transparent;
    text-decoration: none;
}
a:visited  {
    color: #0077aa;
    background-color: transparent;
    text-decoration: none;
}

a:active  {
    color: #0099cc;
    background-color: transparent;
    text-decoration: none;
}

a:hover  {
    color: #0077cc;
    background-color: #eeeeee;
    text-decoration: none;
}
ul  {
            font: normal 0.95em/1.3em "Trebuchet MS", Verdana,
            Arial, sans-serif;
}

li  {
    font: normal 0.95em/1.3em "Trebuchet MS", Verdana,
    Arial, sans-serif;
}
```

Multiple Link Styles Example

What happens if you want to use more than one set of link styles? This might occur if you have a navigation area with a different colored background and would like those links to have different styles than links appearing in the main body text. To accomplish this, you could create a class selector along with the element or pseudo class selector for each link. Examples of these selectors are `a.nav:link`, `a.nav:active`, `a.nav:visited`, and `a.nav:hover`.

Adding Class Selectors

Now that you've got all of the primary elements styled, you can begin creating class selectors to more broadly manage certain features within the document.

In this case, you'll add one class called `small` and another called `smallColor` to enable you to style text within the document as smaller, or smaller and colored differently than other styles within the document:

```
.small  {
    font: 0.75em "Trebuchet MS", Verdana, Arial, sans-
    serif;

}

.smallColor  {
    font: 0.75em "Trebuchet MS", Verdana, Arial, sans-
    serif;
    color: blue;
}
```

 When authoring class names, it's a good idea to make them descriptive but not necessarily specific. For example, I could have named the `smallColor` class `smallBlue`. Later on, however, if I wanted to change the actual color of the class to purple, there'd be a significant discrepancy in any document, site-wide, where `class="smallBlue"` appears. Sticking to descriptive rather than specific names is a much more efficient authoring practice.

Remember, you can add a class to any element using the `class` attribute. For example, if you wanted an entire paragraph within the document to be italicized, you'd style that paragraph as follows:

```
<p class="small">If it weren't for the Burger King, the Holiday Inn, and
the massive Glaxo/Smith Klein complex, I really might have confused it all
for New Jersey.</p>
```

If you'd like to have only one word or series of words within a paragraph affected, you can use the span element, as follows:

```
<p>If it weren't for the Burger King, the Holiday Inn, and the massive
Glaxo/Smith Klein complex, I really <span class="small">might</span> have
confused it <span class="smallColor">all for New Jersey.</p>
```

Figure 3.10 shows these two samples.

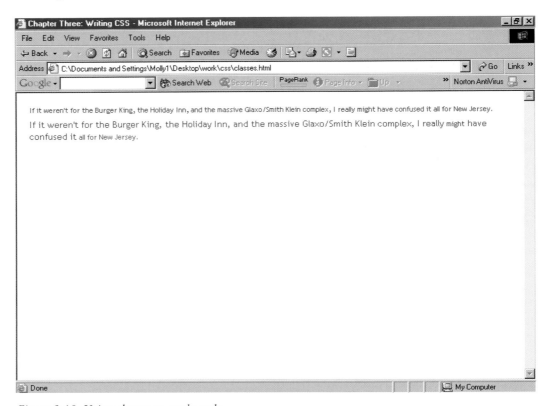

Figure 3.10: Using classes to apply style

Listing 3.7 shows the completed style sheet for this chapter, and Figure 3.11 shows the fully styled document that results.

Listing 3.7: The Completed Style Sheet

```
body   {
     margin: 20px;
     font: normal 0.95em/1.3em "Trebuchet MS", Arial,
     Verdana, sans-serif;
     color: #333333;
     background-color: #FFFFFF;
}

h1   {
     margin: -10px -10px 15px -10px;
     padding: 0px 10px 5px 10px;
     font: 900 2em/1.1em Verdana, Arial, sans-serif;
     color: #aaaaaa;
     background-color: #eeeeee;
     border-bottom: #bbbbbb 1px dashed;
}
```

```
h2   {
      margin: 0px 0px 5px 0px;
      padding: 0px 0px 0px 0px;
      font: bold 1.2em Verdana, Arial, sans-serif;
      color: #666699;
      background-color: transparent;
}

p  {
      margin: 0px 0px 5px 0px;
      font: normal 0.95em/1.3em "Trebuchet MS", Verdana,
      Arial, sans-serif;
}

img   {
      border: none;
}

a:link   {
      color: #0099CC;
      background-color: transparent;
      text-decoration: none;
}
a:visited   {
      color: #0077aa;
      background-color: transparent;
      text-decoration: none;
}

a:active   {
      color: #0099cc;
      background-color: transparent;
      text-decoration: none;
}

a:hover   {
      color: #0077cc;
      background-color: #eeeeee;
      text-decoration: none;
}
ul   {
      font: normal 0.95em/1.3em "Trebuchet MS", Verdana,
      Arial, sans-serif;
}

li   {
      font: normal 0.95em/1.3em "Trebuchet MS", Verdana,
      Arial, sans-serif;
}
```

```
.bold  {
     font-weight: bold;
}

.italic  {
     font-style: italic;
}
```

The result is a well-ordered style sheet that takes its structure directly from the documents for which it's being created.

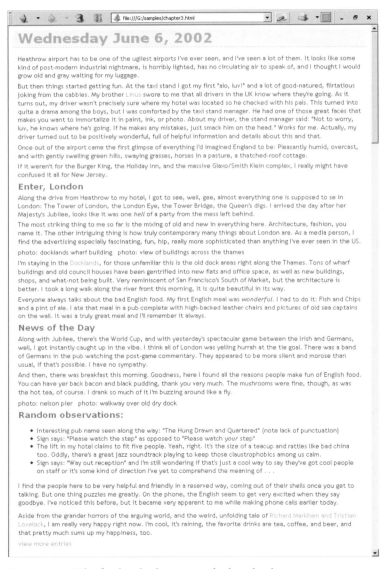

Figure 3.11: The final style sheet as applied to the document

Style Play

To gain a greater sense of style and how it works, create a second instance of this style sheet in which you move rules around (mix the pseudo selectors up and see what happens!), remove rules, and change the values of rules, each time loading the associated document in your browser and making note of the changes.

Validating Your CSS

Just as you validated an HTML document in Chapter 1, "Understanding Structured Markup," here you will validate your CSS document using the W3C's validator. To do so, follow these steps:

1. Point your browser to `http://jigsaw.w3.org/css-validator/` (see Figure 3.12).

Figure 3.12: The W3C's CSS validator

2. As with the HTML and XHTML validator, you can validate in several ways, including by URI (if the document is online), and by upload.
3. Click the option you'd like. If you choose by URI, you'll be asked for the location of the document. If you choose to upload it, you'll be asked to browse for the document or type its path directly into the available text box.
4. Click the Submit This CSS File for Validation button.

The W3C's CSS validator will validate your CSS. As with HTML and XHTML, warnings can be generated. As long as no errors are generated, the CSS document is valid (see Figure 3.13).

NOTE If you do encounter an error, use the information provided to correct your document. A warning can provide helpful information to you, but warnings do not influence the validity of the document.

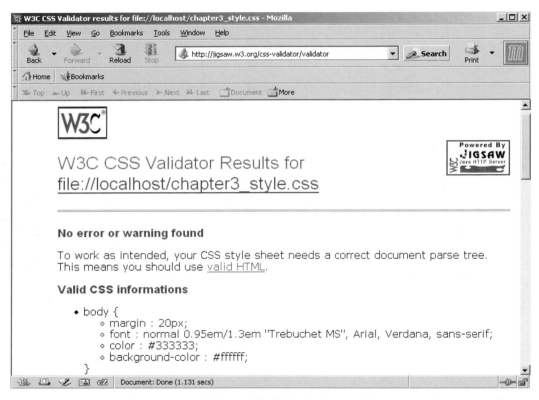

Figure 3.13: The style sheet passes validation! The full style sheet will be displayed as you scroll down the page.

Next Steps

This chapter helped you begin writing style rules in a clear, organized, and effective manner. The next step is to dig deeper into using CSS to create great typographic style.

In Chapter 4, you'll learn general features of CSS type, such as how to use multiple type styles within a document. You'll also gain insight into creating readable, usable pages and learn to control a wide range of typographic features using style.

Design

It's one challenge to learn CSS as a language, it's another test to put it to good use in visual design. That test is yet to be written much less taken—CSS as a language of design is just beginning to emerge.

With a strong foundation of technological principles beneath you, the aesthetic work can now begin. Type, shape, space, color, layout—Design comprises many aspects of the visual realm, and CSS allows you to address many of these aspects with considerable ease.

Learning the design topics discussed in the following chapters will help you be prepared for—and master—the ways you can apply CSS to your pages, making them more innovating and interesting than ever before.

We should welcome typographic variety as the natural consequence of human creativity.

—Sebastian Carter

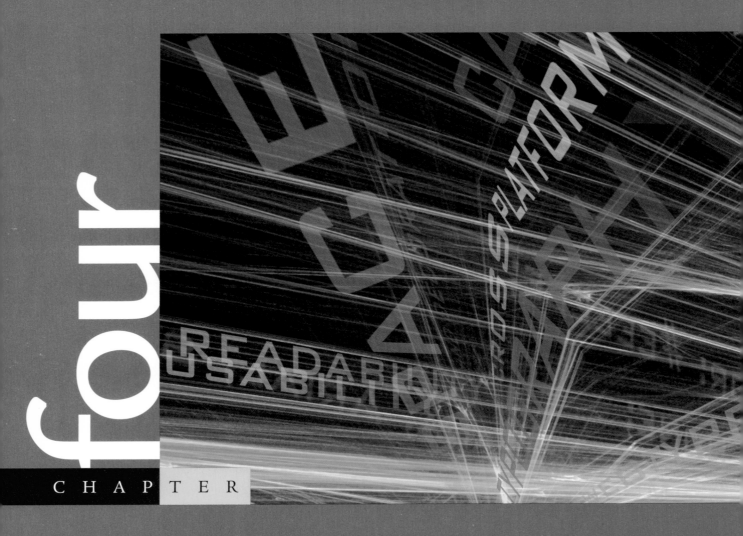

four

CHAPTER

CSS Typography

As noted type designer Sebastian Carter's quote expresses, many type designers and type enthusiasts see typography as an area of design that is nothing short of spiritual. This elevation of typography to such rare air is no mystery: Type is a primary vehicle of human communication.

Setting typographical properties using style sheets is one of the most exciting aspects of contemporary web design. Not only do you have the ability to call for many typographic styles to appear on a page or a site, but you also have access to the detailed control that CSS allows.

In this chapter you will learn:

- How to understand CSS type
- How to use Font Properties
- How to work with Text Properties

Understanding CSS Type

Throughout history, humankind has found ways to express itself using many script and handwriting and—eventually—type styles. Whether the expression is functional (see Figure 4.1), aesthetic (see Figure 4.2), or groundbreaking (see Figure 4.3), type plays an enormous role in visual design.

Many readers of this book are experienced graphic designers and therefore have at least a broad, if not very specific, education when it comes to typography. But, many other readers won't have that advantage. No matter what your background, it's important to recognize immediately that the way CSS specifications deal with type *is unique to CSS.*

While there are certainly relationships between CSS typography and classic print typography, CSS typography must be seen in a distinctive light. To that end, I'll provide information on corollaries within CSS, classic typography, and HTML-based typography. First I will focus in this chapter first on principles as they relate specifically to CSS, and then I will make comments on those concepts analogous to other typographic principles.

 For the majority of this chapter, the focus will be on how CSS typography works on screen, unless otherwise noted.

Control is something that's been lacking for designers, and this is why CSS has become such an exciting topic. Control becomes especially important when you're creating large sites. Instead of having to work with multiple, worrisome font elements and related attributes, CSS allows you to create a single style sheet that defines all the styles required for the entire site, including a variety of link types, specialty links, anchors, and lists. Or, you can use a variety of integration means, just as you would while working with CSS properties in general.

Figure 4.1:
The type on the WaSP home page is easy to read and therefore very functional.

Figure 4.2:
While still readable, the type on this page is used for aesthetics, too.

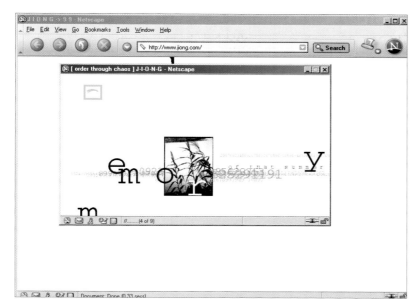

Figure 4.3:
Type within this design is largely experimental rather than specific to verbal communication.

Presentation of Text Using CSS

So now, instead of the dreaded and problematic HTML font element, you can use the style sheet's property font-family to select fonts, and a variety of related font and text properties, including shorthand properties, to style your type. What's more, you can add a wide variety of typographic features to type and text that extend far above and beyond what's available in HTML, providing you with extended options and more refined design results.

In CSS, there are two major groups of properties that help manage typographic presentation. They are:

- Font properties
- Text properties

Font properties are specific to how CSS defines aspects of font presentation. These properties are designed to control type family, style, variants, weight, condensation and expansion of fonts, and the size of the font.

Text properties are a little more global and relate to a variety of text-related concerns: indentation, alignment, decoration, spacing of letters and words, transformation, and white space.

Understanding CSS *font* Specifications

As in classic print typography, there are ways of defining features when it comes to individual fonts and groups of fonts.

The following specifications are the primary font-related properties within CSS. In the following list, the properties follow the description of the specification.

Understand the meanings of each of these specifications and their related properties, and you'll be well on your way to terrific style for your pages:

Font Family (*font-family*) Font families are groups of fonts that contain similar features. The categorization of families is typically broken up in typography by a font's master family (serif), the font's specific family (Times), and members of the font's family, such as bold, italic, or condensed forms (Times bold, Times italic, and so forth). In CSS, there are five generic font families, and the `font-family` property can be used to specify the font's specific family as well as its generic family. See the section "Style Sheet Font Families" later in this section for more details.

Font Style (*font-style*)   The style of a font describes whether the font should be rendered as normal, italic, or oblique. Oblique is a slanted version of a typeface that can be considered is similar to italic but is usually not as slanted as an italicized form, although the distinction is not often clear. Oblique forms are most commonly associated with sans-serif fonts (see Figure 4.4).

Figure 4.4: Examples of font styles

Font Variant (*font-variant*)   A font's variant allows for that font to be displayed in either as normal lowercase letters for lowercase text, or small capitals (often referred to as *small caps*) for lowercase text, which is often referred to as *small caps* (see Figure 4.5).

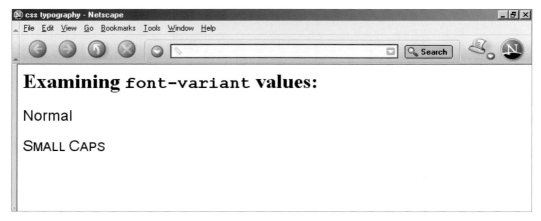

Figure 4.5: Examining font variants

Web browsers are permitted to use all capitals as a substitute for small capitals. Internet Explorer for Windows prior to IE 6.0 is known to make this substitution.

Font Weight (*font-weight*) The weight of a font is the amount of boldness or lightness as it relates to the standard weight within that family (see Figure 4.6). Different font families have different available weights—not every weight available in CSS will be available within a font.

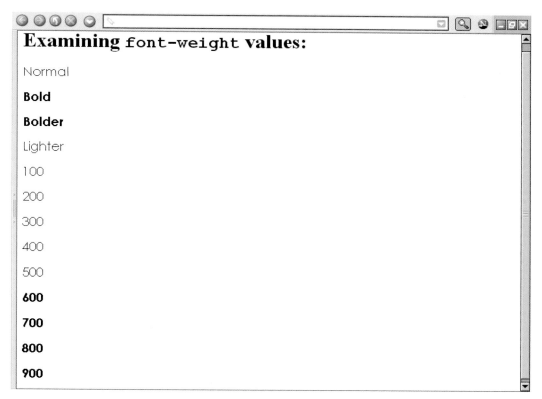

Figure 4.6: Compare these weight samples with the standard weight. Note that many typefaces cannot adequately render the differences in the numeric values.

Font Stretch (*font-stretch*) Stretching refers to the amount of condensing or expansion in a given letter or set of letters. As with weight, stretching is relative to the standard weight of other typefaces within that family. Figure 4.7 shows the *concept* of condensation and expansion in typography, but unfortunately, there is no current support for this property, so it's not possible to replicate this in any browser, despite the fact that the property is in fact a part of the CSS2 specification.

Figure 4.7:
Condensed (top) and
expanded (bottom) examples
using non-CSS glyphs

Font Size (*font-size*) In CSS, `font-size` sets the height of the character boxes in the element. For each character box, some of the box will actually be below the baseline (such as in the case of descenders, parts of letterforms such as is found in a lowercase "g"). There is some confusion as to the exact way that fonts are sized, however, leading to discrepancies in the way the CSS2 specification is written and implemented.

Figure 4.8: Sizing type from baseline to baseline

 W3C's CSS Working Group member David Baron, describes a simple explanation of the concern: `www.people.fas.harvard.edu/~dbaron/css/fonts/explanation`.

Style Sheet Font Families

In an attempt to address the major family groups available in print typography, CSS recognizes five font families, attempting to address the major family groups available in print typography.

Because there's no universally specific means of categorizing type (although there are many conventions used in classification), CSS uses its own means of specifying font characteristics. You'll learn more about these when you study font properties in detail later in this chapter. However, it's important to begin with an understanding of how type families are categorized.

Five font categories, (often referred to in typography as *master families*), are defined within CSS. It's important to recognize that these are considered *generic* families. That is, the category itself can be used as a catch-all means of ensuring that if no specific family, such as "Verdana" is denoted, the browser in question will display the local computer's default font *for that family*. However, within these categories exist numerous specific families. Table 4.1 will explains the generic families and, their features, and also provide examples of fonts found within those generic families.

Table 4.1: CSS Font Families

Generic Family	Description	Example Fonts within the Family
Serif	Serif faces are those faces with strokes (known as serifs, they mimic handwriting flourishes). These strokes are said to aid in readability in print as they provide the effect of subtle tracing lines to guide the eye. Therefore, serif typefaces are often very popular for large amounts of printed text. There is some discussion as to whether serif faces are as readable on-screen; most people think they are not as readable as other forms. Therefore, most web designers prefer using serifs for accent text.	Some examples of serif faces include Times, Times New Roman, Garamond, and Century Schoolbook.
Sans-Serif	These typefaces tend to be rounded and have no strokes. Many sans-serif fonts are excellent for screen readability as they often appear crisper, wider, and clearer on screen than serif fonts.	Common sans-serif faces include Arial, Verdana, Helvetica, Trebuchet, and Tahoma.
Script	A script face is one that looks similar to cursive writing or handwriting.	Common script typefaces include Lucida Handwriting.
Monospace	These faces look like typewriter fonts. They are called monospace fonts because each letter within the face takes up the same width as another. For example, the letter w, which is wider in most faces than an i, is actually the same width in a monospace font. Monospace fonts can be used decoratively for web pages, but mostly they are used to display code samples and preformatted text.	Courier is the common monospace font found on both the Windows and Macintosh platforms.
Fantasy	Referred to by most typographers as decorative, the fonts available in this category are best used for headings and artistic text rather than body text.	Decorative fonts include Whimsy and Comic Sans.

Figure 4.9 shows an example of each of these font types.

 It's best to avoid using the fantasy value because there's a lot less control as to which glyph a browser might substitute for a fantasy font. An example would be that if the initial desired, readable, decorative font were not available on a site visitor's machine, an unreadable font such as Windings might be substituted, completely destroying the message of your page.

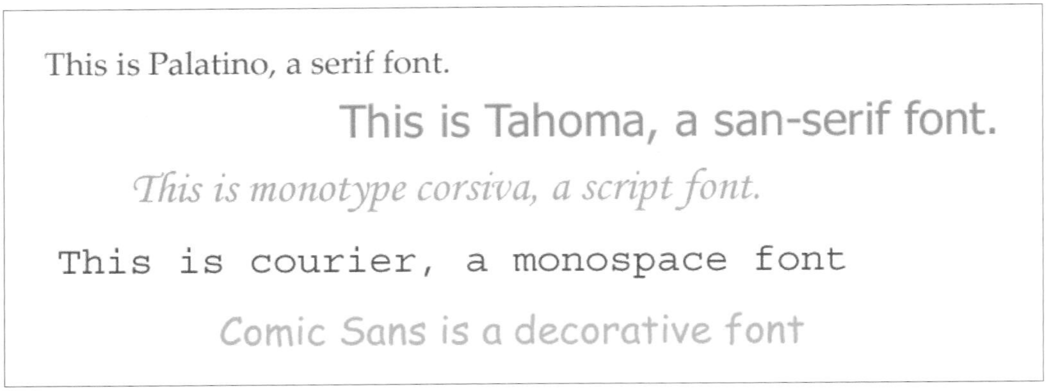

This is Palatino, a serif font.

This is Tahoma, a san-serif font.

This is monotype corsiva, a script font.

This is courier, a monospace font

Comic Sans is a decorative font

Figure 4.9: Exploring font families as defined in CSS

Using Font-Related Properties

In this section, you'll learn to work with font properties to manage your typographic needs. You'll start with font families and continue with the font specifications described so far: size, style, variant, weight, and stretch.

I'll also cover the following:

- How font family names follow a stacking convention such as is found with the font element in versions of HTML and XHTML
- How to use the font property for shorthand

You'll also find tips along the way regarding readability, contrast, and good use of font features.

Begin with Families

A great first step when creating typographic style for the screen is to define the families you'll be using. Even if you modify your style sheets later using grouping, knowing the families you'd like to specify beforehand—both for typeface specification and for the document design itself—provides you with the foundation of your type-related style sheets.

Specifying Type Faces

The reality of font support in style sheets is much the similar to those issues encountered by the designer when employing the font element and its attributes in versions of HTML and XHTML. The specific typeface must be available on the computer viewing your page. And, as with the font element, style sheets do allow you to "stack" any number of typefaces so that you can maximize the chances that your browser will pick up a typeface that you want your audience to see.

By "stacking" typefaces, I just mean listing several so that if your first font choice isn't available, the second listed will display, and so on. For example, if the people viewing Listing 4.1 in a browser don't have Arial, they'll probably have Helvetica and that will be displayed. If they don't have that, the last listing of a generic family name (in this case, sans-serif) will swap in a sans-serif font, and you'll be good to go.

> **NOTE** Although these typefaces have some minor differences, they are similar enough to be considered workable in the context of style sheet design.

Listing 4.1 provides an inline example.

Listing 4.1: Inline Style Example of *font-family* Order

```
<!DOCTYPE html PUBLIC "-//W3C//DTD XHTML 1.0 Transitional//EN"
"http://www.w3.org/TR/xhtml1/DTD/xhtml1-transitional.dtd">

<html xmlns="http://www.w3.org/1999/xhtml">

<head>
<title>Inline Example of font-family Order</title>
</head>

<body>

<p>This paragraph has no style or font information added to it. Therefore,
it relies on the browser's own defaults for a typeface.</p>

<p style="font-family: Arial, Helvetica, sans-serif">In this selection, the
browser will search the user's computer for the Arial font. If it's found,
it will be used to display the element. If Arial isn't found, the browser
will look for Helvetica. If neither is found, the browser will display the
first sans-serif typeface available.</p>

</body>
</html>
```

Figure 4.10 shows the difference between the first paragraph, where the browser defaults determine what typeface to display, and the second paragraph, where the typeface is controlled by CSS.

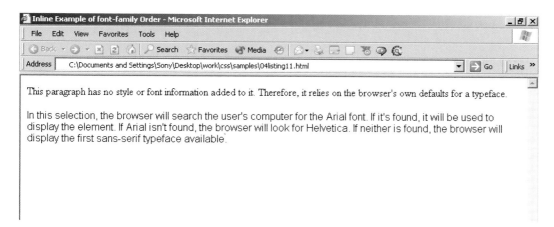

Figure 4.10: The default font compared to the Arial font displayed by one browser and computer

You are always in some danger that you'll lose control when stacking typefaces, particularly those within the Fantasy family. The Fantasy fonts tend to be the ones that are installed by individuals rather than shipped with the computer in question.

Of course, you'll often want style sheets that use a variety of families for an attractive visual look. Depending upon your design and type skills, you may have a range of type ideas already in mind that will help guide your final choices.

For the purposes of learning incrementally, let's keep the process very simple at this point. Begin by using a serif font for headings, and a sans-serif font for paragraphs. The rationale here is that we you want to create a little contrast between the heading font and the body font, but ensure that the body text is easily readable. You'll then add additional features as the chapter progresses.

In print, most people are accustomed to using san-serif fonts for headers, and serif fonts for body text. For the screen, this convention can be reversed if you prefer to use the more rounded letterforms of sans-serif fonts for body text and still would like some visual contrast between the header and body faces.

For now, examine the heading and paragraph CSS rules found in Listing 4.2 to style fonts that are appropriate for easy reading and legibility.

WWW. **Listing 4.2: Styling Heading and Paragraph Fonts Using CSS**

```
<!DOCTYPE html PUBLIC "-//W3C//DTD XHTML 1.0 Transitional//EN"
"http://www.w3.org/TR/xhtml1/DTD/xhtml1-transitional.dtd">

<html xmlns="http://www.w3.org/1999/xhtml">

<head>
<title>Example of Simple Font Styling</title>
<style type="text/css">

h1, h2, h3, h4, h5, h6  {
    font-family: Georgia, Times, serif;
}

p  {
    font-family: Verdana, Arial, Helvetica, sans-serif;
}

</style>

</head>

<body>

<h1>The Laying Of The Monster</h1>
<h2>By Theodosia Garrison</h2>
```

```
<p>Dorothea reposed with her shoulders in the shade of the bulkhead and her
bare feet burrowing in the sun-warmed sand. Beneath her shoulder blades was a
bulky and disheveled volume--a bound year of Godey's Lady Book of the vintage
of the early seventies. Having survived the handling of three generations,
this seemed to take naturally to being drenched with rain and warped by sun,
or, as at the present moment, serving its owner either as a sand-pillow or as
a receptacle for divers scribbled verses on its fly-leaves and margins.</p>

<p>It was with a poem now that Dorothea was wrestling, as she wriggled her
toes in the sand and gazed blankly oceanward. Under the scorching August
sun, the Atlantic seemed to purr like a huge, amiable lion cub.

<p>It was not the amiabilities of nature, however, in which Dorothea found
inspiration. A harp of a single string, she sang as that minstrel might who
was implored to make love alone his theme.</p>

</body>
</html>
```

NOTE At this point there are no defined differences between headings in terms of size, color, and other styles. For this reason, I've grouped them together.

Figure 4.11 shows the results of this simple style sheet.

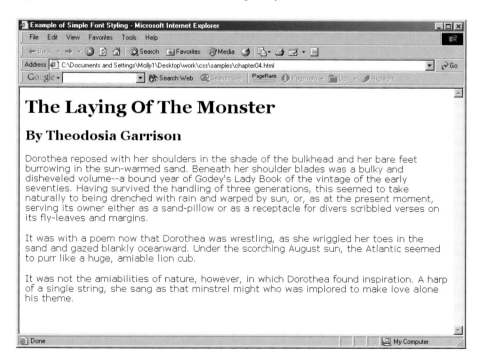

Figure 4.11: The heading style is serif, and the body text in sans-serif, creating a nice contrast between heading and body.

Determine Sizing

You can accomplish sizing by using the font-size property and an associated value.

Value measurements in CSS can be defined using a variety of value measurements, including the following:

- Points
- Pixels
- Inches
- Ems
- Percentages

 For a closer look at additional possible measurements and the definitions of those measurements, please see Appendix A.

The value measurement you choose will depend upon the media with which you are working. For screen, you'll likely want to use a measurement value appropriate for the screen, such as pixels or ems. For print, a measurement such as points or inches may be in order.

Type Measurement for the Screen

It's been a hot debate over which type measurement is best for screen. Many people recommend ems or percentages because they can be made relative to a given value. Other folks, such as Jeffrey Zeldman, highly regarded web designer, standards evangelist, and publisher of A List Apart Magazine, (www.alistapart.com/) recommend using pixels or nothing at all, unless you're concerned with accessibility, in which case ems are thought to be the better choice. One thing all people agree on is avoiding points (unless for use in CSS for print). The sizing discrepancies may occur because of inconsistencies in the way browsers and browser versions manage sizing units. For more information on this issue, please see:

- "Give Me Pixels or Give Me Death," an informative article on sizing at A List Apart, www.alistapart.com/stories/fear4/index.html.
- A good general article about CSS text sizing can be found at hotwired.lycos.com/webmonkey/98/35/index2a.html.

If you take a look at the CSS created in Listing 4.2, you'll notice there is nothing determining at what size the fonts should appear. You can work from the previous style sheet above to expand the headings and paragraphs as follows:

1. Copy the style portion of the sheet from Listing 4.2 as follows:

```
<style type="text/css">

h1, h2, h3, h4, h5, h6  {
    font-family: Georgia, Times, serif;
}

p  {
    font-family: Verdana, arial, helvetica, sans-serif;
}

</style>
```

2. Set up individual rules for each of the headings (I'm going to use h1 - - h3 and leave out h4 - - h6 as I don't need that many headings for this project):

```
<style type="text/css">

h1 {
    font-family: Georgia, Times, serif;
}

h2 {
    font-family: Georgia, Times, serif;
}

h3 {
    font-family: Georgia, Times, serif;
}

p {
    font-family: Verdana, arial, helvetica, sans-serif;
}

</style>
```

3. Add the `font-size` property to each entry, as follows:

```
<style type="text/css">

h1 {
    font-family: Georgia, Times, serif;
    font-size:
}

h2 {
    font-family: Georgia, Times, serif;
    font-size:
}

h3 {
    font-family: Georgia, Times, serif;
    font-size:
}

p {
    font-family: Verdana, arial, helvetica, sans-serif;
    font-size:
}

</style>
```

4. Add values, in pixels, for each. Because you'll want to have your headings incrementally smaller than the last, and the paragraph text appropriately sized for body text, you'll add these values as follows:

```css
<style type="text/css">

h1  {
    font-family: Georgia, Times, serif;
    font-size: 24px;
}

h2  {
    font-family: Georgia, Times, serif;
    font-size: 20px;
}

h3  {
    font-family: Georgia, Times, serif;
    font-size: 18px;
}

p  {
    font-family: Verdana, arial, helvetica, sans-serif;
    font-size: 16px;
}

</style>
```

Figure 4.12 shows the results of using family and sizing for headers and paragraphs.

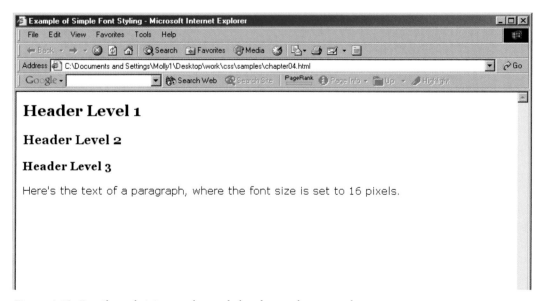

Figure 4.12: Family and sizing used to style headers and paragraphs

Adding a Font Style

Font *style* refers to the slant of a given typeface. The styles available are normal, italic, and oblique. Normal style typically refers to the "Roman" style of the font—the basic font with no adornment. Italic styles are available in most typefaces, so you're pretty safe using it wherever you require italics.

 NOTE Oblique is rare in most fonts and therefore should be used cautiously.

Because the normal value is default, there's no need to use it in this instance. However, I'd like to make the author's name appear in italics. To do so, I'd add the font-style property to the h2 heading styles:

```
h2  {
      font-family: Georgia, Times, serif;
      font-size: 20px;
      font-style: italic;
}
```

 TIP Try to use italics and bold sparingly. Their primary function in body type is to emphasize passages of text. Excessive use of bold or italics looks amateurish and can seriously compromise readability.

Any h2 will now appear in italics. If you wanted to keep the h2 free from the italicized style, you can create a class, h2.italic, and apply the class only where you'd like h2-level headings italicized.

Creating a Font Variant

The font-variant property allows you to create a visual variation to a font. This variation is "small-caps" and places lowercase letters in capital letters, with slightly larger variations for truly capitalized letters. If a font doesn't have this feature within the font itself, most browsers will attempt to simulate the variant.

Since the h1 style in the current document you're using for this chapter could use a little extra panache, you can add it by following these steps:

1. Add the font-variant property within the style rule:

```
h1  {
      font-family: Georgia, Times, serif;
      font-size: 24px;
      font-variant:
}
```

2. Type the small-caps value:

```
h1  {
      font-family: Georgia, Times, serif;
```

```
    font-size: 24px;
    font-variant: small-caps;
}
```

3. Save the changes to your file.

Figure 4.13 shows both the small-caps font variant and the h2 italicized font style.

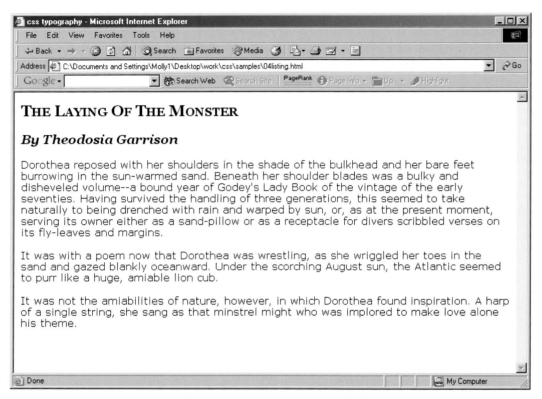

Figure 4.13: Using font-style *and* font-variant *to create styles for headings*

Gaining and Losing Font Weight

Weight is how thick or thin a typeface is. The Arial face, for example, has variations in weight including black (a very heavy face), bold, light, and so forth.

Weight is applied by using the font-weight property and an associated value. Values for the font-weight property are as follows:

- Normal
- Bold
- Bolder
- Lighter
- 100 - 900

Normal is the normal weight of the font before any modification, and it relates to the numeric value of 400. Bold relates to the numeric value 700. Using the "bolder" and "lighter" variations specifies that the font weight is darker or lighter than the inherited value.

If you wanted to make sure that all your strong elements were a weight of 800, you could write a rule as follows:

```
strong  {
     font-weight: 800;
)
```

Of course, you can create classes to help you modify text as well. Let's say you wanted a special light class for certain text. You could create a class of .light, and then apply a rule to it:

```
.light  {
     font-weight: 100;
}
```

 NOTE Because typefaces have different variations, unless you are absolutely sure that visitors to your site have a specific typeface, you generally should apply a value that is going to be available to all typefaces you are using. The one near-global value for typefaces is bold, whereas numeric font weights relate to the fonts themselves. If you use a numeric weight instead of a bold value, and there is no means to display variations within the font itself, then a value of 400 will appear the same as a normal value, and a value of 700 will appear the same as standard bold value.

Listing 4.3 includes all of the property values applied to the document so far.

Listing 4.3: A Document Modified with Font Properties

`WWW.`

```
<!DOCTYPE html PUBLIC "-//W3C//DTD XHTML 1.0 Transitional//EN"
"http://www.w3.org/TR/xhtml1/DTD/xhtml1-transitional.dtd">

<html xmlns="http://www.w3.org/1999/xhtml">

<html>
<head>
<title>css typography</title>
<style type="text/css">

h1  {
     font-family: Georgia, Times, serif;
     font-size: 24px;
     font-variant: small-caps;
}

h2  {
     font-family: Georgia, Times, serif;
```

```
        font-size: 20px;
        font-style: italic;
}

h3  {
        font-family: Georgia, Times, serif;
        font-size: 18px;
}

p  {
        font-family: Verdana, arial, helvetica, sans-serif;
        font-size: 16px;}

strong  {
        font-weight: 800;
)

</style>

</head>

<body>

<h1>The Laying Of The Monster</h1>
<h2>By Theodosia Garrison</h2>

<p>Dorothea reposed with her shoulders in the shade of the bulkhead and
her bare feet burrowing in the sun-warmed sand. Beneath her shoulder blades
was a bulky and disheveled volume—a bound year of <strong>Godey's Lady
Book</strong> of the vintage of the early seventies. Having survived the
handling of three generations, this seemed to take naturally to being
drenched with rain and warped by sun, or, as at the present moment, serving
its owner either as a sand-pillow or as a receptacle for divers scribbled
verses on its fly-leaves and margins.</p>

<p>It was with a poem now that Dorothea was wrestling, as she wriggled her
toes in the sand and gazed blankly oceanward. Under the scorching August
sun, the Atlantic seemed to purr like a huge, amiable lion cub.

<p>It was not the amiabilities of nature, however, in which Dorothea found
inspiration. A harp of a single string, she sang as that minstrel might
who was implored to make love alone his theme.</p>

</body>
</html>
```

Stretching the Limit: Sad Support for the *font-stretch* Property

No major browser supports the `font-stretch` property. You can try it out, but you'll see no results! Still, it's important to know about because it is a part of CSS2, and support for it could appear.

The idea behind font stretching is to enable designers to make their fonts more condensed or more expanded, depending upon the visual effects they'd like for their design. The following is an example of how, if the property were available, you might write a rule using `font-stretch`:

```
.stretch {
    font-stretch: ultra-expanded;
}
```

The value options for the `font-stretch` property are as follows:

- `ultra-condensed`
- `extra-condensed`
- `condensed`
- `semi-condensed`
- `normal`
- `semi-expanded`
- `expanded`
- `extra-expanded`
- `ultra-expanded`

Normal is the standard form of the font with no condensation or expansion occurring.

Working with *text* Properties

Text properties are those properties related to typography that are classified in the CSS specification under text rather than font. While font properties relate to how font glyphs are formatted, text properties tend to influence the way the text itself is arranged. Text properties help you manage a range of text features, as follows:

Indentation (*text-indent*) Indentation allows you to indent the first line of text within a block. Values may be fixed or a percentage and a negative value can be used within reason.

Alignment (*text-align*) Alignment allows you to align the content within a given box. You can use left, right, center, and justify.

 Text alignment is based with respect to the element box rather than the browser window. The `text-indent` and text-align properties only apply to block-level elements.

Decoration (*text-decoration*) The `text-decoration` property lets you add or suppress a variety of decorative elements including underlining, overlining, line-through (more familiar as strike-through to many readers), and blink. Yes, that's right, you read it here—blink.

Letter and Word Spacing (*letter-spacing; word-spacing*) The `letter-spacing` property allows you to set the space between individual characters within a font. The length must be specific, not percentage based, and values may be negative. The length applied is applied in addition (or in subtraction) to the default spacing.

The `word-spacing` property describes the space between words. As with `letter-spacing`, the length must be specific, values may be negative, and the measurements are applied in addition or in subtraction to the default word spacing.

Text Transformation (*text-transform*) Text transformation allows you to control the way text is capitalized. You can make each word capitalized, put all words in upper case or lower case, or suppress capitals completely using this property.

White Space (*white-space*) White space manages the way space within the element's box appears. You can have normal white spacing, where all extra spaces are collapsed (as in normal browser behavior), pre-formatted spacing, where the spacing within the element will take into account your space input, and `nowrap`, which suppresses line breaks.

An additional property important to discuss in this section of the chapter is `line-height`. This is the spacing between lines of text and relates directly to typography but is classified outside of the font and text properties. The property is discussed in the visual model of the CSS2 specification.

Indenting Text

To indent text using the `text-indent` property, follow these steps:

1. Choose a selector to which you'd like to add indentation. In this case, I used p. Add the declaration block:

   ```
   p   {

   }
   ```

2. Add the `text-indent` property:

   ```
   p   {
       text-indent:
   }
   ```

3. Add a value (in this case, I used a specific measurement unit, but you can use percentages, too):

   ```
   p   {
       text-indent: 15px;
   }
   ```

4. Apply this rule to a document and see the results.

   Figure 4.14 shows a series of paragraphs using the `text-indent` property.

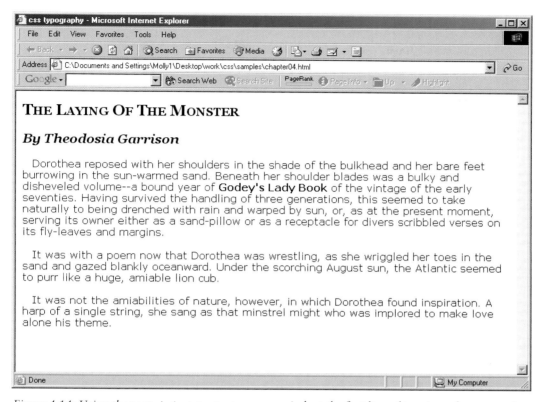

Figure 4.14: Using the `text-indent` *property, you can indent the first line of text in each paragraph.*

Text Alignment

To practice aligning text using CSS, follow these steps:

1. Begin with a series of selectors as follows:

    ```
    p.left {

    }

    p.right {

    }

    p.center {

    }

    p.justify {

    }
    ```

2. Add the `text-align` property to each:

```
p.left  {
     text-align:
}

p.right  {
     text-align:
}

p.center  {
     text-align:
}

p.justify  {
     text-align:
}
```

3. Add the appropriate values as follows:

```
p.left  {
     text-align: left;
}

p.right  {
     text-align: right;
}

p.center  {
     text-align: center;
}

p.justify  {
     text-align: justify;
}
```

4. Add this set of rules to a document with at least four paragraphs. In the document, you'll need to add a class attribute, using one example of each class created here. In Figure 4.15, you'll see the way the paragraphs themselves are styled.

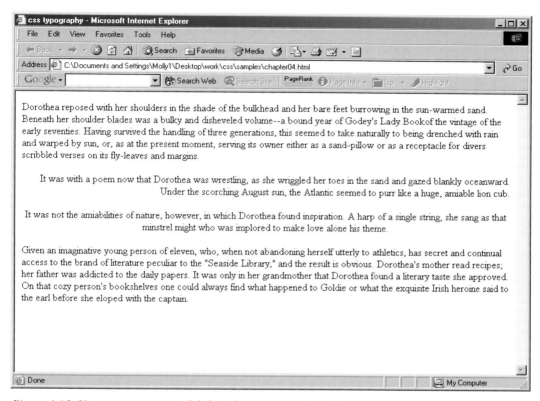

Figure 4.15: Using `text-align` *with left, right, center, and justify values for the paragraphs within our sample*

Decorating Text

Text decoration can be used for a number of reasons including editorial marks (such as with `line-through`) and unusual styling of text for decorative purposes. There are two properties within the decoration section of the CSS2 specs to manage text decoration, `text-decoration` and `text-shadow`. The `text-decoration` has plenty of browser support, but `text-shadow` is currently (and unfortunately) not supported. But, again, as with quite a few CSS properties you've learned in this book, they exist in the specifications and you should be aware of them.

The specific decorations values for text-decoration are as follows:

- `none` (no decoration)
- `underline` (line under text)
- `overline` (line over text)
- `line-through` (line through text)
- `blink`

 The `text-decoration` property is extremely useful for turning off link underlining within an anchor. To do so, set `text-decoration` for anchors to a value of none.

The specific values for the text-shadow property are as follows:

- color (defines the color of the shadow)
- length (defines the length of aspects of the shadow)

You can use shadowing to create some unusual effects. A simple drop shadow using the default color for h1 (in this case, black) that is to the right by 5 pixels and down by 5 pixels could be created using the following CSS:

```
h1 {
    text-shadow: 5px 5px;
}
```

If you'd like to add a blur to your shadow, add a value measurement for the blur:

```
h1 {
    text-shadow: red 5px 5px 5px;
}
```

The preceding rule will create a red shadow that is 5 pixels right, 5 pixels down, and has a 5 pixel glow.

Using Letter and Word Spacing

Designers often want the opportunity to modify the spacing between characters within words, and between words themselves. CSS2 offers two properties that allow you to modify these aspects of text. The values available for each are normal and length, where the length is specified using a CSS measurement value.

Listing 4.4 shows the document from earlier in the chapter with letter and word spacing rules set in the style sheet.

WWW.

Listing 4.4: Letter and Word Spacing in Action

```
<!DOCTYPE html PUBLIC "-//W3C//DTD XHTML 1.0 Transitional//EN"
"http://www.w3.org/TR/xhtml1/DTD/xhtml1-transitional.dtd">

<html xmlns="http://www.w3.org/1999/xhtml">

<html>
<head>
 <title>css typography</title>
<style type="text/css">

h1 {
    font-family: Georgia, Times, serif;
    font-size: 24px;
    font-variant: small-caps;
}

h2 {
    font-family: Georgia, Times, serif;
    font-size: 20px;
```

```
        font-style: italic;
}

h3  {
        font-family: Georgia, Times, serif;
        font-size: 18px;
}

p  {
        font-family: Verdana, arial, helvetica, sans-serif;
        font-size: 16px;
        letter-spacing: 2px;
        word-spacing: 10px;}

strong  {
        font-weight: 800;
)</style>

</head>

<body>

<h1>The Laying Of The Monster</h1>
<h2>By Theodosia Garrison</h2>

<p>Dorothea reposed with her shoulders in the shade of the bulkhead and
her bare feet burrowing in the sun-warmed sand. Beneath her shoulder blades
was a bulky and disheveled volume—a bound year of <strong>Godey's Lady
Book</strong> of the vintage of the early seventies. Having survived the
handling of three generations, this seemed to take naturally to being
drenched with rain and warped by sun, or, as at the present moment, serving
its owner either as a sand-pillow or as a receptacle for divers scribbled
verses on its fly-leaves and margins.</p>

<p>It was with a poem now that Dorothea was wrestling, as she wriggled her
toes in the sand and gazed blankly oceanward. Under the scorching August
sun, the Atlantic seemed to purr like a huge, amiable lion cub.

<p>It was not the amiabilities of nature, however, in which Dorothea found
inspiration. A harp of a single string, she sang as that minstrel might
who was implored to make love alone his theme.</p>

</body>
</html>
```

Figure 4.16 shows the spacing in effect.

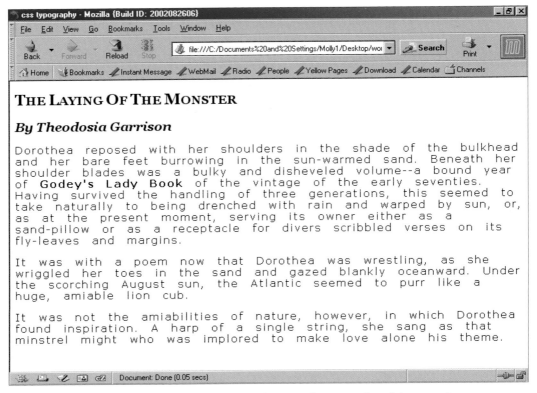

Figure 4.16: Letter and word spacing. Compare this to earlier examples of the same document without the spacing rules in place.

 Many CSS authors prefer to use ems for letter and word spacing because ems will allow the font to scale automatically when you make a change to the font's size.

Transforming Text

You can modify the way text is capitalized using the `text-transform` property.

Here's a snippet that shows a selector and rule for a variety of available `text-transform` values:

```
h1 {
    text-transform: capitalize;
}

h2 {
    text-transform: uppercase;
}

h3 {
    text-transform: lowercase;
}
```

NOTE A value of none will ensure that no capitalization effects are applied.

Figure 4.17 shows examples of how these transformations apply.

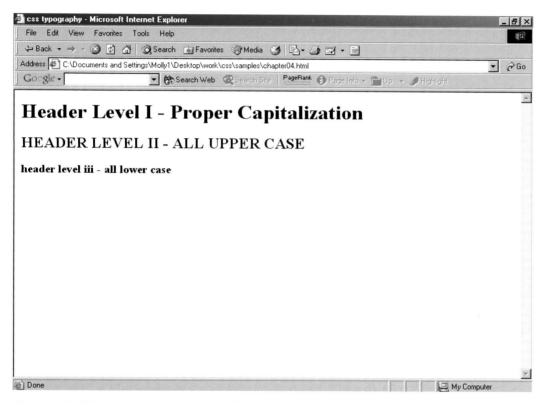

Figure 4.17: Using text-transform *on headings to control capitalization.*

Managing White Space

You can manage aspects of white space using the white-space property.

To mimic normal browser behavior where any additional white space between tags or characters is collapsed down to one space, use the normal property:

```
p {
    white-space: normal;
}
```

To prevent collapse of white space and preserve your line breaks, use the pre property:

```
p {
    white-space: pre;
}
```

Finally, you can suppress line breaks in text by using the nowrap property:

```
td.nowrap  {
      white-space: nowrap;
}
```

Try out these properties and values within a document of your own, and look at the differences between values.

Working with Line Height

In typography, *leading* is the space between individual lines of text. The term comes from the days of typesetting, when lead was used to ensure the proper spacing between lines.

Normal leading is usually the same or very near to the size of the type being used. For example, when you have 12 pixel type, the leading is going to look very natural at 12 pixels, too.

To control leading with style sheets, you can use the line-height property. Its value is numeric, in whatever measurement you're using:

```
p  {
      font-family: Verdana, Arial, Helvetica, sans-serif;
      font-size: 16px;
      line-height: 22px;
}
```

To give you and idea of how line-height works, Listing 4.5 shows a document with inline line-height properties and values.

Listing 4.5: Working with *line-height*

```
<!DOCTYPE html PUBLIC "-//W3C//DTD XHTML 1.0 Transitional//EN"
"http://www.w3.org/TR/xhtml1/DTD/xhtml1-transitional.dtd">

<html xmlns="http://www.w3.org/1999/xhtml">

<html>
<title>css typography</title>

<style type="text/css">

h1  {
      font-family: Georgia, Times, serif;
      font-size: 24px;
      font-variant: small-caps;
}

h2  {
      font-family: Georgia, Times, serif;
      font-size: 20px;
      font-style: italic;
}
```

```
h3  {
    font-family: Georgia, Times, serif;
    font-size: 18px;
}

p  {
    font-family: Verdana, arial, helvetica, sans-serif;
    font-size: 16px;
    letter-spacing: 2px;
    word-spacing: 10px;
    line-height: 26px;
}

strong  {
    font-weight: 800;
)

</style>

</head>

<body>

<h1>The Laying Of The Monster</h1>
<h2>By Theodosia Garrison</h2>

<p>Dorothea reposed with her shoulders in the shade of the bulkhead and
her bare feet burrowing in the sun-warmed sand. Beneath her shoulder blades
was a bulky and disheveled volume—a bound year of <strong>Godey's Lady
Book</strong> of the vintage of the early seventies. Having survived the
handling of three generations, this seemed to take naturally to being
drenched with rain and warped by sun, or, as at the present moment, serving
its owner either as a sand-pillow or as a receptacle for divers scribbled
verses on its fly-leaves and margins.</p>

<p>It was with a poem now that Dorothea was wrestling, as she wriggled her
toes in the sand and gazed blankly oceanward. Under the scorching August
sun, the Atlantic seemed to purr like a huge, amiable lion cub.</p>

<p>It was not the amiabilities of nature, however, in which Dorothea found
inspiration. A harp of a single string, she sang as that minstrel might
who was implored to make love alone his theme.</p>

</body>
</html>
```

Figure 4.18 shows a document using line-height values. Compare this figure to one
of the earlier figures of the same document to see the difference.

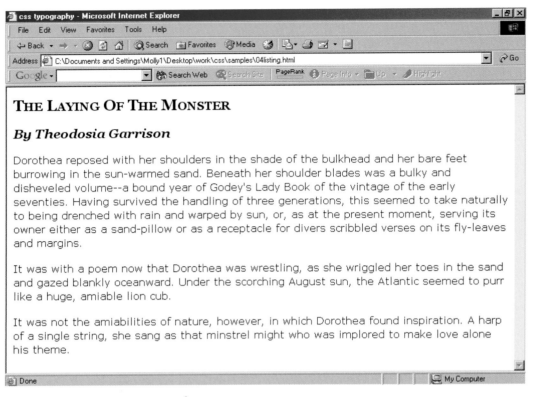

Figure 4.18: Using line-height *values*

Using the Shorthand *font* Property

Just as with so many properties, font-related properties can be condensed into a shorthand form using the font property. Here's an example:

```
p {
      font: italic bold small-caps 16px/22px Verdana, Arial, Helvetica, sans-serif;
}
```

Order is crucial when working with shorthand font properties. First comes style, then weight, then any variants. This is followed by font size and size value, followed by a slash (/) and the line height with its size value, followed by any font names you'd like to use.

Next Steps

This chapter has given you a lot to work with when it comes to CSS typography. Of course, the examples here are only a small sampling of what can be done with type. In the following chapters, you'll see rules relating to fonts and text used in a variety of ways on a range of sites and designs.

Next up is Chapter 5, "Color, Backgrounds, and Borders," in which you'll get a taste of working with CSS to add interesting effects to various elements within a document.

*Artists can color the sky red
because they know it's blue.*

—Jules Feiffer

five

Color, Backgrounds, and Borders

Some of the greatest flexibility you'll encounter when designing with CSS is the way you can apply color to a page and its elements, use backgrounds to add interest and texture to designs, and make use of an element's borders to create visual interest.

Of course, the exciting parts about CSS are the properties that let you control specific aspects of design elements, unlike those options in HTML or XHTML presentational markup.

In this chapter, you will learn:

- How to use color to style elements
- How to work with background properties
- How to use border properties to add interest to your visual designs

Using Color

Color is a profoundly important part of design, largely because it affects people in a visceral, emotional way. The colors you choose for your site will significantly impact the way your visitors interpret your message.

Color can be exciting, calming, persuasive, elegant, uplifting. What's more, perspectives related to culture, language, geography, and gender complicate the meaning of color, too.

Consider the following:

- Death is represented by black in most of Western society, whereas in many Eastern cultures, death is represented by white.
- For the Yup'ik Eskimo, there are 15 variations on the word "snow." Many of the subtleties within these definitions are based on features specific to color: hue, opacity, lightness, and darkness.
- It appears that women are capable of naming many more color names than men. This is likely due to more of an awareness of color variations rather than a physiological difference, although interestingly, color blindness is more predominant in males.

Color is a rather astonishing blend of science and art, physiology and human perception. Using CSS, designers are empowered to do things with color that will really bring a fresh perspective to contemporary web design.

With CSS, you can apply color not just to an element but also to specific portions of that element, such as a particular border style on a specific border. The flexibility of CSS gives us countless options as designers—options we've only barely tapped in the short time we've actually been able to enjoy CSS's powers.

Color and the Web

Before you dig too deeply into CSS color, it's important to know a few things. If you're trained in computer-related or design technology, you might be aware of color models. If you have a background in design or web design, you've undoubtedly heard about web-safe colors. If not, this section will provide information on both, some of which you might find surprising.

Color Models

There are several color models in graphic design. These models exist to manage various aspects of how color is managed and ultimately seen in a range of media.

Color models are based on color theories. Color theory is an extremely complicated topic, and with the exception of the generalities I'll be discussing here, its details are far beyond the scope of this book. Take a look at the "Learn More About Color" sidebar for some ideas on where to get more information.

Color theory, for our needs here, can be broken down into two general groups: subtractive synthesis and additive synthesis. Subtractive synthesis is the idea that what you see in the real world and how you recreate organic color via dyes and inks is based on how much or little light interacts with the given pigment. The familiar color wheel is an example of subtractive synthesis (see Figure 5.1).

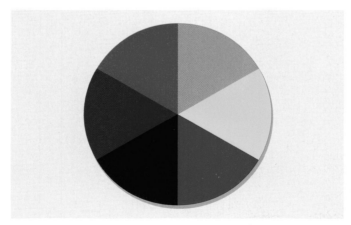

Figure 5.1:
The familiar color wheel

The color model known as CMY—Cyan, Magenta, Yellow—is a means used by computers for expressing colors in subtractive synthesis. With the addition of black, which creates the color model CMYK, this is the means by which colors are reproduced in print (see Figure 5.2).

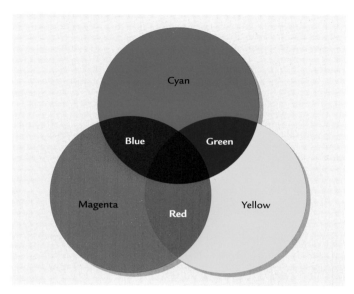

Figure 5.2:
CMYK color

But computers are different when managing screen color because they rely on additive synthesis to create that color (Figure 5.3). Computers generate light. There are three colors of light that computers generate: Red, Green, and Blue. To create a given color on screen, varying amounts of Red, Green, and Blue are mixed. White is the total amount of Red, Green, and Blue respectively, and Black is the absence of Red, Green, or Blue.

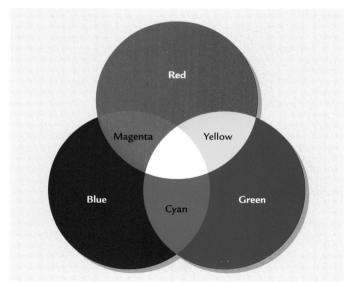

Figure 5.3:
RGB color

 How well color is replicated onscreen is based upon not only a requested value but also how effectively the unique combination of hardware and software can reproduce that color.

When you use hexadecimal or color name values in HTML or XHTML, those values all relate to RGB. In hexadecimal (base 16) the numeric values of red, green, and blue are respectively represented by the base 16 alphanumeric string of six characters. While color names are more obvious, they, too, are simply another means of representing a color within the RGB color model. Ultimately, these hex and name values ask that a computer display the related RGB value.

 CSS naturally uses the RGB model because it is predominantly a screen-based technology. Values in CSS are quite a bit more flexible than those presentational attribute values available in HTML and XHTML.

Web-Safe Color

Web-safe color came about because of specific problems between the ways different platforms manage color. By limiting the palette to 216 colors (see Figure 5.4), the idea was that dithering—the computer attempting to create a close approximation of a color it couldn't quite support—would be avoided.

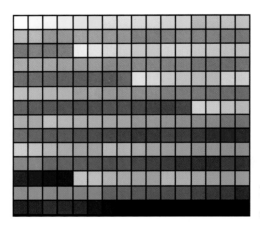

Figure 5.4:
The 216 colors of the
web-safe palette

These 216 colors were considered the common denominator between Windows and Macintosh during a time when most Web users had limited color support via hardware and software anyway.

 Bring Unix and Linux into the mix and you find that there are even fewer colors available that *probably* won't dither in limited color support situations.

There is no such thing as truly consistent color on a computer screen. This is due to what I mentioned earlier—color reproduction on a screen is not just at the mercy of the RGB color model, it's also at the mercy of the hardware and software that individual computer is using. Other issues, such as a computer's ability to manage Gamma, the intensity produced by specific monitors, also influence this issue. When you think of how many possible combinations of video cards, video monitors, operating systems, and operating system versions exist, it's easy to see why color reproduction onscreen is so inconsistent.

Add to that complicated mix the fact that different web browsers and browser versions manage color differently, and you really end up with a lot of possibilities. In my office there are currently three computers with different configurations, and all of them are displaying the same web page with significant differences in the display of the supposedly "safe" colors.

Because of this, I believe that there is no such thing as web-safe color. If you can't have color consistency between individual configurations, how can you possibly have color consistency when you add browsers into the soup? The fact is, you cannot.

What may be closer to reality is web-*safer* color.

 There's been some web-safe color testing that demonstrates different viewpoints. See www.visibone.com/colorlab/colortest.html and http://hotwired.lycos.com/webmonkey/00/37/index2a.html for more information.

So what does this mean to you? Should you not use web-safe colors? Well, that's going to mostly depend upon your audience. If you're dealing with an audience that is largely using older computers, you may have more impetus to avoid dithering.

But the majority of designers have little to worry about for most of their site visitors. Consumer computers now ship with fairly high-end color management for all platforms, so even if a given user doesn't optimize their system for color management, their default is going to be able to manage almost any color. Will that color look the same on that computer configuration as on mine? Probably not. But it's the best we can get, and so it must do.

As a result, you'll see a mix of colors used throughout this book. Some of these colors fall into the web-safe category, while others do not.

Learn More About Color

Color means a lot to me, so I've written a bit about it. Here are three articles and a book to help you learn more about web color.

Satisfying Customers with Color, Shape, and Type
Originally written for *Web Techniques Magazine*, this article describes using color effectively on the Web: www.molly.com/articles/webdesign/1999-11-customers.php

Color My World
This article focuses on international color design for the Web: www.molly.com/articles/webdesign/2000-09-colormyworld.php

True Colors
In this article, you'll take a deeper look at web color technology, and what is "safe" or "unsafe" color: www.molly.com/articles/webdesign/2001-05-truecolors.php

Color for Websites
The name says it all! This is a large-format, hard-cover book that takes a close look at color for the web, in full color, hardback, from Rotovision: www.rotovision.com/description.asp?bookid=500#

Applying Color

Color is applied in CSS by combining appropriate properties with color values. There exist numerous properties related to color, but the core color property I'll begin with is, simply, color.

The color property specifically defines the *foreground* of an element's text-based content. So, if you write this rule:

```
body: {
    color: #000000;
}
```

it means that all text elements, unless other rules are provided for them, will be black.

To work through the examples in this section—and for many of the examples in the rest of the chapter—you'll begin with a simple listing and style sheet. I've embedded the sheet so that everything is kept in one document here, but you can certainly separate the style sheet out into a linked sheet should you so desire.

Listing 5.1 shows the basic document.

WWW.

Listing 5.1: A Document with Some Basic Styles

```
<!DOCTYPE html PUBLIC "-//W3C//DTD XHTML 1.1//EN"
        "http://www.w3.org/TR/xhtml11/DTD/xhtml11.dtd">

<html xmlns="http://www.w3.org/1999/xhtml" xml:lang="en">

<head>
    <title>Chapter Five</title>

<style type="text/css">

body {
    font: 16px Verdana, Arial, Helvetica, sans-serif;
    margin: 20px;
}

h1 {
    font: bold 28px Verdana, Arial, Helvetica, sans-serif;
}

h2 {
    font: bold 24px Verdana, Arial, Helvetica, sans-serif;
}

</style>

</head>

<body>

<h1>color my world</h1>
```

```
<p>The way color is used in a worldwide context is a profound issue that's
often misunderstood or overlooked by Web designers. How it's used on the
screen is made more challenging by the fact that the perception of color
depends not only upon our ability to see that color, but also on our
ability to interpret it within the context of our emotional and cultural
realities.</p>

<h2>gender and color</h2>

<p>Another issue often missed when determining color is gender. Men's and
women's reactions to color are significantly different and, when combined
with cultural issues, the challenge becomes quite complex.
</p>

<p>"In our culture, real men don't eat quiche and they don't use color
terms like 'mauve' and 'teal,'" quips Morton. "I don't think men are as
sensitive as women to color."</p>

<p>"The Meaning of Color for Gender" by Natalia Khouw points out some
interesting theories derived from academic studies about color and gender,
including the following:</p>

<ul>

<li>Blue stands out for men much more than for women</li>

<li>Men prefer blue to red, women red to blue</li>

<li>Men prefer orange to yellow, women yellow to orange</li>

<li>Women's color tastes are thought to be more diverse than men's</li>

</ul>

<p>One of the studies cited in the paper was done in Nepal, where men and
women were asked to list all of the colors they could think of. Women were
able to consistently list more colors than men could. A similar study in
England had similar results, with women identifying many more colors than
men could.</p>

<hr />

</body>
</html>
```

Figure 5.5 shows the document as it appears prior to the styles you'll be adding in this chapter.

color my world

The way color is used in a worldwide context is a profound issue that's often misunderstood or overlooked by Web designers. How it's used on the screen is made more challenging by the fact that the perception of color depends not only upon our ability to see that color, but also on our ability to interpret it within the context of our emotional and cultural realities.

gender and color

Another issue often missed when determining color is gender. Men's and women's reactions to color are significantly different and, when combined with cultural issues, the challenge becomes quite complex.

"In our culture, real men don't eat quiche and they don't use color terms like 'mauve' and 'teal,'" quips Morton. "I don't think men are as sensitive as women to color."

"The Meaning of Color for Gender" by Natalia Khouw points out some interesting theories derived from academic studies about color and gender, including the following:

- Blue stands out for men much more than for women
- Men prefer blue to red, women red to blue
- Men prefer orange to yellow, women yellow to orange
- Women's color tastes are thought to be more diverse than men's

One of the studies cited in the paper was done in Nepal, where men and women were asked to list all of the colors they could think of. Women were able to consistently list more colors than men could. A similar study in England had similar results, with women identifying many more colors than men could.

Figure 5.5: The simply styled document

Color values in CSS are quite a bit more flexible then those in HTML and XHTML. You can apply color values in the following ways:

Color names   There are 16 valid color names that you can use in CSS2. CSS2.1 adds the color orange for a total of 17 valid names. There's a table in Appendix A that you can refer to when you need a quick look at these colors, but because it's a short list, I'll provide them here also for the purpose of our discussion. The color names you can use are: aqua, black, blue, fuchsia, gray, green, lime, maroon, navy, olive, purple, red, silver, teal, white, and yellow.

An example using a color name:

```
body  {
     color: black;
}
```

This would cause all the text within the body (and any children of the body) to have the color black unless other rules are specified.

 NOTE   The 16 color names in CSS come from the HTML 4 specification. It's interesting to note that most of the colors in this list are not considered to be web safe.

Hexadecimal values (long form) You can use any hexadecimal value you like with CSS. The correct form is to use the octothorpe, also known as a hash mark (#), followed by the correct hexadecimal equivalent of the RGB value that you'd like to use:

```
#663366;
```

Here's an example for a heading level 1:

```
h1  {
     color: #663366;
}
```

If you add this rule to a style sheet for the example described in Figure 5.1, the h1 turns a dark purple hue (see Figure 5.6).

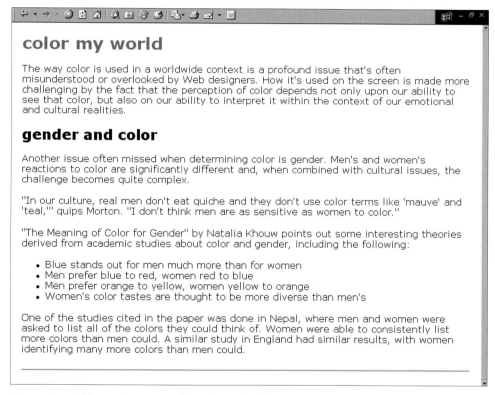

Figure 5.6: Adding color using a hexadecimal value

Hexadecimal shorthand values Any hexadecimal value that contains double characters can be written in shorthand. In other words, if you take the value #cc99cc, you'll notice the red, green, and blue values are represented by a value pair of either letters (CC) or numbers (99). You can shorthand this type of hexadecimal value as follows:

```
#c9c
```

You'll notice that I still use the octothorpe, and I shortened each pair to its singular value. Here's a sample as applied to a heading level 2.

```
h2   {
     color: #c9c;
}
```

Figure 5.7 shows that the h2 is now lavender.

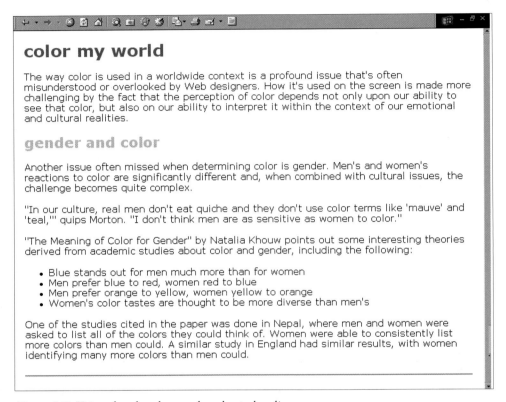

Figure 5.7: Using shorthand to apply color to headings

It's important to keep in mind that shorthand values are only available for paired values as described here. If you have a hexadecimal value that is not paired, such as #B03060, you cannot make it shorthand because the interpretation is based on pairing.

RGB numeric values You can use the literal number value for red, green, and blue in sequence. This is done by denoting that you're using the RGB value and then placing the values, separated by commas, into parentheses:

```
rgb(051, 051, 102)
```

To style the bulleted list using this subtle blue RGB value, you would do the following:

```
ul   {
     color: rgb(051, 051, 102);
}
```

Figure 5.8 shows the results.

The way color is used in a worldwide context is a profound issue that's often misunderstood or overlooked by Web designers. How it's used on the screen is made more challenging by the fact that the perception of color depends not only upon our ability to see that color, but also on our ability to interpret it within the context of our emotional and cultural realities.

gender and color

Another issue often missed when determining color is gender. Men's and women's reactions to color are significantly different and, when combined with cultural issues, the challenge becomes quite complex.

"In our culture, real men don't eat quiche and they don't use color terms like 'mauve' and 'teal,'" quips Morton. "I don't think men are as sensitive as women to color."

"The Meaning of Color for Gender" by Natalia Khouw points out some interesting theories derived from academic studies about color and gender, including the following:

- Blue stands out for men much more than for women
- Men prefer blue to red, women red to blue
- Men prefer orange to yellow, women yellow to orange
- Women's color tastes are thought to be more diverse than men's

One of the studies cited in the paper was done in Nepal, where men and women were asked to list all of the colors they could think of. Women were able to consistently list more colors than men could. A similar study in England had similar results, with women identifying many more colors than men could.

Figure 5.8: Using specific RGB values

RGB percentage values Another means of writing RGB values is to use percentages. The percentage relates to how much red, green, or blue is used to create the color: 100 percent of each color creates white, whereas 0 percent of each creates black. The syntax for RGB percentage values is as follows:

```
rgb(0%, 50%, 100%)
```

You can get creative and use this light blue color to style the horizontal rules within the document:

```
hr  {
     color: rgb(0%, 50%, 100%);
}
```

 While most common browsers do, not all browsers support the color property to style horizontal rules. If you do decide to use this method, be sure to test in those browsers that do. Another approach would be to style a bottom border, which you will learn how to do later this chapter.

Listing 5.2 shows all of the color styles created here in a style sheet together. It's not a problem to combine value methods as I've done here, as long as the syntax for each rule is correct.

Usually, for quick mockups, sticking to color names is very handy. My own preference is to use RGB values, because these can be most easily matched to any existing RGB value guidelines without having to convert to hexadecimal.

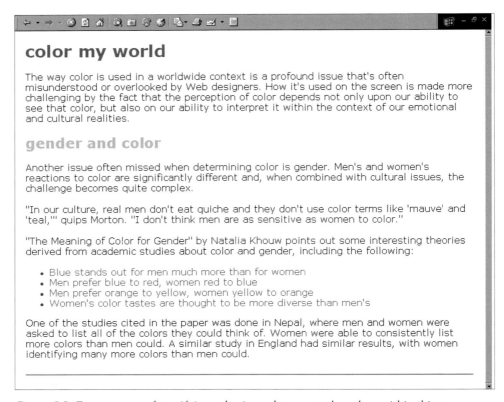

Figure 5.9: Every means of specifying color is used to create the colors within this page.

WWW.

Listing 5.2: The Style Sheet Using Multiple Color Values

```
body  {
      font: 16px Verdana, Arial, Helvetica, sans-serif;
      margin: 20px;
      color: black;
}

h1  {
      font: bold 28px Verdana, Arial, Helvetica, sans-serif;
      color: #663366;
}

h2  {
```

```
      font: bold 24px Verdana, Arial, Helvetica, sans-serif;
      color: #c9c;
}

ul {
      color: rgb(051, 051, 102);
}

hr {
      color: rgb(0%, 50%, 100%);
}
```

Figure 5.9 shows the colorful results.

Working with Backgrounds

You can apply a background property to any element. Whether it's a division, a table, a paragraph, a heading—whatever you like—you can add color or graphics to enhance the appearance of that element.

In the CSS2 specifications, background refers to the background of the content *and* padding areas for the element. This means any property you apply to a background will include the padding as well as the background.

 Background properties are not inherited.

Adding a Background Color

To add a background color to any element, use the `background-color` property. Here's a perfect opportunity to use color!

There are two values available for this property, `<color>` and `transparent`.

A value of `<color>` is any color value: Hexadecimal, Hex shorthand, RGB, and color names. A value of transparent makes the background of the element transparent so that the color or images behind it can show through.

 The `transparent` value is especially helpful because background properties are not inherited. Also, the `background-color` property, while not inherited, will show through to children elements in compliant browsers because the `transparent` value is considered the default for that property.

If you add the following rules to the headings in the earlier document, you'll see the effect of the background color and how it's applied to the complete element:

```
body {
      font: 16px Verdana, Arial, Helvetica, sans-serif;
      margin: 20px;
```

```
    color: black;
    background-color: #FFFFCC;
}


h1  {
    font: bold 28px Verdana, Arial, Helvetica, sans-serif;
    color: #663366;
    background-color: #CCC;
}


h2  {
    font: bold 24px Verdana, Arial, Helvetica, sans-serif;
    color: #c9c;
}
```

Figure 5.10 shows the document with updated changes.

Figure 5.10: Adding a few background colors starts to perk this page up.

Inserting a Background Image

Background images are a great way to add color, texture, and visual interest to your designs. Backgrounds for use with CSS are created with many of the same design ideals in mind as those created for use with conventional HTML.

- Backgrounds can be wallpaper tiles or watermark style.
- File sizes should be kept as small as possible.
- Backgrounds should contrast with foreground text colors as much as possible to encourage readability.

 While background images can be made to tile to fill the browser window exactly as they do using conventional HTML, CSS does offer more control over backgrounds. Because you can determine whether they should repeat or be fixed, you have more flexibility in how your background images are designed.

Background images can be inserted into any element using the `background-image` property (or the `background` property; see the "CSS Shorthand for Backgrounds" section later in this chapter). The image can then be positioned or modified in a variety of ways. The general syntax is as follows:

```
background-image: url(my_image.gif)
```

To add a background image that will tile the entire body of your design, follow these steps:

1. Be sure your background image is placed in the proper directory. For the purposes of this exercise, I placed the image (`flower-tile.gif`) in the same directory as the sample document (grab the file from the book's web page for a close-up look as the file is quite small). The image is 40x40 pixels and purposely designed to create a seamless tile design (see Figure 5.11).

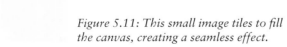

Figure 5.11: This small image tiles to fill
the canvas, creating a seamless effect.

2. In the style sheet, add the `background-image` property to the body selector:

```
body   {
     font: 16px Verdana, Arial, Helvetica, sans-serif;
     margin: 20px;
     color: black;
     background-color: #FFFFCC;
     background-image: url(flower-tile.gif);
}
```

3. Save and view your file.
   Figure 5.12 shows the results.

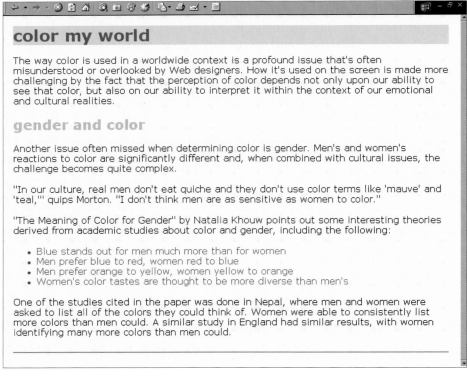

Figure 5.12: Adding the background to the document

To see how an image can be applied to a specific element, follow these steps:

1. Begin by commenting out the background image in the body. This is so you can leave the image in the style sheet, but disable it for the time being:

    ```
    body   {
           font: 16px Verdana, Arial, Helvetica, sans-serif;
           margin: 20px;
           color: black;
           background-color: #FFFFCC;
           /* background-image: url(flower-tile.gif); */
    }
    ```

2. In the style sheet, add a paragraph selector and declaration block below the h2 selector entry:

    ```
    h2   {
           font: bold 24px Verdana, Arial, Helvetica, sans-serif;
           color: #c9c;
    }

    p   {

    }
    ```

3. Add the declaration:

```
p {
    background-image: url(flower-tile.gif);
}
```

Save your file and view in your browser (see Figure 5.13). The tiles will now only be applied to the paragraph elements (5.13A), but any others elements (5.13B) remain unaffected by the rule.

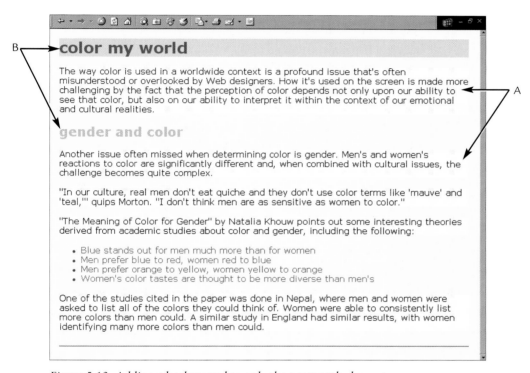

Figure 5.13: Adding a background to only the paragraph elements

Applying suitable mix-and-match backgrounds to different page elements is one area where designers have a terrific opportunity to be innovative and unique using CSS.

 As with HTML, it's recommended that you include a background color that's as close to the main color within your background graphic *as well as* the background graphic in your style sheet. This way, if a background does not load, your site visitor will still see the intended color.

Modifying Background Features

There are several features with which you can manage background graphics to create clever as well as functional design opportunities:

Repeating With the `background-repeat` property, you can define how a background repeats, or if it repeats at all.

Positioning Using the `background-position` property and a range of values, you can position your background graphics in context of the element for which they are defined.

Scrolling The `background-attachment` property allows the background image to scroll with the content (behavior you're used to with HTML backgrounds) or remain fixed in place while the rest of the document scrolls in front of it.

 Fixed background images are placed with respect to the browser window, not the element to which they're assigned.

Repeating a Background Image

You can define the way a background image will repeat, or not repeat, depending upon your needs.

Using the `background-repeat` property, you can modify a background's repetitions using the values described in Table 5.1.

Table 5.1: Values Associated with Background Repetition

Value	Description
repeat	Causes the background to tile as you'd expect if you were using conventional HTML.
repeat-x	Causes the background to be repeated along the left and right of the x-axis.
repeat-y	Causes the background to be repeated up and down along the y-axis.
no-repeat	Suppresses repetition completely. The background will be placed into the element, but no repeating will occur.

To make the background graphic repeat along the x-axis, follow these steps:

1. In the style sheet, replace any existing background graphic within the body selector as follows:

```
body   {
        font: 16px Verdana, Arial, Helvetica, sans-serif;
        margin: 20px;
        color: black;
        background-color: #FFFFCC;
        background-image: url(background-square.gif);
    }
```

2. Add the repeat declaration:

```
body  {
      font: 16px Verdana, Arial, Helvetica, sans-serif;
      margin: 20px;
      color: black;
      background-color: #FFFFCC;
      background-image: url(background-square.gif);
      background-repeat: repeat-x;
}
```

3. Save your file and view the changes in your browser (see Figure 5.14).

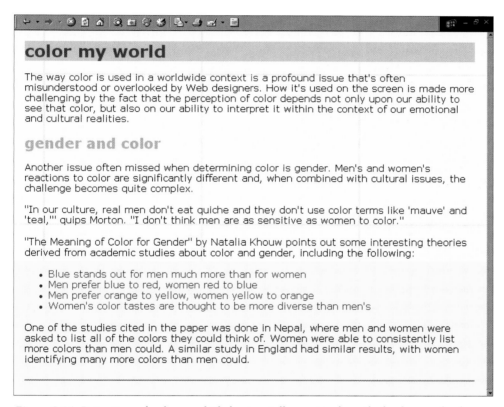

Figure 5.14: Repeating a background tile horizontally—notice how the background color appears where the background ceases to tile.

You can now play with the available values to see how they will affect the behavior of the repetition.

To repeat an image along the y-axis, modify the above style sheet within the document as follows:

```
body  {
      font: 16px Verdana, Arial, Helvetica, sans-serif;
      margin: 20px;
```

```
    color: black;
    background-color: #FFFFCC;
    background-image: url(background-square.gif);
    background-repeat: repeat-y;
}
```

Figure 5.15 shows the results.

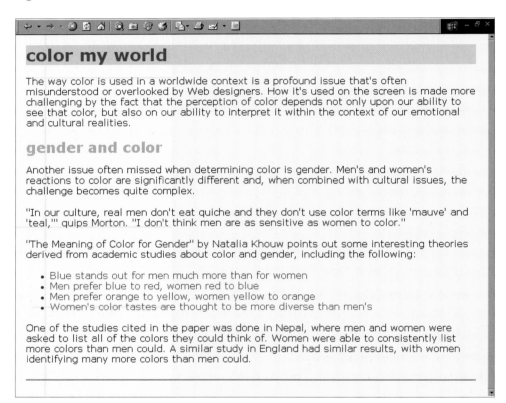

Figure 5.15: Repeating the background along the y-axis only

To fix the image so it doesn't repeat, modify the style using the no-repeat value:

```
body  {
    font: 16px Verdana, Arial, Helvetica, sans-serif;
    margin: 20px;
    color: black;
    background-color: #FFFFCC;
    background-image: url(background-square.gif);
    background-repeat: no-repeat;
}
```

View the document in your browser, and you'll see that the image does not repeat at all. Rather, it is fixed to the upper-left and right of the element for which it is defined, in this case, the body (see Figure 5.16).

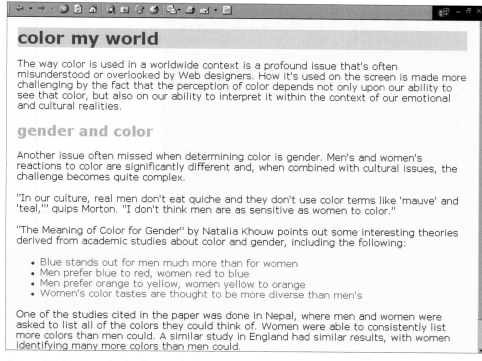

Figure 5.16: Here, the background doesn't repeat.

By now, you've probably noticed that the way you manage repeating a background image influences its position to a certain degree. You can get even greater control at this point by adding background positioning for the image.

Positioning a Background Image

Positioning determines the point or points within the element in use where the tiling of your image begins.

Table 5.2 shows the values and a description of their results.

Table 5.2: Value Meanings for Background Positioning

Value	Meaning
percentage	You can use one or two percentage values. If you use a single value, that value will place the background in relation to the padding edge of its element for both the x- and y-axes. If you use two percentage values, the first denotes the x-axis location, the second, the y-axis.
length	Defines the relationship of the background image from the top left corner of the element's padding edge. You can use one length value for both axes. If you use two values, the first is the horizontal (x) axis, and the second is the vertical (y).

Table continues on next page

Table 5.2: Value Meanings for Background Positioning *(continued)*

Value	Meaning
top	Causes the top edge of the originating position within the element to be aligned with the top edge of the background graphic. Note that you can combine the keywords top, bottom, left, and right to achieve different effects.
bottom	Causes the bottom edge of the originating position within the element to be aligned with the bottom edge of the background.
left	Causes the left edge of the originating position to be aligned with the left edge of the graphic.
right	Causes the right edge of the originating position to be aligned with the right edge of the graphic.
center	Allows the center of the originating position and the center of the image to be aligned.

NOTE You can't mix keywords and values. For example, "top 50%" is not acceptable, where "0px 50%" is.

Because you've made a lot of modifications for the first listing, you'll start with a new listing to learn about positioning backgrounds, Listing 5.3.

WWW.   **Listing 5.3: The Sample Document, Cleaned Up for the Following Exercises**

```
<!DOCTYPE html PUBLIC "-//W3C//DTD XHTML 1.1//EN"
     "http://www.w3.org/TR/xhtml11/DTD/xhtml11.dtd">

<html xmlns="http://www.w3.org/1999/xhtml" xml:lang="en">

<head>
    <title>Chapter Five: Positioning Backgrounds</title>

<style>

body  {
    font: 16px Verdana, Arial, Helvetica, sans-serif;
    margin: 20px;
    color: black;
    background-color: #FFFFCC;
}

h1  {
    font: 24px Verdana, Arial, Helvetica, sans-serif;
    margin: 20px;
    padding: 35px;
    border: 2px solid;
}
```

```
h1.background   {
    background-image: url(position-test.gif);
    background-repeat: no-repeat;
}

</style>

</head>

<body>

<h1>pristine &amp; clean</h1>

<h1 class="background">background action</h1>

</body>
</html>
```

Figure 5.17 shows the results.

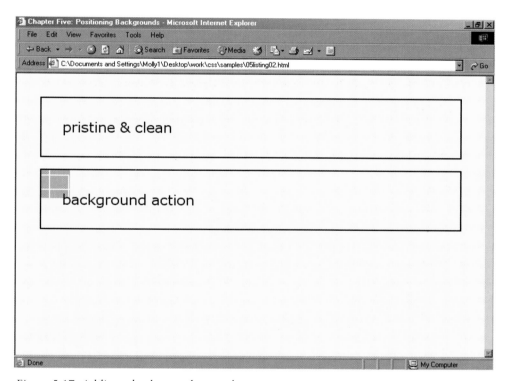

Figure 5.17: Adding a background to an element

A few things to note:

• I've added a padding value to the h1 selector of 35 pixels and a border of 2 pixels solid (see "Working with Borders" later in this chapter, for more information on border options).

- I've added a `background` class for the `h1` selector that includes a background image for the example and a value of `no-repeat`. This is to show the sample image once so you can see how it is influenced by the various positioning values.

Positioning with Percentages

Using percentages allows you to denote a position on your graphic that you'll align in relation to the element for that background.

To position your background using one equal percentage value, follow these steps:

1. In the `h1.background` rule, add the `background-position` property:

```
h1.background  {
      background-image: url(position-test.gif);
      background-repeat: no-repeat;
      background-position:
}
```

2. Add the positioning. Set the value as a percentage. Because you're basing your positioning on equivalent values for both the x- and y-axes, you need only use the one value:

```
h1.background  {
      background-image: url(position-test.gif);
      background-repeat: no-repeat;
      background-position: 35%;
}
```

3. Save your changes and view the results (see Figure 5.18).

The background image has been placed 35 percent along the x-axis (5.18A) of the element box, and 35 percent along the y-axis of the element (5.18B).

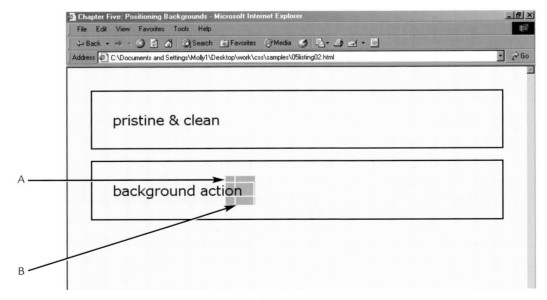

Figure 5.18: Positioning a background using a percentage

You may also use two values, as follows:

```
background-position: 35% 50%;
```

In this case, the first value relates to the x-axis and the second to the y-axis.

 Percentage values may not be mixed with keyword values available when using the background-position property. However, percentage values may be mixed with length values.

Positioning with Length Values

You may prefer to use length values because you can use pixels, precisely positioning your background within its element box.

Length values work a bit differently. Length values describe an offset between the top left corner of the viewing area and the top left corner of the image. Percentages line up the percentage point within the image itself to the same position within the viewing area. For example, if you use a percentage of 50%, the midpoint of the image is aligned to the midpoint of the viewing area.

If only one length is given, that value is applied to the measurement for the x- and y-axes:

```
h1.background  {
     background-image: url(position-test.gif);
     background-repeat: no-repeat;
     background-position: 25px;
}
```

This markup will cause the background to be neatly positioned 25 pixels along the horizontal axis and 10 pixels along the vertical. If two are given, the first one is for the x-axis, the second value for the y-axis:

```
h1.background  {
     background-image: url(position-test.gif);
     background-repeat: no-repeat;
     background-position: 25px 10px;
}
```

Figure 5.19 shows the results. Notice the image is still positioned 25 pixels along the horizontal (5.19A) and is 10 pixels along the vertical axis (5.19B).

 You can combine length with percentage values. If you want a background image to be 25 pixels along the horizontal and 10 percent along the vertical axis, you would write background-position: 25px 10%; for the declaration. You cannot combine length values with keywords, however.

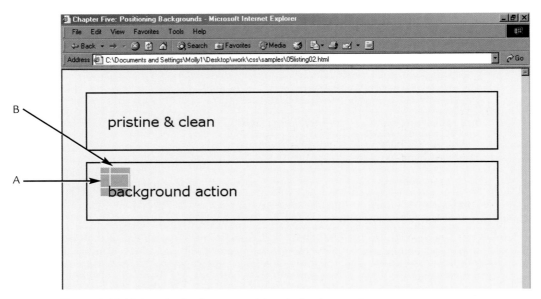

Figure 5.19: Using pixel values to position the background

Positioning with Keywords and Keyword Combinations

As you read at the beginning of this "Positioning a Background Image" section, there are several keyword positioning options available. Keywords can exist by themselves or can be combined into pairs to position the background more effectively within the element box.

Listing 5.4 shows a style sheet that defines and applies a class position for each of the h1 selectors, demonstrating the location of each individual named keyword.

WWW.

Listing 5.4: Demonstrating Background Positioning with Keywords

```
<!DOCTYPE html PUBLIC "-//W3C//DTD XHTML 1.1//EN"
        "http://www.w3.org/TR/xhtml11/DTD/xhtml11.dtd">

<html xmlns="http://www.w3.org/1999/xhtml" xml:lang="en">

<head>
   <title>Chapter Five: Positioning Backgrounds</title>

<style>

body  {
      font: 16px Verdana, Arial, Helvetica, sans-serif;
      margin: 20px;
      color: black;
      background-color: #FFFFCC;
}

h1  {
```

```
        font: 24px Verdana, Arial, Helvetica, sans-serif;
        margin: 20px;
        padding: 35px;
        border: 2px solid;
}

h1.left  {
        background-image: url(position-test.gif);
        background-repeat: no-repeat;
        background-position: left;
}

h1.right  {
        background-image: url(position-test.gif);
        background-repeat: no-repeat;
        background-position: right;
}

h1.bottom  {
        background-image: url(position-test.gif);
        background-repeat: no-repeat;
        background-position: bottom;
}

h1.center  {
        background-image: url(position-test.gif);
        background-repeat: no-repeat;
        background-position: center;
}

</style>

</head>

<body>

<h1>pristine &amp; clean</h1>
<h1 class="left">background-position: left;</h1>
<h1 class="right">background-position: right;</h1>
<h1 class="bottom">background-position: bottom;</h1>
<h1 class="center">background-position: center;</h1>

</body>
</html>
```

Figure 5.20 shows how the background is positioned using these rules.

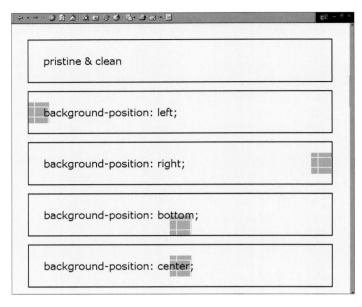

Figure 5.20:
Positioning backgrounds
using keywords

Combining keyword values gets you more options. You can use the following combinations:

- top left
- top center
- top right

- center center
- right center
- bottom left

- bottom center
- bottom right

> **NOTE** You can write these the other way, too. That is, top left can be written left top and it is interpreted the same way. Netscape 6 has a noted bug in this regard; you can read more about it at http://devedge.netscape.com/viewsource/ 2002/background-position-keyword/.

In Listing 5.5, I've created a new document containing styles that demonstrates these combinations.

WWW. **Listing 5.5: Document Describing Paired Keyword Positions**

```
<!DOCTYPE html PUBLIC "-//W3C//DTD XHTML 1.1//EN"
    "http://www.w3.org/TR/xhtml11/DTD/xhtml11.dtd">

<html xmlns="http://www.w3.org/1999/xhtml" xml:lang="en">

<head>
    <title>Chapter Five: Positioning Backgrounds</title>

<style type="text/css">
body {
    font: 16px Verdana, Arial, Helvetica, sans-serif;
    margin: 20px;
```

```
        color: black;
        background-color: #FFFFCC;
}

h1  {
        font: 24px Verdana, Arial, Helvetica, sans-serif;
        margin: 20px;
        padding: 35px;
        border: 2px solid;
}

h1.topLeft  {
        background-image: url(position-test.gif);
        background-repeat: no-repeat;
        background-position: top left;
}

h1.topRight  {
        background-image: url(position-test.gif);
        background-repeat: no-repeat;
        background-position: top right;
}

h1.centerCenter  {
        background-image: url(position-test.gif);
        background-repeat: no-repeat;
        background-position: center center;
}

h1.rightCenter  {
        background-image: url(position-test.gif);
        background-repeat: no-repeat;
        background-position: right center;
}

h1.bottomLeft  {
        background-image: url(position-test.gif);
        background-repeat: no-repeat;
        background-position: bottom left;
}

h1.bottomCenter  {
        background-image: url(position-test.gif);
        background-repeat: no-repeat;
        background-position: bottom center;
}

h1.bottomRight  {
        background-image: url(position-test.gif);
```

```
      background-repeat: no-repeat;
      background-position: bottom right;
}

</style>

</head>

<body>

<h1>pristine &amp; clean</h1>
<h1 class="topLeft">top left</h1>
<h1 class="topRight">top right</h1>
<h1 class="centerCenter">center center</h1>
<h1 class="rightCenter">right center</h1>
<h1 class="bottomLeft">bottom left</h1>
<h1 class="bottomCenter">bottom center</h1>
<h1 class="bottomRight">bottom right</h1>
</body>
</html>
```

Figure 5.21 clearly demonstrates the keyword positioning results.

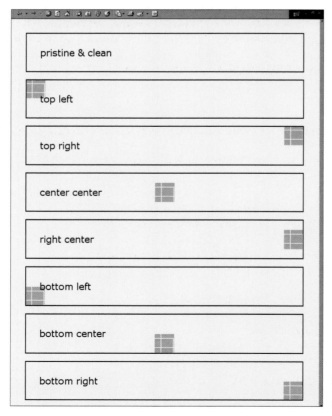

Figure 5.21:
Using paired keywords for
background positioning

It's important to note that keyword and keyword pairs relate directly to specific percentage values. Table 5.3 shows how this works and illustrates how both keywords and percentages relate the background to the x- and y-axes of the element block.

Table 5.3: Keywords and Related Percentage Values in Background Positioning

Keyword/Keyword Pair	Percentage Value
top left	0% 0%
top, top center	50% 0%
right top	100% 0%
left, left center	0% 50%
center, center center	50% 50%
right, right center	100% 50%
bottom left	0% 100%
bottom, bottom center	50% 100%
bottom right	100% 100%

Modifying Scroll

With the `background-attachment` property you can control whether your background scrolls or is fixed. Scrolling backgrounds mimic the behavior you're used to seeing on HTML pages using a background defined with the `background` attribute in the body tag. In HTML, there's no way to modify the scrolling of backgrounds. In CSS, however, you can do so to provide some unique visual effects.

There are two values for the `background-attachment` property:

- `scroll`
- `fixed`

These are pretty self-explanatory, but here's an example of each to clearly differentiate the behavior.

Listing 5.6 describes a simple page with a background image set to scroll.

Listing 5.6: Creating a Background Scroll   WWW.

```
<!DOCTYPE html PUBLIC "-//W3C//DTD XHTML 1.1//EN"
      "http://www.w3.org/TR/xhtml11/DTD/xhtml11.dtd">

<html xmlns="http://www.w3.org/1999/xhtml" xml:lang="en">

<head>
   <title>Chapter Five: Positioning Backgrounds</title>

<style type="text/css">

body  {
      font: 16px Verdana, Arial, Helvetica, sans-serif;
      margin: 20px;
```

```
        color: black;
        background-color: #FFFFCC;
        background-image: url(background-square.gif);
        background-attachment: scroll;
    }

</style>

</head>

<body>


<p>Look well into thyself; there is a source of strength which will always
spring up if thou wilt always look there.</p>

<p><em>Marcus Aurelius</em></p>


</body>
</html>
```

Now, you'll have to fill the page up with enough text so that it does create a vertical scroll. I've used a placeholder quote here to avoid additional pages of just text within the listing, but you can copy and paste any amount of text into this document to test the scrolling. What you'll see is that the background image scrolls along *with* the text; they are attached to one another and act in a dependent way.

To set the contents of the document to scroll over the background while the background remains in a fixed position, replace the scroll value with fixed:

background-attachment: fixed;

Save the document and view it again in a web browser. Now you'll see the content move over the fixed background.

 Browser support is a bit odd for the background-attachment property. While most browsers support the property itself, the majority of available browsers properly support fixed backgrounds only when used with the body element, despite the fact that the CSS2 specification does express that the property should apply to all elements.

CSS Shorthand for Backgrounds

As with quite a few of the properties you've explored in this book, you can write rules for backgrounds using shorthand.

The shorthand property for backgrounds is background. All of the properties and values discussed in this section relate to this property, but of course you only need to define the properties you need to achieve your desired results.

You can set only the background color with a background:

```
p {
    background: yellow;
}
```

A background with a color and an image:

```
p {
    background: yellow url(floral-tile.gif);
}
```

A background with a color, an image, positioning, repeat, and scroll values:

```
p {
    background: yellow url(floral-tile.gif) left bottom repeat-y scroll;
}
```

As always, shorthand properties make for more concise and manageable style sheets. However, using shorthand is an entirely personal choice, and you can mix both longhand and shorthand forms within a style sheet without any problems.

 Since both longhand and shorthand forms are acceptable, when you're working in a larger organization it can be in your best interest to have a style guide describing how authors should write their rules.

Working with Borders

CSS is especially interesting when you realize that you can control element borders quite specifically. This way, you can style a wide range of visual aspects via the element border edge using color, line style, and width. The mere fact that you can style a specific border of a specific element (the left border of one paragraph, the right border of an h2, and so on) means that you can create interesting and appealing visuals by styling portions rather than entire aspects of your element borders.

Borders are a bit complex as a result, and CSS provides several ways to help you manage that complexity:

- As with many CSS properties, the border category of properties has a primary short-hand property that allows you to manage style, color, and width of an element's border.
- Shorthand properties exist for each of an element's four borders (top, bottom, left, right) so that you can manage the style, color, and width of just that element border.
- Complete, individual properties allow you to set specific styles for specific aspects of a border.

So you can get a taste of how all of these properties work, I'll explain each of them. I'm going to go backward from this bulleted list though, starting with the individual styles, then moving on to examples of shorthand properties so you can refine your syntax.

Working with Individual Border Properties

In addition to shorthand border properties, there are 14 individual border properties. In this section, you'll examine each property, its associated values, and some additional properties related to borders that aren't used for width, style, or color.

Border Properties for Border Style

Each individual element has four sides. These are, of course, top, right, bottom, and left. Style in this case is the design style applied to these specific borders.

The individual (nonshorthand) properties specific to border style are as follows:

- `border-top-style`
- `border-right-style`
- `border-bottom-style`
- `border-left-style`

Table 5.4 describes the values related to border styling and their related meaning.

Table 5.4: Border Values and their Meanings

Value	Description
none	No border.
hidden	Like none but refers to border conflict resolution for table elements.
dotted	A series of dots.
dashed	A series of short line segments.
solid	A single line segment.
double	Two solid lines, with the lines plus the space between them equivalent to the defined width.
groove	Appears as a groove carved into the canvas.
ridge	The opposite of groove, appears as a ridge on the canvas.
inset	The border makes the box look as though it were inset into the canvas.
outset	The border makes the box look as though it were coming out of the canvas.

Figure 5.22 shows each of the visible styles (none and hidden are not visible!) applied to all borders within an element.

To add style to individual borders, combine the specific border with a suitable value or values into a rule for a selector. The following will create a dotted border to the left of each paragraph:

```
p {
    border-left-style: dotted;
}
```

You can add width and color to these styles, giving you even more design possibilities.

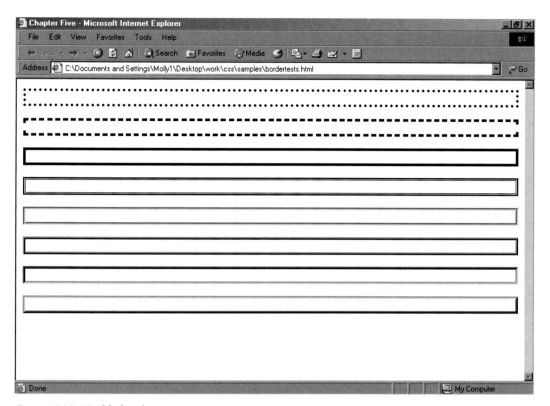

Figure 5.22: Visible border options

Border Properties Related to Width

Within each individual border properties are width properties related to each of these borders.

The properties specific to border width are as follows:

- `border-top-width`
- `border-right-width`
- `border-bottom-width`
- `border-left-width`

There are four possible values for each of these properties:

- The `thin` value creates a thin border.
- The `medium` value creates a medium border.
- The `thick` value creates a thick border.
- You can also define a length value in any available measurement, but not percentages.

Listing 5.7 shows a sample document with a style sheet describing these border properties and values.

Listing 5.7: Examining Individual Border Properties for Width

```
<!DOCTYPE html PUBLIC "-//W3C//DTD XHTML 1.1//EN"
        "http://www.w3.org/TR/xhtml11/DTD/xhtml11.dtd">

<html xmlns="http://www.w3.org/1999/xhtml" xml:lang="en">

<head>
    <title>Chapter Five</title>

<style type="text/css">

body  {
        font: 24px Verdana, Arial, Helvetica, sans-serif;
        color: black;
        background-color: #FFFFCC;
}

h1  {
        border-style: solid;
        border-top-width: thin;
        border-right-width: medium;
        border-bottom-width: thick;
        border-left-width: 25px;
}

</style>

</head>

<body>

<h1>i've got a stylin' border!<h1>

</body>
</html>
```

It's important to note that I added the `border-style: solid;` declaration for the purposes of this example. I needed to provide a style for the entire border before applying widths to demonstrate the concept.

NOTE The color here is taken from the element's color value.

The border in Figure 5.23 is comprised of four values. The border to the top is thin (5.23A). The right border is medium (5.23B). The bottom border is thick (5.23C), and the left, chunky border was achieved by using a length value of 25 pixels (5.23D).

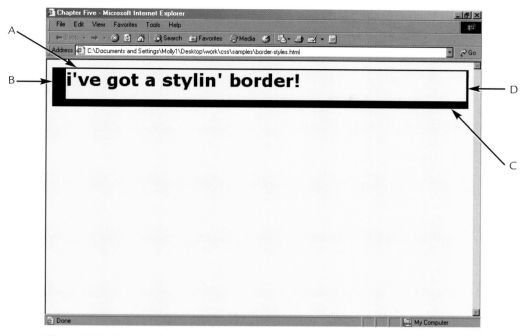

Figure 5.23: Creating border styles

Border Properties for Color

The four properties for styling color for specific borders are as follows:

- `border-top-color`
- `border-right-color`
- `border-bottom-color`
- `border-left-color`

There are two available values:

- Any CSS2 color value (hex, named color, RGB, percentages)
- `transparent`

To color a specific border within an element, follow these steps:

1. Add a selector or class and declaration block to your style sheet to which you'd like to add border color:

   ```
   blockquote  {

   }
   ```

2. Create a border style:

   ```
   blockquote  {
       border-left-style: dashed;

   }
   ```

3. Add a border color:

```
blockquote {
    border-left-style: dashed;
    border-left-width: 4px;
    border-left-color: #ffcc00
}
```

Any instance of a blockquote within a document will now have a 4-pixel dashed yellow border. Listing 5.8 shows a styled document using border color, width, and style.

WWW.   **Listing 5.8: Individual Border Properties for Style, Width, and Color**

```
<!DOCTYPE html PUBLIC "-//W3C//DTD XHTML 1.1//EN"
        "http://www.w3.org/TR/xhtml11/DTD/xhtml11.dtd">

<html xmlns="http://www.w3.org/1999/xhtml" xml:lang="en">

<head>
   <title>Chapter Five</title>

<style>
body {
    font: 24px Verdana, Arial, Helvetica, sans-serif;
    color: #ffffff;
    background-color: #ff6633;
}

h1 {
    border-style: solid;
    border-top-width: thin;
    border-right-width: medium;
    border-bottom-width: thick;
    border-left-width: 25px;
    border-right-color: #ffcc33;
    border-top-color: #33ff33;
}

p {
    font: 20px Verdana, Arial, Helvetica, sans-serif;
    color: black;
}

blockquote {
    border-left-style: dashed;
    border-left-width: 4px;
    border-left-color: #ffcc00;
    padding: 20px;
}
```

```
</style>

</head>

<body>

<h1>i've got a stylin' border!</h1>

<p>Do you now?</p>

<p><blockquote>I've heard it said that a design with a stylin' border can
really pep up the way one's web designs look.</blockquote></p>

<p>Did you now?</p>

</body>
</html>
```

Figure 5.24 shows the results.

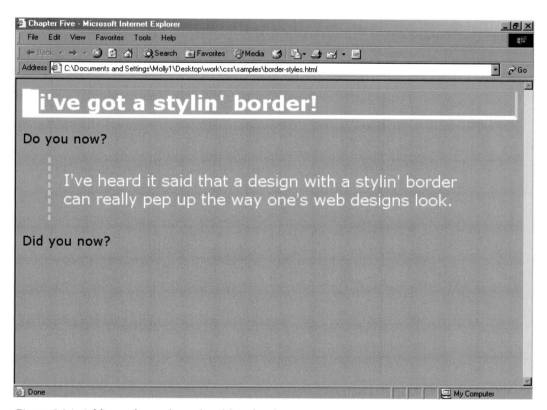

Figure 5.24: Adding color, style, and width to borders

Additional Individual Border Properties

There are two additional nonshorthand border properties of which to be aware: `border-collapse` and `border-spacing`. Both of these properties manage borders in tables.

There are two layout methods available in CSS2. In the collapsing border method, adjacent cells in a table share the same border; this is the default method used by most browsers. In the separate border method, each cell has its own border—none are shared.

To set the method, you begin with the `border-collapse` property and either a `collapse` value:

```
table  {
    border-collapse: collapse;
}
```

or a separate value:

```
table  {
    border-collapse: separate;
}
```

Now, you can continue styling your tables. Obviously, in the `collapse` method, adjacent borders will share whichever styles you use for your border width, style, or color based on a hierarchy of rules. With the `separate` method, every cell has its own border, which can be styled individually.

The `border-spacing` property comes into play when using the separate method. You can control the space between cells using lengths. If you define one length, it provides the value for both the horizontal and vertical spacing of a table. If you specify two lengths, the first is for horizontal and the second is for vertical:

```
table  {
    border-collapse: separate;
    border-spacing: 10px 10px;
}
```

If your table has empty cells, in the `separate` border model, you can choose to determine whether these cells are displayed are not using the `empty-cells` property along with a value of `show` or `hide`, respectively.

 Support for these properties is still more limited than desirable. The `border-collapse` property is only available in IE for Windows versions 5.5 and 6, along with some buggy implementation in Opera 5. The `border-spacing` property is available in IE for Windows versions 5.5 and 6, Netscape 6+ for all platforms, and Opera 5 for all platforms. The `empty-cells` property is only available in Netscape 6+ for all platforms and Opera 5 for all platforms. This limitation makes using these properties unwise for general audiences.

Shorthand Border Properties

You can manage your borders quite effectively using shorthand border properties. I showed you the individual properties first to demonstrate the level of design control you really have over various elements.

The shorthand border properties and their actions are listed in Table 5.5.

Table 5.5: Shorthand Border Properties

Property	Action	Examples
border	Shorthand property to set the same width, color, and style to all four borders of an element.	```h2 { border: 2px dotted magenta; }```
border-top	Shorthand property to set the same width, color, and style to the top border of an element.	```p.note { border-top: 0.25em double black; }```
border-right	Shorthand property to set the same width, color, and style to the right border of an element.	```.caution { border-right: thick solid red; }```
border-bottom	Shorthand property to set the same width, color, and style to the bottom border of an element.	```blockquote { border-bottom: thin dashed #3F3; }```
border-left	Shorthand property to set the same width, color, and style to the left border of an element.	```p.block { border-left: medium solid white; }```

Next Steps

At this point, I hope to have convinced you that it's a really fun, flexible, and creative way of adding presentation to pages that didn't exist prior to the advent and more progressive support of CSS. You can now write CSS rules efficiently modify your type and text using CSS typography and text-related properties. Adding visual interest to pages with color, backgrounds, and borders will help you be more creative than ever when it comes to your designs.

Now comes the truly exciting part: CSS layout. This is not an easy topic, largely due to the fact that support has been quite inconsistent for many layout-related properties. But times are changing, and progressive websites are making the most out of CSS for layout and positioning. You'll learn the properties and methods used to design the layout of pages and also examine some of the workarounds available to manage graceful degradation of CSS-based layouts for older browsers, or those without appropriate CSS support.

The position of the artist is humble.
He is essentially a channel.

—Piet Mondrian

Working with CSS Layouts

The full promise of style sheets is finally coming to fruition. While Opera and Internet Explorer have each had some support for CSS positioning over the past several years, Netscape was slow to the plate, providing only certain aspects of position within its version 4 browsers. However, all new releases of popular web browsers have good support for positioning in general.

This means that you can turn to style sheets for more than just styling text. We can begin to look at the true separation of presentation and document formatting in the context of CSS layout.

In this chapter you'll learn:

- How to position elements using absolute positioning
- How to position elements using relative positioning
- How to float elements
- How to design layouts with positioning
- Workarounds for display of layouts

About CSS Positioning

In the past few years, the primary problem with positioning was that properties for positioning had inconsistent browser support. With more sophisticated browsers, it isn't the positioning that's the problem, but ensuring that sites built with CSS layout methods gracefully degrade for browsers with limited or no CSS support.

Tables have long been the de facto method by which to create layouts, and probably will remain so for some time to come—at least for many designers. Nevertheless, the power of CSS is coming into its own, and many designers are making the daring switch.

Even if you're not instantly able to apply CSS layouts to your professional work, it's a good idea to begin incorporating CSS layouts into your portfolios as much as you can.

Positioning Schemes

Positioning schemes relate to the aspects of how content is presented on a canvas using CSS. First I'll define each scheme, and then I'll provide helpful visual examples of each.

There are several schemes for positioning:

Normal Flow Normal flow content is unpositioned, unfloated content that follows the normal way a browser manages that content. Normal flow works on the principles of block and inline boxes (discussed in Chapter 2, "Learning CSS Theory"). Block boxes are comprised of a containing block and its descendant block boxes. Inline boxes are boxes that are placed along the horizon of a block box, beginning at the top of that block.

Floats While not specific to positioning in the purest sense, floats are a method of laying out boxes. In the float scheme, boxes are first laid out by the normal flow rules. Then, they are removed from the flow and shifted to the left or right. You'll read more about how this works in the "About Floats" section later in the chapter.

Absolute Positioning In this model, a given box is removed from the normal flow, so it doesn't follow the same principles. This means that there is no relationship to that box to any of its sibling boxes. However, it is positioned specifically within its containing block. Unlike normal flow and float schemes, absolutely positioned elements are positioned based on the containing block, not the location where the element actually resides within the normal flow.

Relative Positioning While relative positioning is considered to be part of the Normal Flow positioning scheme in the CSS2 specification, from a design standpoint it's best to describe it as a unique scheme. Using relative positioning means that whatever element you are positioning will be positioned relative to where it would normally fall in normal flow, and *then* moved into the position defined.

Positioning schemes are applied using two CSS properties, position and float, and any associated values. Since floating is quite a bit different than positioning, I'll discuss floating in its own section, "About Floats" in just a bit. For now, I'll focus on the position property.

Understanding the *position* Property

The position property offers four possible values, each with different uses. Table 6.1 describes these properties and their meanings.

Table 6.1: Positioning Values and Their Meanings

Value	Meaning
Static	A normal box within the normal flow. This is the default value prior to positioning.
Relative	A positioned box that is first positioned according to normal flow, then offset relative to that position using offset values (see "Box Offsets" later in this chapter).
Absolute	A positioned box offset to box offset values. An absolute box is not positioned within the normal flow.
Fixed	The box is positioned using the absolute method (and therefore does not use the normal flow scheme). The box is, however, fixed with respect to the viewport—in a browser, this is the browser window.

To write a positioning rule, follow these steps:

1. Type in a selector and declaration block. I'm going to create an ID rule so I can position whatever element bears that ID value.

   ```
   #content     {


   }
   ```

2. Add the position property:

   ```
   #content     {
        position:
   }
   ```

3. Add a value:

   ```
   #content     {
        position: relative;
   }
   ```

Of course, you'll need to add other properties and values for any positioning rules you create. These rules will depend upon the whether you choose to position an item relatively, absolutely, fixed, or floated.

Box Offsets

If you'd like to position an element using the position property, you have to first create a position rule as you've just done. Then, you'll want to use a box property and associated value or values to define the offset of that box.

 You can only use box offsets with relative, absolute, or fixed property values.

The four box offset properties, their values, and their meanings are in Table 6.2.

Table 6.2: Box Offset Properties, Values, and Meanings

Property	Values	Meaning
Top	Length Measurement Percentage Measurement auto	Specifies how far a box's top edge is offset *below the top* of the containing block.
Right	Length Measurement Percentage Measurement auto	Specifies how far a box's right edge is offset *to the left of the right edge* containing block.
Bottom	Length Measurement Percentage Measurement auto	Specifies how far a box's bottom edge is offset *above the bottom* of the containing block.
Left	Length Measurement Percentage Measurement auto	Specifies how far a box's left edge is offset *to the right of the left edge* of the containing block.

 A value of auto will offset the position in question with regards to the vertical measurements of an absolutely positioned element. This measurement has no visual effect on relatively positioned elements.

To get a better idea of how this works, I've provided a series of visuals to help you see what the differences between these somewhat complicated ideas are. Figure 6.1 shows a box, positioned relatively (within normal flow) and then offset 100 pixels from the top (6.1A).

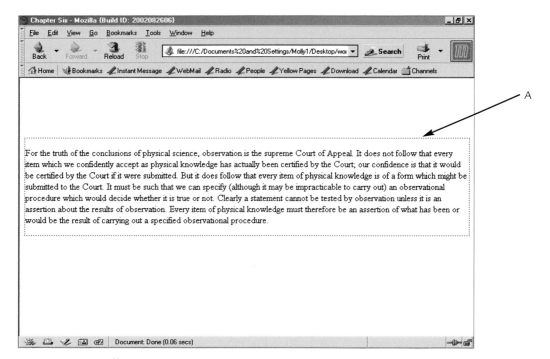

Figure 6.1: Box offset: top

Figure 6.2 is a box, relatively positioned and offset from the bottom a total of 10 pixels from the normal flow (6.2A). You can see how this causes the box to push up above the viewport (6.2B).

In Figure 6.3, you see a relatively positioned box offset to the right at 10 pixels (6.3A).

Finally, in 6.4, a relatively positioned box is offset to the left 100 pixels (6.4A).

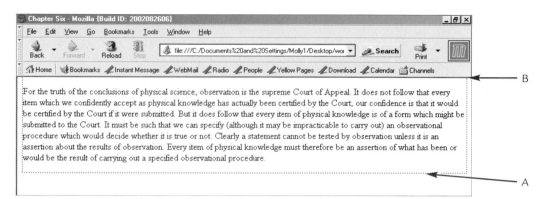

Figure 6.2: Box offset: bottom

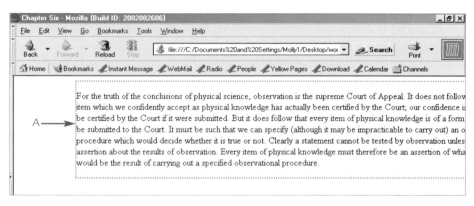

Figure 6.3: Box offset: right

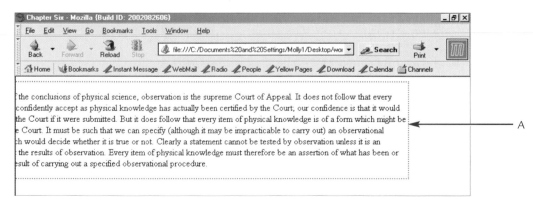

Figure 6.4: Box offset: left

Remember, any relatively positioned box will first fall into the normal flow and *then* be positioned according to these values. An absolutely positioned box is offset to the containing block itself.

Of course, you can (and will) combine offsetting values when positioning. Listing 6.1 describes an absolutely positioned box of text. I've included the border property so you can envision the box itself (6.5A).

Listing 6.1: Absolute Positioning with Box Offsets

```
<!DOCTYPE html PUBLIC "-//W3C//DTD XHTML 1.0 Transitional//EN"
    "http://www.w3.org/TR/xhtml1/DTD/xhtml1-transitional.dtd">

<html xmlns="http://www.w3.org/1999/xhtml" xml:lang="en">

<head>

<title>Positioning</title>

<style type="text/css">

#quote   {
    position: absolute;
    border: 2px dotted red;
    top: 100px;
    left: 50px;
    right: 100px;
}

</style>

</head>

<body>

<h1>Sir Arthur Eddington said:</h1>

<p id="quote">"For the truth of the conclusions of physical science,
observation is the supreme Court of Appeal. It does not follow that every
item which we confidently accept as physical knowledge has actually been
certified by the Court; our confidence is that it would be certified by the
Court if it were submitted. But it does follow that every item of physical
knowledge is of a form which might be submitted to the Court. It must be
such that we can specify (although it may be impracticable to carry out) an
observational procedure which would decide whether it is true or not. Clearly
a statement cannot be tested by observation unless it is an assertion about
the results of observation. Every item of physical knowledge must therefore
```

```
be an assertion of what has been or would be the result of carrying out a
specified observational procedure."</p>

</body>
</html>
```

Figure 6.5 shows the positioned box.

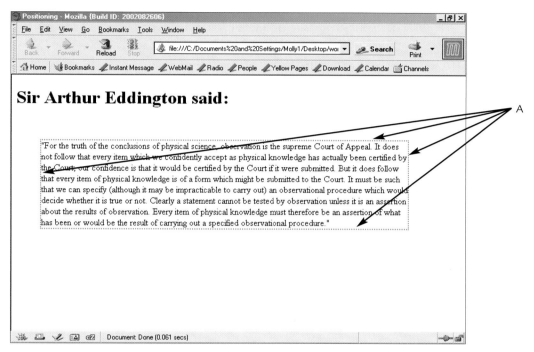

Figure 6.5: An absolutely positioned box

Changing a Box's Display

The display property is a powerful CSS property that allows you to control whether a box is block or inline, giving you some choice in the way a box is positioned in or out of the flow by changing the way it behaves normally within the box model. Other values are available for display as well, including a means of controlling lists and tables. Unfortunately, these values are rather limited in their support.

About Floats

Floating begins with a pretty basic premise: shift a box to the left or the right on the current line. To demonstrate float simply, consider Listing 6.2, which floats two images, one to the left, and one to the right.

Listing 6.2: A Simple Float Example

```
<!DOCTYPE html PUBLIC "-//W3C//DTD XHTML 1.0 Transitional//EN"
    "http://www.w3.org/TR/xhtml1/DTD/xhtml1-transitional.dtd">

<html xmlns="http://www.w3.org/1999/xhtml" xml:lang="en">

<head>

<title>Positioning</title>

<style type="text/css">

#logoMain  {
    float: left;
}

#logoSub  {
    float: right;
}

</style>

</head>

<body>

<img id="logoMain" src="header.gif" width="300" height="100" alt="supah
industries" />

<img id="logoSub" src="footer.gif" width="200" height="50" alt="supah
industries" />

</body>
</html>
```

Figure 6.6 shows the two floated images.

Figure 6.6: Floating images

Flowing Content

Floating is especially helpful when you want to flow other content around the side of a floated box.

In a sense, this is analogous to marking up an image using the align attribute and a right or left value in HTML or XHTML Transitional. In HTML or XHTML Transitional, you can further modify with hspace and vspace attributes:

```
<img src="my.gif" width="50" height="50" align="left" hspace="10" vspace="10">
```

This will cause any content to flow to the right and bottom of the image.

In CSS, using float enables you to do the same thing, but with much more precision and detail because you can use margins, padding, and borders with specific values to control the look.

Listing 6.3 shows an example of a floated logo image and content flowing to the right. You'll notice I provided padding for the image to the right and bottom, so the text flows around the image with some needed white space in between. Without the padding, the text would jut right up against the image, which makes reading difficult.

 Many designers prefer to use margins for images, as not all browsers honor padding set to images. This problem is particularly apparent in Internet Explorer for Windows. But, from a strict perspective, padding is the appropriate property to use.

Listing 6.3: Flowing Content around a Floated Image

```
<!DOCTYPE html PUBLIC "-//W3C//DTD XHTML 1.0 Transitional//EN"
    "http://www.w3.org/TR/xhtml1/DTD/xhtml1-transitional.dtd">

<html xmlns="http://www.w3.org/1999/xhtml" xml:lang="en">

<head>

<title>Positioning</title>

<style type="text/css">

#logoMain  {
    float: left;
    padding-right: 20px;
    padding-bottom: 10px;
}

p  {
                font: 14px Arial;
}

</style>

</head>
```

```
<body>

<p><img id="logoMain" src="header.gif" width="300" height="100" alt="supah
industries" /></p>

<p>Welcome to Supah Cool Industries. The goal of this web site is to
provide you with up-to-date information about all the Supah Cool things we
do. We like to make logos, especially in blue and orange. We like to start
the day with coffee and end it with a nice red wine. We like to make
photos, especially of memorable images. We travel when we can to talk to
other Supah Cool Industry groups around the world. We prefer meeting in
places such as Hawaii, Greece, and off the coast of Spain. We probably
don't sell a lot of stuff, but we are supah cool, which is really all that
matters to us, anyway. If you are interested in joining up with Supah Cool
Industries, you'll want to check the employment page. Which we haven't put
up just yet. We think our webmaster went to the donut shop, but we're not
quite sure.</p>

</body>
</html>
```

You can see the results of using float in Figure 6.7.

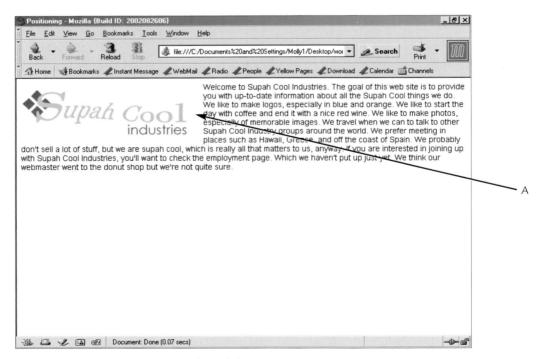

Figure 6.7: Flowing text around a floated element

To help you visualize how the padding provides specific amounts of white space to the right and bottom of the image, I created an outline within the graphic itself (Figure 6.8). The white space you see between the outline on the image and the text itself (6.8A) is the result of the padding property and associated values.

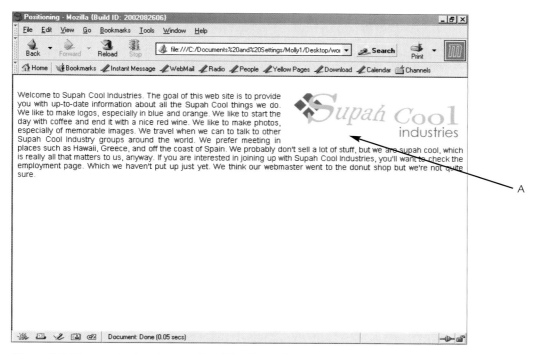

Figure 6.8: Demonstrating the use of padding for white space

Of course, you can create the opposite effect by floating the image to the right. In that case, the content will flow to the left. You'll also want to alter the padding options to pad to the right and bottom rather than the left and bottom (Listing 6.4).

Listing 6.4: Floating to the Right, Flowing to the Left

```
<!DOCTYPE html PUBLIC "-//W3C//DTD XHTML 1.0 Transitional//EN"
    "http://www.w3.org/TR/xhtml1/DTD/xhtml1-transitional.dtd">

<html xmlns="http://www.w3.org/1999/xhtml" xml:lang="en">

<head>

<title>Positioning</title>

<style type="text/css">

#logoMain   {
    float: right;
padding-left: 20px;
```

```
padding-bottom: 10px;
}

p {
font: 14px Arial;
}

</style>

</head>

<body>

<p><img id="logoMain" src="header-stroke.gif" width="300" height="100"
alt="supah industries" /></p>

<p>Welcome to Supah Cool Industries. The goal of this web site is to
provide you with up-to-date information about all the Supah Cool things we
do. We like to make logos, especially in blue and orange. We like to start
the day with coffee and end it with a nice red wine. We like to make
photos, especially of memorable images. We travel when we can to talk to
other Supah Cool Industry groups around the world. We prefer meeting in
places such as Hawaii, Greece, and off the coast of Spain. We probably
don't sell a lot of stuff, but we are supah cool, which is really all that
matters to us, anyway. If you are interested in joining up with Supah Cool
Industries, you'll want to check the employment page. Which we haven't put
up just yet. We think our webmaster went to the donut shop but we're not
quite sure.</p>

</body>
</html>
```

I left the outlined image in place so you can see the effect. It's somewhat different because the text content that's flowing around the image creates what is referred to as *ragged right.*

Figure 6.9 shows the edgy results.

Instead of a tight padding between the right edge of the text and the left edge of the image, it's more free-form. This is perfectly okay for many designers, but if you justify the text, you can regain that straight edge:

```
p {
    font: 14px Arial;
    text-align: justify;
}
```

Figure 6.10 shows the smoother results.

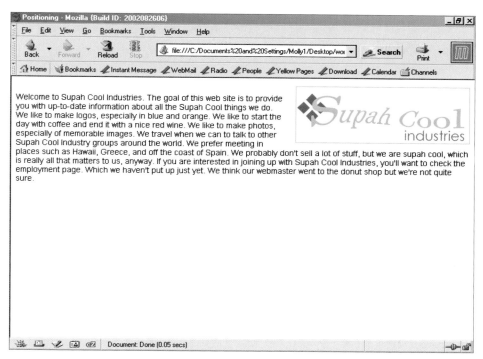

Figure 6.9: Floating can create a ragged-right margin.

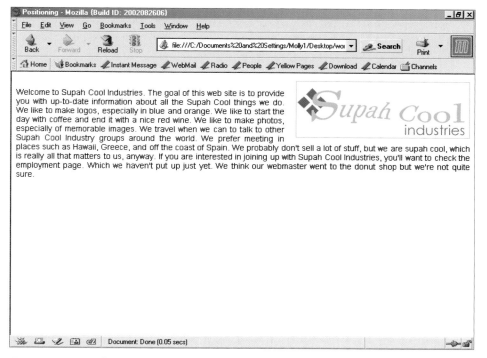

Figure 6.10: Justifying text to avoid a ragged right

Modifying Flow

Despite the obvious value that flow provides, you may wish to prevent content from flowing around a float. You can do this using the clear property and any one of its values, described in Table 6.3.

Table 6.3: Clear Property Values and Their Meanings

Value	Description
Left	The top margin of a nonfloated box is increased so that its top border edge is below the bottom margin edge of a left-floated box.
Right	The top margin of the box is increased so that its top border edge is below the bottom margin edge of any right-floated boxes.
Both	The box is moved below all floating boxes.
None	There are no constraints on the box whatsoever.

Here, I've cleared to the left and right of a paragraph, using the both value for the clear property:

```
#logoMain  {
      float: right;
      padding-right: 20px;
              padding-bottom: 10px;
}


p  {
      font: 14px Arial;
      clear: both;
}
```

Figure 6.11 shows how the resulting paragraph is moved all the way below the box containing the logo.

Using a value of none will look the same as the original float sample without the use of clear.

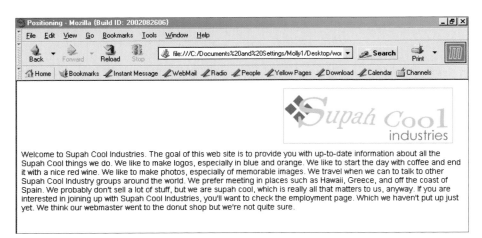

Figure 6.11: Clearing to both sides of a float

Positioning Along the Third Axis

Along with positioning along the x and y axes, there is a third axis defined in CSS. This is called z-axis, and refers to a stacking order that you can visualize by imagining boxes overlapping. The box that is closest to the front of the screen is considered to be in front of or on top of the stack, and the box farthest away is considered to be the bottom of the stack.

This kind of positioning is especially helpful in creating browser-based dynamic content using DOM technologies and scripting (DHTML). Z-axis positioning is controlled by the z-index property, which has the following values and meanings:

- **Auto** A value of auto will keep the generated box's stacking order as its parent.

```
.logo {
    position: absolute;
    left: 25px;
    top: 25px;
    z-index: auto;
}
```

- **Integer** An integer value will position a box within a stacking context.

```
.logo {
    position: absolute;
    left: 25px;
    top: 25px;
    z-index: 1;
}
```

In Listing 6.5, I created three ID selectors. In each division, I added a blank graphic and styled borders for each of the divs to help you with the visualization of z-axis positioning with z-index.

Listing 6.5: Visualizing Z-Axis Positioning

```
<!DOCTYPE html PUBLIC "-//W3C//DTD XHTML 1.0 Transitional//EN"
http://www.w3.org/TR/xhtml1/DTD/xhtml1-transitional.dtd">

<html xmlns="http://www.w3.org/1999/xhtml" xml:lang="en">

<head>

<title>Z-Axis Positioning</title>
<style type="text/css">

#bottom {
    position: absolute;
    left: 100px;
    top: 25px;
    z-index: 1;
    border: 1px solid black;
}

#middle {
```

```
        position: absolute;
        left: 90px;
        top: 25px;
        z-index: 2;
        border: 1px dotted red;
    }

#top   {
        position: absolute;
        left: 80px;
        top: 25px;
        z-index: 3;
        border: 1px dashed green;
    }

</style>

</head>

<body>

<div id="top"><img src="white.gif" width="300" height="300" alt=""
border="0"></div>
<div id="middle"><img src="white.gif" width="300" height="300" alt=""
border="0"></div>
<div id="bottom"><img src="white.gif" width="300" height="300" alt=""
border="0"></div>

</body>
</html>
```

Figure 6.12 shows the order. The top division has a black outline (6.12A), the middle division has a red dotted outline (6.12B), and the bottom division has a dashed green outline (6.12C).

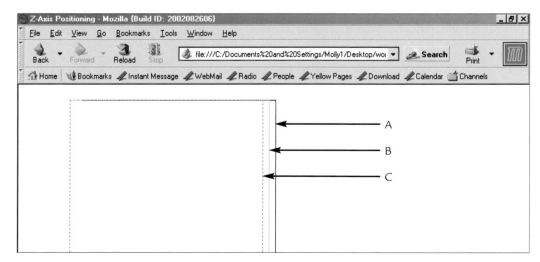

Figure 6.12: Visualizing boxes along the z-axis

Experimenting with Layouts

In this section, you'll design two different layouts. The first uses positioning, the second uses float. When you're finished with the exercises, you can save your results as templates and begin to use your newfound awareness of positioning to create even more complicated layouts.

Designing a Three-Column Layout

In this case, you'll create a layout that has three columns, a very popular approach to layout. The left and right columns are going to be positioned absolutely, while the center "content" layout will be fluid, adjusting to resolution and browser sizing.

 This example relies on the assumption that there are no padding and no margins to the body element.

This example will use an embedded style sheet, but you can also use a linked sheet if you prefer.

1. Begin with an HTML or XHTML document:

    ```
    <?xml version="1.0" encoding="UTF-8" ?>

    <!DOCTYPE  html PUBLIC "-//W3C//DTD XHTML 1.1//EN"
          "http://www.w3.org/TR/xhtml11/DTD/xhtml11.dtd">

    <html xmlns="http://www.w3.org/1999/xhtml">

    <head>

    <title>CSS Layout Techniques</title>

    </head>

    <body>


    </body>
    </html>
    ```

2. Add the style element and ID selector to the head portion of the document:

    ```
    <style type="text/css">

    #left

    </style>
    ```

3. Create a rule to position the column absolutely, using the `position` property with a value of `absolute`:

```
<style type="text/css">

#left {
    position: absolute;
}

</style>
```

4. Add the positioning information, in pixels:

```
#left {
    position: absolute;
    left:10px;
    top:50px;
    width:200px;
}
```

You've now created a left column set to a width of 200 pixels that will be positioned in a compliant browser at 50 pixels from the top and 10 pixels from the left. You can change these values to suit your needs.

Next, you'll create the fluid center. To do so, follow these steps:

1. Create an ID selector for the center column:

```
#center
```

2. Now create a rule for the left margin value:

```
#center {
    margin-left: 200px;
}
```

3. And a rule for the right margin value:

```
#center {
    margin-left: 200px;
    margin-right: 200px;
}
```

Save your file before continuing.

You'll now want to create the style rules for the right column.

1. Create an ID selector to denote the right column:

```
#right
```

2. Position the column using an absolute value:

```
#right {
    position: absolute;
}
```

3. Add the position values:

```
#right {
    position: absolute;
    right:10px;
    top:50px;
    width:200px;
}
```

To implement the layout within your document, you'll employ the div element along with the appropriate ID. Listing 6.6 shows the completed markup and style. I've added some dummy content so you can see the results in Figure 6.13.

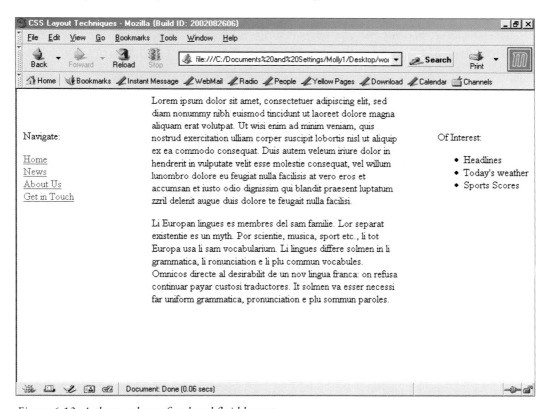

Figure 6.13: A three-column fixed and fluid layout

Listing 6.6: A Three-Column Layout with a Dynamic Center

```
<?xml version="1.0" encoding="UTF-8" ?>
<!DOCTYPE  html PUBLIC "-//W3C//DTD XHTML 1.1//EN"
     "http://www.w3.org/TR/xhtml11/DTD/xhtml11.dtd">

<html xmlns="http://www.w3.org/1999/xhtml">
<head>

<title>CSS Layout Techniques</title>
```

```
<style type="text/css">

#left {
    position: absolute;
    left:10px;
    top:50px;
    width:200px;
}
#center {
    margin-left: 200px;
    margin-right: 200px;
}
#right {
    position: absolute;
    right:10px;
    top:50px;
}

</style>


</head>

<body>

<div id="left">
<p>Navigate:</p>
<p><a href="index.html">Home</a><br />
<a href="news.html">News</a><br />
<a href="about.html">About Us</a><br />
<a href="contact.html">Get in Touch</a></p>
</div>


<div id="center">

<p>Lorem ipsum dolor sit amet, consectetuer adipiscing elit, sed diam
nonummy nibh euismod tincidunt ut laoreet dolore magna aliquam erat
volutpat. Ut wisi enim ad minim veniam, quis nostrud exercitation ulliam
corper suscipit lobortis nisl ut aliquip ex ea commodo consequat. Duis
autem veleum iriure dolor in hendrerit in vulputate velit esse molestie
consequat, vel willum lunombro dolore eu feugiat nulla facilisis at vero
eros et accumsan et iusto odio dignissim qui blandit praesent luptatum
zzril delenit augue duis dolore te feugait nulla facilisi.</p>

<p>Li Europan lingues es membres del sam familie. Lor separat existentie es
un myth. Por scientie, musica, sport etc., li tot Europa usa li sam
vocabularium. Li lingues differe solmen in li grammatica, li ronunciation e
```

```
li plu commun vocabules. Omnicos directe al desirabilit de un nov lingua
franca: on refusa continuar payar custosi traductores. It solmen va esser
necessi far uniform grammatica, pronunciation e plu sommun paroles.</p>
</div>

<div id="right">

<p>Of Interest:</p>

<ul>
<li>Headlines</li>
<li>Today's weather</li>
<li>Sports Scores</li>
</ul>

</div>
</body>
</html>
```

Exploring a Two-Column Layout Using *float*

This technique was first described by Jeffrey Zeldman (see the sidebar "Related Resources" earlier in this chapter for his URL) and is now gaining widespread popularity as a simple way to lay out pages using CSS. It's based on the float concepts described earlier in this chapter, and it provides a really nice, flexible means of laying out content without having to rely on absolute positioning.

You'll define the left and right columns using ID selectors and the float property to anchor the design. In this example, you'll create a style sheet that is external so it can be linked or imported. You can, however, embed the style if you so desire.

1. Open a new document to create the external style sheet, and add a class ID for the left portion (which in this case is being used as a content portion) to the document:

   ```
   #content
   ```

2. Create a rule using the float property with a value of left:

   ```
   #content    {
        float:left;
   }
   ```

3. Set the width (in percentages, making it dynamic) of the column, along with a right margin to create a gutter between the content column and the right-hand column:

   ```
   #content {
        float:left;
        width:70%;
        margin-right: 25px;
   }
   ```

4. Go ahead and create an ID selector and rule for the right column, adding any additional rules you desire. In this case, I simply added some padding to the top of the column:

```
#right {
    padding-top: 20px;
}
```

Listing 6.7 shows the complete CSS listing, and Listing 6.8 shows the XHTML document.

Listing 6.7: CSS Syntax for Two-Column Layout

```
#content {
        float:left;
        width:70%;
        margin-right: 25px;
}

#right {
        padding-top: 20px;
}
```

Listing 6.8: XHTML Document Linked to the Layout CSS

```
<!DOCTYPE html PUBLIC "-//W3C//DTD XHTML 1.0 Transitional//EN"
      "http://www.w3.org/TR/xhtml1/DTD/xhtml1-transitional.dtd">

<html xmlns="http://www.w3.org/1999/xhtml">

<head>

<title>Working with Style</title>

<link rel="stylesheet" type="text/css" href="layout2.css" />

</head>

<body>

<div id="content">

<h3>Quotations</h3>
<p>"Brain researchers estimate that your unconscious data base outweighs
the conscious on an order exceeding ten million to one. This data base is
the source of your hidden, natural genius. In other words, a part of you is
much smarter than you are. The wise people regularly consult that smarter
part."</p>
```

```
<p>"Crazy people who are productive are geniuses. Crazy people who are rich
are eccentric. Crazy people who are neither productive nor rich are just
plain crazy. Geniuses and crazy people are both out in the middle of a deep
ocean; geniuses swim, crazy people drown. Most of us are sitting safely on
the shore. Take a chance and get your feet wet."</p>
</div>

<div id="right">
<p>Navigate:</p>
    <p><a href="index.html">Home</a><br />
    <a href="news.html">News</a><br />
    <a href="about.html">About</a><br />
    <a href="contact.html">Get in Touch</a></p>
    </div>
</body>
</html>
```

You now have a two-column, dynamic layout suitable for getting creative with on
your own. Figure 6.14 shows the results.

Figure 6.14: An example of a two-column layout using `float`

CSS Workarounds

Ever since CSS became prevalent enough for widespread use yet still remained problematic in terms of browser support, one of the most difficult CSS problems to address has been making sure that people with partial or no CSS can get to your content. This isn't so much of a problem if you're still using tables for layout or sticking to simple HTML structures. But if you're using CSS positioning and floating, you end up having to provide some workarounds to ensure that your site visitors are getting to the goods.

This section outlines two important workarounds, the box model hack and the @import trick, both useful in better rendering and graceful degradation.

Hack or Workaround?

Web authors and programmers are discussing whether these methods are hacks, workarounds, or justifiable uses of CSS. Using @import to seemingly trick Netscape 4.x browsers into graceful degradation is not an actual misuse of the rule. The box model hack, however, is thought by some people to misuse properties to fake out the browser, although other experts feel this is acceptable because the CSS used does in fact validate... The bottom line is that at least for the foreseeable future, workarounds for CSS implementation problems are going to be in use for some time.

The Box Model Hack

Tantek Çelik, lead developer for Microsoft IE for Macintosh, defined this workaround. The problem is this. The box model, which was described in detail in Chapter 3, "Writing CSS," is misinterpreted in a number of browsers, including IE 5 for Windows. This means that there's significantly different rendering of boxes between browsers.

 Tantek Çelik's original description of this workaround is at www.tantek.com/CSS/ Examples/boxmodelhack.html.

The problem, which I'll paraphrase from Çelik's explanation, has to do with the differences in the way user agents calculate borders and padding. Consider the following:

```
#box1  {
    border: 10px solid red;
    padding: 20px;
    background: blue;
    width: 300px;
}
```

This CSS would create a box that has a 10-pixel border to each four sides, padding around the entire box to a measurement of 20 pixels, and a set width of 300 pixels. If you're calculating the box model properly, you would add border and padding measurements to the 300-pixel content area, not subtract from them, making the content area small. To properly calculate the total width, including content, border, and padding:

- 10 pixels left border +
- 20 pixels left padding +
- 300 pixels content area +
- 20 pixels right padding +
- 10 pixels right border =

The box should be a total of 360 pixels wide, as shown in Figure 6.15. The border constitutes the 10 pixels in red and there's padding between the border and the text, but the actual text box itself is still 300 pixels for the content area.

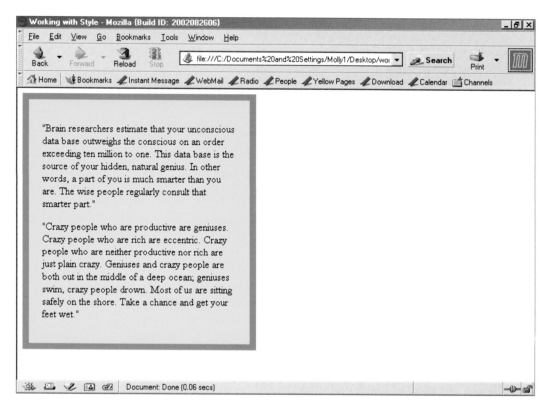

Figure 6.15: Anatomy of a correctly interpreted box

Misinterpretations of the box model place the border and padding *inside* the defined content width. As you can immediately see, if you define a box to have 300 pixels and then any borders and padding are subtracted from your content area, that area is unfairly minimized. A browser that improperly manages this will calculate the box as follows:

- 300 pixels content area –
- 20 pixels left padding –
- 10 pixels left border –
- 20 pixels right padding –
- 10 pixels right border =

The content area of the box is now 240 pixels wide, and the total width of the box is 300 pixels.

The workaround that Çelik describes styles the box with the original parameters except instead of the proper width measurement, it uses the misinterpreted measurement of the desired box.

```
#box1  {
       border: 10px solid red;
       padding: 20px;
       background: blue;
       width: 360px;
}
```

Then, by adding two properties from Aural style sheets (not covered in this book), this workaround takes advantage of a CSS parsing bug in IE 5 and 5.5 for Windows, allowing compliant browsers to read an instance of the correct width:

```
#box1  {
       border: 10px solid red;
       padding: 20px;
       background: blue;
       width: 360px;
       voice-family: "\"}\"";
       voice-family:inherit;
       width: 300px;
}
```

Çelik also adds another rule to help correct rendering in those browsers with CSS2 support:

```
html>body #box  {
       width: 300px;
}
```

 If you are using the XML prolog in your documents, IE 6 for Windows switches to "quirks" mode. Because compliance mode in IE 6 has corrected box model support, developers should leave the XML prolog off for the most consistent rendering between browsers possible.

Using @import

Because of Netscape 4.*x*'s problematic implementation of style sheets, CSS layouts aren't very effective for that browser. However, designers have combined a flaw in the browser and a CSS technique to help gracefully degrade the layout so that the page is at least readable.

This is done using the @import workaround, which exploits the fact that Netscape 4.*x* doesn't understand the @import rule. As a result, you can link to one style sheet with styles that Netscape 4.*x* *does* understand and use the @import method to bring in another style sheet for the layout. This will create a readable page in Netscape 4.*x* and allow browsers that can interpret both the @import rule and the layout styles to properly lay out the document. Without this workaround, the page could be completely unreadable in Netscape 4.*x*.

The following snippet shows the @import rule at work alongside a linked style sheet to display styles supported by Netscape 4.*x*.

```
<head>

<title> Welcome</title>

<!- begin style sheet for site-wide styles supported by many browsers ->

<link rel="stylesheet" type="text/css" href="site.css" />
<!- begin style sheet for positioning. it is imported so Netscape 4.x
excludes it and displays the content in readable format ->

<style type="text/css" media="all"> @import "position.css";</style>

</head>
```

> **NOTE** Another advantage to using the @import rule is that browsers that do not support CSS will also be able to view the unstyled document.

Figure 6.16 shows a web page from a site using CSS layout in Netscape 7 for Windows. Compare this figure to Figure 6.17, which is a shot of the page as viewed in Netscape 4. As you can see, the layout is lost.

However, the information is still logically structured, readable, and accessible, even if it doesn't look too pretty.

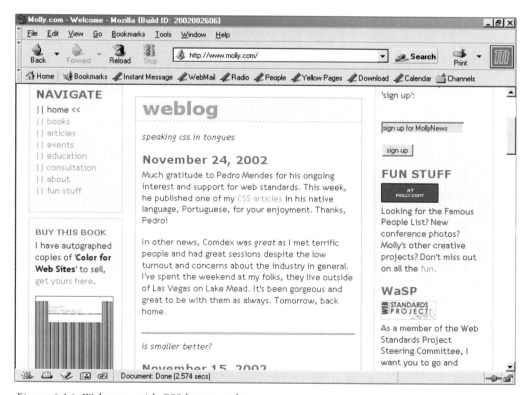

Figure 6.16: Web page with CSS layout styles

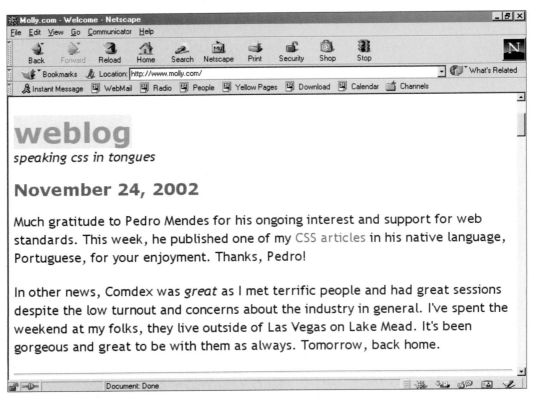

Figure 6.17: No layout, but some styles, and the logically structured text is completely readable in Netscape 4.x.

Next Steps

Now that you've got plenty of details on how to style your pages, you'll spend the next several chapters looking at a variety of sites that will serve to educate and inspire.

In the following chapter, you'll work through the deconstruction of a working, table-based site. You'll first refashion it using minimal tables and CSS, and then take it all the way—getting rid of the tables and using only CSS for presentation.

Vision

It's well and good to understand CSS technology and aesthetics, but it's going to be difficult to put together great pages without being inspired by the progressive work of other designers and developers using CSS. This part opens with the deconstruction of a working website. The site is then reconstructed, first using a combination of transitional structured markup and CSS, and then going to a complete CSS design with no table-based layouts used whatsoever.

I'll continue by giving you a tour of great CSS sites; you'll also see code and get comments and insight from top designers using CSS. Finally, you'll be inspired by the daring move that Wired News took to help spotlight web standards in general and move CSS specifically into the forefront of contemporary web design.

*Correct the nuisance problems when
you can, but remember that you'll get
the biggest improvements by fixing
the exasperation problems.*

—Jared Spool

seven

Reconstructing a Table-Based Site

This chapter will help reinforce your understanding of the relationship between structured markup and style. The process used here will be to take an existing, working website designed in the conventional way, deconstruct it by removing all proprietary and overly complex markup, restructure the markup, and rebuild the page using CSS. This exercise of deconstructing and reconstructing a table-based website can be applied to any site you currently have or know of, and it provides an excellent means of helping you clearly see how CSS can vastly improve aspects of a design.

The goal here is not to encourage redesigning table-based sites by reconstructing them with CSS, but rather to show the benefits that occur when table-based designs are left behind in favor of a transitional approach with minimal tables and CSS in combination, or even a completely table-free approach. Study the exercise, walk through it using the code samples available from the book's web page, or take a table-based site of your own and perform the same process on it.

The example serves as a compare-and-contrast exercise regarding what happens when presentation and proprietary tags and attributes are removed from an existing design and converted to transitional and pure CSS designs. You can also apply this general process if you're looking to reconstruct legacy pages.

In this chapter, you will learn:

- How to strip a conventionally designed page down to its structure
- Some of the major concerns when structure and presentation are not separated
- How to convert the page to valid XHTML
- How to prepare the document for styling with CSS
- How to add some accessibility features
- How to style the document using a simple layout table and CSS
- How to remove all tables, using only CSS for layout

Exploring the Original Document

This example was developed by me and Eric A. Meyer (technical editor of this book) as a demonstration for attendees of the User Interface 7 conference, using the UI7 conference home page (Figure 7.1). All the markup examples described in this chapter can be downloaded from the book's web page.

The example was such a good choice for an exercise of this nature that we both knew we should include it in this book to demonstrate the way that structure and style relate to one another in contemporary web design.

The original page uses fairly complicated tables as well as font tags and style to create the ultimate look. The page is heavy with graphics and uses many spacer GIFs to position page elements within the layout tables.

Figure 7.2 shows the document with table borders styled so you can see the complexity of the nested tables. The table borders are red (7.2A), the cells borders are green (7.2B).

Figure 7.1: *The original page*

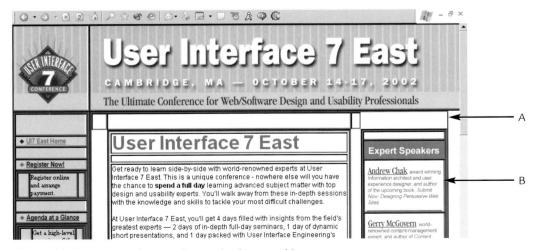

Figure 7.2: *Examining the nested, complex layout tables*

Another problem with the document is that it is filled with proprietary elements and attributes for presentation, as well as scripting and elements proprietary to Adobe GoLive.

As the chapter progresses, you'll see how overly complex and weighty this kind of design is—not to mention invalid. As the page is converted to a more structured document using CSS and following web standards in general, the page becomes far more manageable and lighter in file size. The page also validates and will retain its general look and feel within most browsers.

Deconstructing the Document

After examining the document carefully, the deconstruction process can begin. The following items will need to be dealt with specifically:

- Use of font elements and attributes
- Problematic use of span elements
- Removal of all proprietary, nonstandard markup
- Removal of any markup used specifically for presentation
- Replacement of all scripting and current CSS with better methods

As the deconstruction progresses, a deterioration of the visual design of the document occurs. However, after the document is deconstructed, it will be reconstructed in two different ways, and the overall layout and design of the page will be restored.

Removing *font* Elements and Related Attributes

One of the first things to do is to remove all font elements. Because font elements are wholly presentational in nature and typographic concerns can be addressed using CSS, stripping the font elements and their related attributes out of the document is the first step to clearing the clutter. Go ahead and look through the markup and see if you can find all the font elements that I did.

After doing a search, 39 font elements and variations were found and removed. Here's a list of the font elements and attribute variations I found:

- `<font face="times new roman,Georgia"> . . . </font>`
- `<font color="black" face="arial,helvetica,verdana"> . . . </font>`
- `<font color="#cc203c" face="Arial,Helvetica,Verdana"> . . . </font>`
- `<font face="arial,helvetica,verdana"> . . . </font>`
- `<font color="#cc203c"> . . . </font>`
- `<font color="#4253b2" face="Arial,Helvetica,Verdana"> . . . </font>`

Because the page is currently relying on a style sheet along with all of these font elements, few visual differences result when they're removed (see Figure 7.3).

 The document weight was reduced by 1KB as a result of removing all the font elements.

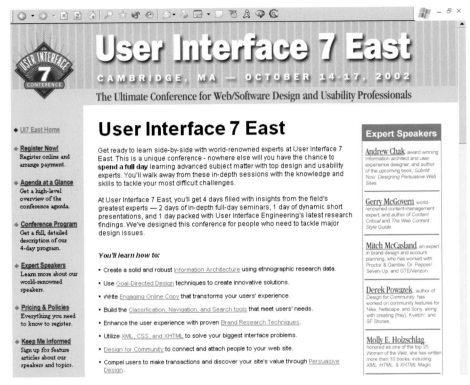

Figure 7.3: Even with all the font *elements gone, the page looks basically the same.*

Removing *span* Elements

While the span element can be useful for applying style inline, improper use of the span element is a common problem. Some of the concern arises from document authors who are as yet unaware of the importance of document structure (see Chapter 1, "Understanding Structured Markup"), but most of the problem is the result of the markup generated by visual editors. Again, check out the document on your own and try to find the problems, as I did.

Two of the most common problematic uses of span are:

- Adding style to headers instead of using structural headers h1–h6; for example, using

    ```
    <span class="h1">Welcome!</span>
    ```

    instead of the structurally and concise

    ```
    <h1>Welcome!</h1>
    ```

- Styling nested presentational elements; for example, using

    ```
    <span class="bold"><b><i>go to next entry</i></b></span>
    ```

    instead of a better option:

    ```
    <span class="boldItalic">go to next entry</span>
    ```

Another problem in this particular document involves the use of span to style bullets:

```
<span class="bullet">&#149;</span>
```

instead of using the structurally correct method for bulleted items: an unordered list.

So, time to get rid of all the span elements and related attributes. Here's what I found:

- `<span class="subhead1"> . . . </span>`
- `<span class="bottomlinks">. . . </span>`
- `<span class="arcatext"> . . . </span>`
- `<span class="menu-subhead"> . . . </span>`
- `<span class="bodygen1rg"> . . . </span>`
- `<span class="heading-super"> . . . </span>`
- `<span class="bullet"> . . . </span>`

 I took the subhead1 class out at this point to fully strip the document down to its structure. However, it will be added back later, although it will be styled differently.

After a complete search, there were a total of 41 span elements and related attributes in the document.

Significant differences now appear, particularly to the fonts (see Figure 7.4A). And, guess what? Another 2KB was shaved off of page weight!

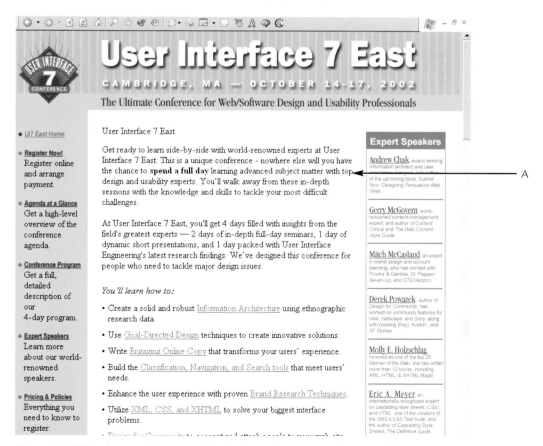

Figure 7.4: With the span *elements and related attributes gone, changes to fonts (A) appear.*

Removing Nonstandard Markup

Whether you're working with a favorite visual editor or writing your markup by hand, many HTML elements and attributes you're using may not be valid according to specifications.

In specific instances, tools employ both proprietary and unique markup. In the case of the UI7 website, both are true.

Here's an overview of the proprietary markup in the document:

- body margins:

  ```
  <body onload="CSScriptInit();" background="uie-7/images-uie/
  tile-1600-yellow.gif" link="#4253b2" vlink="#4253b2"
  leftmargin="0" marginheight="0" marginwidth="0" topmargin="0">
  ```

- GoLive-generated JavaScript elements in body and head:

  ```
  <csscriptdict import> . . . </csscriptdict>
  <csobj> . . . </csobj>
  ```

- Non-SGML character entities:

  ```
  &#151;
  &#149;
  &#146;
  ```

Further decomposition of the page is noticeable now that I've removed scripting and the margin-related proprietary attributes in the body tag (see Figure 7.5). Specifically, the body margins have caused shifting at the top (7.5A), left margin (7.5B), and bottom (7.5C), and the mouseover effects are disabled due to the removal of portions of the document's scripting.

Ready for Validation

With nonstandard markup removed, it becomes possible to add a DOCTYPE declaration for HTML. Because the font and presentational elements and attributes have been removed, I decided to aim high and try for a strict document (see Chapter 1), so I added an HTML 4 strict DOCTYPE declaration to the page, and validated it. The document might not look like much at this point, but it validates as HTML 4 Strict, meaning that all proprietary and most presentational markup within the document is gone.

Waste Removal

At this point, a lot of stuff is still left in the document that can be addressed by better methods. Specifically, remaining presentational markup, including the following:

- Alignment attributes within table cells not picked up in validation
- Spacer GIFs
- All remaining JavaScript
- External style sheet reference

With these features gone, the page layout and presentation has almost completely deteriorated (see Figure 7.6). The layout is no longer precise (7.6A), and all the fonts have reverted to default (7.6B).

Figure 7.5: Further deconstruction occurs at this stage.

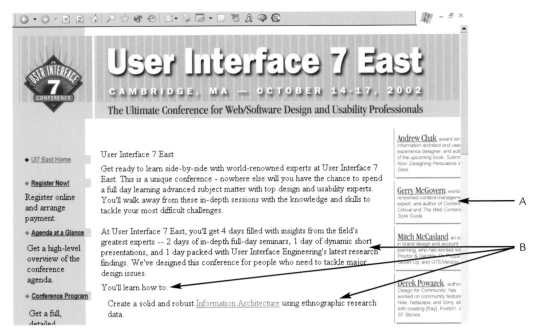

Figure 7.6: With all presentation and spacer graphics within the table gone, the layout deteriorates.

Preparing for Reconstruction

Before the reconstruction specific to CSS can begin, a few more steps can be taken to improve the design. The first step is to examine the remaining table and re-engineer it to be as simple as possible. The rationale for this is to keep a basic table for layout in order to address cross-browser concerns.

As you are already aware, layout using only CSS is going to be problematic in Netscape 4 and any other browser with no or partial CSS support. Leaving this main table in allows for the primary structure to remain intact, but the majority of presentation will be shifted to CSS. This is considered a transitional technique, useful when you must provide for a wide audience.

In this step, the following occurs:

- You'll examine the nested tables
- You'll redesign and optimize graphics for weight concerns as well as easier layout
- You'll re-engineer the primary table layouts and removed nests

WWW.   The resulting markup (available on the website) demonstrates some of the visual layout returning to the page (see Figure 7.7).

Figure 7.8 shows the page with table borders turned on. Compare this figure with Figure 7.2 to see how streamlined this approach is. There are two tables, one for the masthead (7.8A), and one for the main layout (7.8B). These tables are so basic, it seems confusing in contrast to the original design. The use of two simple tables with no nests at all provide you with a structural container to which you can further add CSS to deal with presentational details. The red borders demonstrate the table, and the green borders show the table cells (7.8C). Quite a difference from the original, indeed!

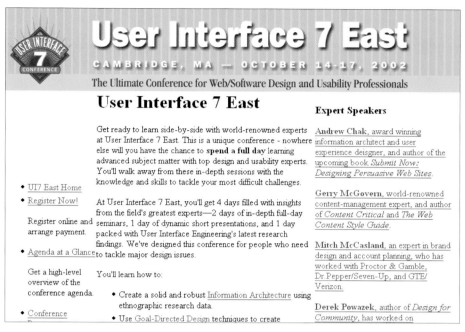

Figure 7.7: The re-engineered layout using simple tables with no nests

Figure 7.8: Examine the re-engineered tables in this screenshot. The layout is incredibly simplistic compared to the original.

Conversion to XHTML 1.1

Because part of the goal is to bring the document up to date and make it as strict as possible, I took the re-engineered document and converted it from HTML 4.0 to XHTML 1.1. To accomplish this, I did the following:

- Replaced the HTML 4.0 DOCTYPE declaration with the XHTML 1.1 DOCTYPE
- Converted all syntax to XHTML
- Made sure all elements and attribute names appeared in lowercase
- Checked that all attribute values are quoted
- Checked for any minimized attributes and expanded them where necessary

 See Chapter 1 for more information on XHTML syntax.

Once completed, I validated the document as XHTML 1.1.

Added Accessibility Features

Before beginning to style the document I also wanted to ensure that some basic accessibility issues were handled. The original document was interesting in this regard: it had alt attributes *only* in the spacer images. Other images had no alt attributes or descriptive text. Furthermore, no other accessibility features had been added to the document.

I added the following:

- Table summaries. These summaries assist those using screen readers or other devices to better understand the content and context of the two tables in the document:

```
<table border="0" cellspacing="0" cellpadding="0" id="masthead"
summary="conference masthead: user interface 7 east">
```

and:

```
<table border="0" cellspacing="0" cellpadding="0" id="main"
summary="main layout table">
```

- alt attribute descriptions to all images, as in these examples:

```
<img src="http://www.uiconf.com/uie-7/images-uie/logo-01.gif"
alt="user interface conference logo" height="150" width="129" />
```

and:

```
<img src="http://www.uiconf.com/uie-7/images-uie/uie-hostedby-logo.gif"
alt="hosted by user interface engineering" height="80" width="129" />
```

- Titles in anchors:

```
<a href="http://www.uiconf.com/uie-7/conference_program.htm"
title="conference program">Conference Program</a>
```

While additional accessibility features could be added to this document, these features easily and quickly address the most common concerns.

Reconstructing the Site Using Transitional Means

At this point, the document is ready to be reconstructed in a transitional sense. Style will be created in external and embedded style sheets along the way, but I placed all styles into the external style sheet. This decision was based on organization—I didn't require more than one style sheet. However, depending upon the size and scope of a website you might be creating styles for, using just one external style sheet might not be the best way to go. These styles will address, for this section, issues pertaining to the visual presentation and behaviors of the original document.

 A good way to develop is with a single file with an embedded style sheet, so you can do quick comparisons of style to markup; once you're done, you can take the style sheet and move it to an external file.

At this point, go ahead and add the link to the external style sheet you'll be creating in this portion of the chapter:

```
<link rel="stylesheet" type="text/css" href="uiconf-style workspace.css" />
```

This will go in the head portion of the document, of course.

Visualizing Structure

To visualize the structure of the page as you work on it, you can employ style to gain borders or colored fields that define the style areas.

This technique is much akin to adding a border to a table to see how that table works. Using CSS, you can assign border values to all kinds of aspects of the document, allowing you to effectively visualize the work you are doing, and where you are doing it.

Listing 7.1 shows a CSS style sheet that you can place in your working document to assist you with visualizing document elements with borders.

Listing 7.1: Temporary Style Sheet for Visualizing Element Borders   `WWW.`

```
/* styles to visualize with borders */
table {
    border: 1px solid red;
    margin: 2px;
}

th {
    border: 1px dashed red;
    padding: 2px;
}

td {
    border: 1px dashed purple;
    padding: 2px;
}
```

```
div {
    border: 1px dashed #888;
    padding: 2px;
}

div div {
    border: 1px dotted #888;
}

div div div {
    border: 1px dashed #BBB;
}

div div div div {
    border: 1px dotted #BBB;
}

div div div div div {
    border: 1px dashed #DDD;
}
```

Figure 7.9 shows the current document with these temporary styles applied. Using borders is a good approach for visualization, but it can modify your layout somewhat.

Figure 7.9: Applying temporary styles to visualize the layout effectively

As an alternative, you can try using background colors to create fields for visualizing page elements (see Listing 7.2).

Listing 7.2: Temporary Field Styles for Visualizing Page Elements

WWW.

```
/* styles to visualize with backgrounds */

table {
    background: red;
    margin: 2px;
}

th {
    background: #FCC;
    padding: 2px;
}

td {
    background: #FCF;
    padding: 2px;
}

div {
    background: #CBC;
    padding: 2px;
}

div div {
    background: #BAB;
}

div div div {
    background: #A9A;
}

div div div div {
    background: #989;
}

div div div div div {
    background: #878;
}

div div div div div div {
    border: 1px dotted black;
}
```

Figure 7.10 shows the effects. Backgrounds won't affect layout as borders will, but depending upon your color choices, it can be jarring.

For fun, you can use both, as shown in Figure 7.11.

How you use this method of visualizing layout is up to you—I find it helpful, especially when working with complex tables or pure CSS layout because it's harder for me to visualize the structure being created or modified in those instances.

User Interface 7 East

CAMBRIDGE, MA — OCTOBER 14-17, 2002

The Ultimate Conference for Web/Software Design and Usability Professionals

User Interface 7 East

Get ready to learn side-by-side with world-renowned experts at User Interface 7 East. This is a unique conference - nowhere else will you have the chance to **spend a full day** learning advanced subject matter with top design and usability experts. You'll walk away from these in-depth sessions with the knowledge and skills to tackle your most difficult challenges.

- UI7 East Home
- Register Now!

Register online and arrange payment.

- Agenda at a Glance

Get a high-level overview of the conference agenda.

- Conference

At User Interface 7 East, you'll get 4 days filled with insights from the field's greatest experts—2 days of in-depth full-day seminars, 1 day of dynamic short presentations, and 1 day packed with User Interface Engineering's latest research findings. We've designed this conference for people who need to tackle major design issues.

You'll learn how to:

- Create a solid and robust Information Architecture using ethnographic research data.
- Use Goal-Directed Design techniques to create

Expert Speakers

Andrew Chak, award winning information architect and user experience deisgner, and author of the upcoming book *Submit Now: Designing Persuasive Web Sites.*

Gerry McGovern, world-renowned content-management expert, and author of *Content Critical* and *The Web Content Style Guide.*

Mitch McCasland, an expert in brand design and account planning, who has worked with Proctor & Gamble, Dr.Pepper/Seven-Up, and GTE/Verizon.

Derek Powazek, author of *Design for Community*, has worked on

Figure 7.10: Using backgrounds to denote areas of the page

User Interface 7 East

CAMBRIDGE, MA — OCTOBER 14-17, 2002

The Ultimate Conference for Web/Software Design and Usability Professionals

User Interface 7 East

Get ready to learn side-by-side with world-renowned experts at User Interface 7 East. This is a unique conference - nowhere else will you have the chance to **spend a full day** learning advanced subject matter with top design and usability experts. You'll walk away from these in-depth sessions with the knowledge and skills to tackle your most difficult challenges.

- UI7 East Home
- Register Now!

Register online and arrange payment.

- Agenda at a Glance

Get a high-level overview of the conference agenda.

At User Interface 7 East, you'll get 4 days filled with insights from the field's greatest experts—2 days of in-depth full-day seminars, 1 day of dynamic short presentations, and 1 day packed with User Interface Engineering's latest research findings. We've designed this conference for people who need to tackle major design issues.

You'll learn how to:

- Create a solid and robust Information Architecture using ethnographic research data.
- Use Goal-Directed Design techniques to create

Expert Speakers

Andrew Chak, award winning information architect and user experience deisgner, and author of the upcoming book *Submit Now: Designing Persuasive Web Sites.*

Gerry McGovern, world-renowned content-management expert, and author of *Content Critical* and *The Web Content Style Guide.*

Mitch McCasland, an expert in brand design and account planning, who has worked with Proctor & Gamble, Dr.Pepper/Seven-Up, and GTE/Verizon.

Derek Powazek, author of *Design for Community,* has worked on

Figure 7.11: Combining both temporary style sheets for border and field shading

NOTE You'll notice that in these style examples, the shorthand notation for hexadecimal color values is used. This is a perfectly acceptable means of writing hex colors. Just remember that the technique is based on doubles only, so 878 is shorthand for 887788, and so on. You cannot shorthand hex values that are not represented by doubles in this way. All web-safe colors are doubles, so all web-safe colors can be written in shorthand, as can any doubled hex value outside of the safe palette. A mixed hexadecimal value, such as cc203c, cannot be shortened. See Appendix A for more details on color values.

Choosing Class and ID Names

To begin applying styles to the document, it's important to begin creating classes and IDs (see Chapter 2, "Learning CSS Theory").

At this point in the reconstruction process, class names are created for all things that have common aspects including:

- External links
- Captioned pictures

IDs will be applied to unique elements, including:

- Navigation sidebars
- Masthead
- Footer

In general, classes are more commonly used because they were a little better supported in old browsers, but IDs are quite safe, and woefully underused.

Most of this document will use IDs because those in combination with regular element names will handle almost all the document's needs.

Table 7.1 shows the IDs created to manage main sections of the page.

Table 7.1: IDs and Document Portions

Document	Portion #ID
Top masthead	#masthead
Main table	#main
Left-side navigation	#nav
Current page link	#current
Main content	#content
Expert List	#expertlist
First	#first
Hosted	#hosted
Bottom Links	#bottomlinks
Credits	#credits

Here's a snippet showing the main, nav, and current IDs in use:

```
<table border="0" cellspacing="0" cellpadding="0" id="main">
<tr>
<td id="nav">
<ul>
<li id="current"><a href="index.html">UI7 East Home</a></li>
```

Global Styling

In this section, the original document is examined, and certain aspects of the document are organized by common features, specifically:

- Document width (comparing original to newly re-engineered)
- Setting vertical alignment of table cells
- Reducing the page background
- Styling for fonts
- Styling for links
- Styling for image borders

To style the body:

```
body  {
      background: url(body-bg.gif); margin: 0; padding: 0;
}
```

This CSS provides the URL of the background graphic and sets the margins originally intended for the page. These margins were set using proprietary attributes. Those are long gone and are replaced here with CSS.

To set the width on the tables, which are the same width, incorporate this rule within your style sheet:

```
#main, #masthead  {
      width: 800px;
}
```

To regain a background of white for the main content area, style it as follows:

```
#main  {
      background: white;
}
```

 Note that instead of the 56KB background image used to create the white background in the original design, the background graphic was redesigned as a repeating 143-byte image, and the white background is set on the relevant table cell itself.

Finally, with one CSS rule, all table cells within the #main section will be set to a vertical alignment of top.

```
#main td  {
      vertical-align: top;
}
```

This last rule alone demonstrates how efficient styling with CSS can be. Instead of 25 or more table cells containing the `align="top"` attribute and value, all of that markup is removed from the document and replaced with *one* simple rule within the CSS.

Styling the Left Navigation Bar

If you find yourself trying to recreate a page in this way, one of the decisions you will undoubtedly have to make is whether or not precise recreation of the look is really necessary. Working with style and structure does change the approach designers and developers have to take. In many instances, precision control is lost with CSS, but a richer variety of options and better means of managing documents emerges.

In this case, you can't recreate the exact original look, but you can use intelligent markup and CSS to properly structure and style the left navigation bar.

The issues to be managed include the following:

- Replace image and JavaScript link effects with regular text links
- Set a width and background color
- Boldface the links; normalize the paragraphs
- Kill off paragraph margins
- Note line height's effect on spacing
- Remember to leave some indentation room

The resulting CSS is in Listing 7.3.

Listing 7.3: Styling the Left Navigation Bar

```
#nav   {
     width: 125px;
     padding: 16px 1px 3px;
     background: #F4D532;
}

#nav ul   {
     margin: 0;
     padding: 0 0 0 15px;
}

#nav li   {
     margin: 22px 0 0;
     text-indent: -15px;
     font: bold 11px/12px Arial, Verdana, sans-serif;
     list-style-type: none;
}

#nav li p   {
     margin: 0;
     font: 11px "Times New Roman", Georgia, Garamond;
     text-indent: 0;
}
```

If you examine the nav ID, you'll notice that an explicit width in pixels is set for the navigation bar itself. A percentage width would make more sense for flexible design—adjustments are harder if everything's in pixels. Similarly, the vertical separations are set in pixels to emulate the spacing created by the long-gone spacer GIFs.

Figure 7.12 shows the progress on the document design, with emphasis on the navigation bar.

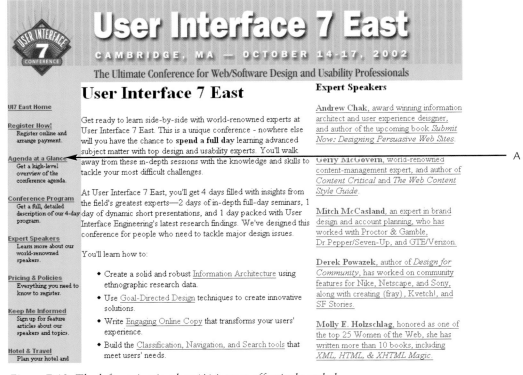

Figure 7.12: The left navigation bar (A) is now effectively styled.

 You'll notice that "Times New Roman" appears with quotations, whereas single-name fonts do not (Georgia, Garamond, etc.). If there is ever a space between words in a font name, use quotation marks around the full name.

Bullet Time

While CSS makes it easy to style bullets, the bullets are turned off in this case. Instead, images will be used, but these will specifically be dropped into the link backgrounds. Using images rather than bullets, you can recreate the hover effects in the original document.

Some padding is required to accommodate the images, and the creation of a hanging indent will push the images into their proper place. Then the hover and link styles can be added to manage the rollover effects.

Listing 7.4 shows the CSS that manages these concerns.

Listing 7.4: Managing Bullets and Hover Effects

```
#nav li a  {
    color: black;
    padding-left: 15px;
    word-spacing: -1px;
    background: #F4D532 url(nav-bull.gif) 3px 50% no-
    repeat;
}


#nav #current a, #nav a:hover  {
    color: #CC203C;
    background-image: url(nav-bull-cur.gif);
}
```

Figure 7.13 shows a link within this navigation bar, and Figure 7.14 shows the link as the mouse passes over it.

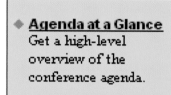

Figure 7.13: A link within the navigation bar

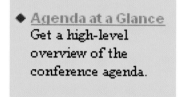

Figure 7.14: A link as the mouse passes over it

One of the advantages to getting rid of pure images to do these rollovers is that text is easier to maintain. Let's say you wanted to later change the rollover color. Instead of having to generate more graphics, you need only change the hover color within the style sheet, and voila! The color changes. What's more, you reduce page overhead and interpretation time because there's no JavaScript involved—the style is created using CSS.

Styling the Bulleted List in the Body

There's a bulleted list in the main section. To preserve the look, images will be used for the bullets, but no link effects are required. Some of the necessary features for styling this list include the following:

- Providing a default bullet style should the image not load
- Ensuring padding and vertical space for the bullet image
- Properly styling the font within the list

Listing 7.5 shows the required style to accomplish these goals.

Listing 7.5: Styling Bulleted Lists in the Main Section of the Document

```
#content ul  {
    list-style: square url(red-dot.gif);
    margin: 0 0 1.25em; padding: 0 10px;
}
```

```
#content ul li  {
      margin: 10px 0;
      font: 11px Arial, Helvetica, Verdana, sans-serif;
}
```

At this point, styling the rest of the content in the main area is needed.

 NOTE Because there's no way to vertically align a bullet image to the text line in the list item, a few extra pixels at the top of the image might be necessary to properly align the bullet with the text.

Styling the Content

To style the main content area, some decisions have to be made. First, the specific width of the content area can be set, although it's not entirely necessary. With a fixed pixel option, the page isn't as fluid as if the width were left unset, which helps keep more to the original look of the table-based design. Using no specified width, you also may lose some of the integrity of the page's design. As with most things in web design, compromise is necessary, so in this case I decided to fix the main content width.

Because padding is necessary to recreate the gutters originally managed by spacer GIFs, padding will be important to add to retain the general look:

```
#content   {
      padding: 25px;
      width: 460px;
}
```

Paragraph features including font size, font faces, and paragraph margins are also set:

```
#content p  {
      font: 12px Arial, Helvetica, Verdana, sans-serif;
      margin: 1.25em 0;
}
```

Headers level 1 and 2 are styled with font features and margins:

```
h1  {
      font: bold 34px/33px sans-serif;
      word-spacing: -2px;
      letter-spacing: 0.4px;
      margin: 0.1em 0 0;
}

h2  {
      font: bold 18px sans-serif;
      word-spacing: 1px;
      margin: 2em 0 0;
}
```

And finally, you must set features for all headings, including color and font family:

```
h1, h2, h3, h4, h5, h6  {
     color: #CC203C;
     font-family: Arial, Helvetica, Verdana, sans-serif;
}
```

 NOTE The spacer GIFs that held open the vertical space between "columns" is recreated by applying padding to the #content ID (applied to the table cell itself). Padding, as with many aspects of CSS, is not well supported in Netscape 4. If you're creating websites using CSS for Netscape 4 and still want to use aspects of style, you may need to use workarounds. See Chapter 6, "Working with CSS Layouts."

In this portion of the style sheet, you're going to create the styles for all links. Naturally, the specialty links created earlier for the left navigation will apply to those areas, but these links will be the default for the entire document unless you specify another style.

The link colors were taken from the body element in the original document. Note that the visited and link color are the same:

```
a:link  {
     color: #4253B2;
}

a:visited  {
     color: #4253B2;
}

a:hover  {
     color: #CC203C;
}
```

These rules technically apply to every link in the entire document, even those that are linked images. The specificity of the rules for the left navigation bar is higher than for these rules, so those rules override these.

 TIP Remember, to work properly, link pseudo selectors must appear in a specific order: link, visited, focus, hover, active (LVFHA). While you can leave a specific pseudo selector out of the order, you should still maintain the proper order, or your links will most likely not work in the manner you expect.

Styling Specialty Areas

The original document had several classes already defined, including .subhead1, regbasetext, and regsubtext. To make things a little easier, keep these classes and style them appropriately, in this case applying the styles only within the content area.

Listing 7.6 shows the class styles created for various text within the content.

Listing 7.6: Class Styles for the Content Section

```
#content .subhead1  {
     font-weight: 800;
     font-style: italic;
     margin-top: 2em;
}


#content .regbasetext {
     font: bold 22px "Times New Roman", Georgia, Garamond,
     serif;
     text-decoration: none;
     text-align: center;
     margin-bottom: 0;
}


#content .regsubtext  {
     font-size: 11px;
     text-align: center;
     margin-top: 0;
}
```

Figure 7.15 shows the content area styles, minus the styles you'll be creating for the expert speakers list. The speaker list is very long at this point because it remains unstyled.

Figure 7.15: Here, the majority of the content area has been restyled, with the primary exception of the speaker list (A).

Recreating the Expert Speakers List

Originally created using images and JavaScript, the expert speakers list will, in this case, be recreated in text with no JavaScript to manage the rollover effects.

There is one disadvantage: text on images can be better controlled in terms of anti-aliasing. Because a small font is used, some readability might be lost when converting this section to text. However, the advantages are many: reduced page weight, a page that's easier to modify, and the removal of cumbersome JavaScript within the document.

You'll recall that an ID was created earlier for this section, called #expertlist. The list is within its own table cell, but to control it more effectively and style it with ease, wrapping it in a div element sets it off as a specific division and gives you more power.

First, the division itself will be styled with a colored border, margins, and a specific border width for the bottom border, as follows:

```
#expertlist div  {
    border: 1px solid #467CC2;
    border-bottom-width: 10px;
    margin: 40px 40px 0 0;
}
```

Then, the h3 is styled to create the title for the box:

```
#expertlist h3  {
    margin: 0;
    padding: 10px 1px 4px;
    background: #467CC2;
            color: white;
    font-size: 14px;
    text-align: center;
}
```

In this case, it's better to not style the table cell directly, as a border on the table cell could throw off the width calculations of the entire table. Using a div within the table cell is somewhat like nested tables, except with style, you don't have to nest two tables just to get a border—the border is created with CSS.

Setting Up the Links

Upon examination of the expert speaker list, it's easy to see that each link has its own paragraph. This is fine; in fact, keeping this intact makes it easier to address concerns with consistency. But there's spacing and indentation within paragraphs, and the separators between each—originally images—will now be styled using CSS.

If you examine Figure 7.16, you'll notice that the top of the list is a little funky because it has the white space around its border (7.16A).

This can be taken care of using an ID to remove the borders from the first separator, which will make it flush:

```
#expertlist p#first  {
    border-width: 0;
}
```

Now, the paragraphs themselves will be styled for fonts, margins, padding, top border, color, and letter spacing:

```
#expertlist p  {
     font: 9px Verdana, sans-serif; margin: 0 3px;
     padding: 1em 2px;
     border-top: 2px solid  #467CC2;
     letter-spacing: -1px;
     color: #666;
}
```

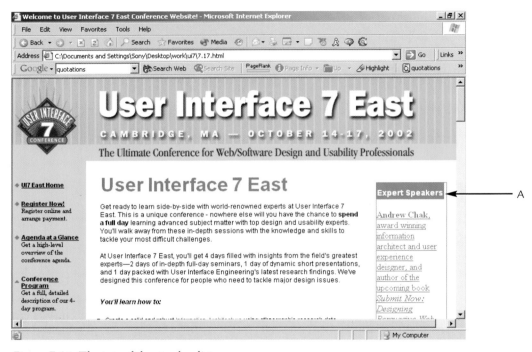

Figure 7.16: The top of the speaker list

The strong element, already in the text, can be used as a selector to create more specific style:

```
#expertlist strong  {
     font: bold 13px Times, "Times New Roman", serif;
     text-decoration: underline;
     color: #444;
     letter-spacing: 0;
}
```

Finally, the color for the link is set, along with the removal of underlines using the text-decoration property with a value of none:

```
#expertlist a  {
     color: #666;
     text-decoration: none;
}
```

The recreated expert speaker list can be seen in Figure 7.17.

Using CSS instead of images for this section has its limitations: there's no anti-aliasing, there's unpredictable line-wrapping, and there are definite limits on how small in text size you can go. On the other hand, the text is far easier to resize now, both for you the designer, when you use the style sheet to resize the document, and for the end user, who can resize the text via their browser.

Adding the Hover Effect

Creating the hover effect is easy using the a:hover pseudo selector. First, the base color of the links was set as #666 in the previous section.

Next, add the hover style:

```
#expertlist a:hover  {
    color: #375E8F;
}
```

Interestingly, as you pass your mouse over the linked text (see Figure 7.18), you'll notice that the speaker names *do not change color*. This behavior mimics the original and is the result of the strong element not inheriting the style because it already has a color value assigned to it directly via the #expertlist strong rule.

Figure 7.19 shows the document tree for this division, showing which styles are inherited and where they are blocked at the level of strong.

Expert Speakers

Andrew Chak, award winning information architect and user experience deisgner, and author of the upcoming book *Submit Now: Designing Persuasive Web Sites*.

Figure 7.18: The speaker name stays the same color during hover, despite the fact that it is part of the link.

Expert Speakers

Andrew Chak, award winning information architect and user experience deisgner, and author of the upcoming book *Submit Now: Designing Persuasive Web Sites*.

Gerry McGovern, world-renowned content-management expert, and author of *Content Critical* and *The Web Content Style Guide*.

Mitch McCasland, an expert in brand design and account planning, who has worked with Proctor & Gamble, Dr.Pepper/Seven-Up, and GTE/Verizon.

Derek Powazek, author of *Design for Community*, has worked on community features for Nike, Netscape, and Sony, along with creating {fray}, Kvetch!, and SF Stories.

Molly E. Holzschlag, honored as one of the top 25 Women of the Web, she has written more than 10 books, including *XML, HTML, & XHTML Magic*.

Eric A. Meyer, an internationally-recognized expert on cascading style sheets (CSS) and HTML, one of the creators of the W3C's CSS Test Suite, and the author of *Cascading Style Sheets: The Definitive Guide*.

Figure 7.17: The expert list is recreated with some compromise to text quality and size.

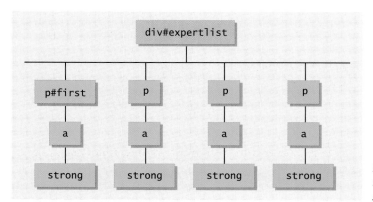

Figure 7.19: The document tree for the #expertlist section

Fixing the Footer

At this point, the look of the page has really come a long way toward the original. However, the footer section is missing styles to wrap up this portion of the reconstruction (see Figure 7.20).

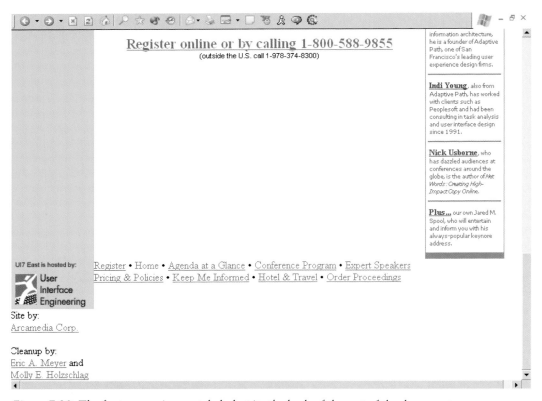

Figure 7.20: The footer remains unstyled, despite the look of the rest of the document.

The following tasks need to be performed to reconstruct the footer:

- Add background colors where needed
- Add text styles for the links
- Pad the credits table cell to produce some extra space at the bottom of the design, smoothing the design out

In this case, the style will be applied to the table cell itself (rather than a division, as demonstrated with the expert speakers list). Listing 7.7 shows the CSS rules to add to the style sheet.

WWW.

Listing 7.7: Styling the Footer

```
#hosted  {
    background: #F4D532;
}
```

```
#bottomlinks  {
     font: 12px Arial, Helvetica, Verdana, sans-serif;
     text-align: center;
     padding-top: 1em;
     color: #4253B2;
}
#credits  {
     font: 500 10px Arial, Helvetica, Verdana, sans-serif;
     word-spacing: 1px;
     padding: 10px 2px 50px 10px;
     background: #F4D532;
}
```

Figure 7.21 shows the newly styled footer, which you can compare with the unstyled version in Figure 7.20.

Figure 7.21: The styled footer

Compare and Contrast

At this point, the document has been re-engineered using simple tables for layout and lots of style to recreate the visual look (Figure 7.22).

Here are some comparisons regarding this approach:

- With the styles, the page weight is about 13KB.
- Changes are a snap. Want to make the expert speaker links purple on gold with an orange hover effect? Just change the style sheet—there's no need to redo numerous graphics and scripting.
- The markup itself is much more simple to read and therefore to edit.
- If you view the page using a CSS-browser without style sheet support, the un-styled view is perhaps not as visually nice, but is still attractive and readable (unstyled, the page looks exactly as it does in Figure 7.7), making the content at least backward-compatible.

Figure 7.22: The completed, simplified table and CSS design

Altogether, the page and its dependencies have gone from its original138KB to 57KB total; even without considering the images, it went from 32KB to 13KB in markup reduction alone.

A Case for Bandwidth Savings

Assuming that this page gets 100,000 views a month, the bandwidth savings is 1.9GB for that page; on a site with 100 pages, that's a savings of 190GB per month. Even on small sites, bandwidth of this nature adds up; a page that gets 5000 visitors a month that's reduced by 10KB will save 50MB per month, and that's for that single page! If you're paying for bandwidth by volume, this can significantly affect the total cost, depending upon what you're paying and how active your site is.

Of course, benefits of doing a site this way go far beyond the savings in kilobytes, which saves you bandwidth and your site visitors load time. With the flexibility that CSS provides, elements can be quickly and conveniently changed in almost any way, using a compact notation that makes sense. When you have one style sheet (or a set of style sheets) controlling an entire website, site-wide changes become a breeze.

 The font styling in this approach was created to demonstrate each important step. Now that the styling of the page is done, it's easy to see that most pieces of the layout use the same font families, so you can reduce the number of times the font is set throughout the style sheet. For those cases where the fonts don't match the "global" styles, just leave the styles as they are now, and those will override the inherited styles from the "global" rule.

Going the Distance: Pure CSS

The real question is, how far can this design be pushed into the realm of pure CSS layout? The answer is that some of the design will work well in a pure CSS layout situation, whereas other aspects of the design will be lost. This is why, ideally, you will be designing pure CSS layouts from the get-go. However, it's a good exercise to learn what will be lost and what benefits will be gleaned from pushing this exercise to the limits.

With CSS, browser compatibility becomes more of a concern, of course, and any browser that has problems with CSS layout features will be compromised. Accessibility increases, however, because all tables will have been removed and the document is therefore easy for screen readers to interpret effectively.

Converting Tables to *divs*

At this point, the tables will all be converted to div elements, with some cells becoming div elements as well. This provides you a way to define which areas need to be laid out using CSS.

Listing 7.8 shows the structure within the body portion of the document. All the tables are gone, but the divisions remain with their appropriate IDs.

Listing 7.8: Removing the Tables and Preparing for Layout Styles

```
<body>
<div id="masthead">...</div>
<div id="main">
 <div id="nav">...</div>
 <div id="expertlist">...</div>
  <div id="content">
   ...
   <div id="bottomlinks">...</div>
 </div>
 <img id="hostedby">
 <div id="credits">...</div>
</div>
</body>
```

> **NOTE** One thing to watch out for is "div soup," which is not too much better than table soup! If you find yourself nesting div elements more than two or three deep, you're probably overdoing it and need to look for a simpler solution.

Placing the Pieces Using *float*

Within the "main" div, there are three "columns." Conceivably, these could be floated or positioned, but that could raise problems. Floats are dependent on source order—a float can't be above another floated element that comes before it in the document source. So, to get the desired effect, the document has to be rearranged accordingly. One of the advantages to using float over position is that floating has somewhat better browser support than positioning.

> **NOTE** You can see a source order rearrangement in the previous section, where the expertlist ID came *before* the content ID. This allowed you to float the following pieces more effectively.

For this exercise, the sidebar will be floated, and the main column will be left in the normal flow. The footer will require attention in terms of margins and widths. Listing 7.9 shows the style sheet for the page layout.

Listing 7.9: Laying Out the Page Using float

```
<style type="text/css">
<!-
div#masthead, div#main  {
    width: 800px;
}

div#masthead img  {
    vertical-align: bottom;
}
```

```
div#nav  {
     float: left;
     width: 140px;
}
div#expertlist  {
     float: right;
     width: 160px;
}

div#expertlist  {
     border: 1px solid #467CC2;
     border-bottom-width: 10px;
     margin: 40px 40px 0 0;
}

div#content  {
     margin: 0 200px 0 145px;
}

div#credits  {
     width: 788px;
}

img#hostedby  {
     margin-top: -120px;
}
->
</style>
```

It's important to point out that in this example, the content section is not floated, but the content div is given margins large enough to give the floated columns room to live without overlap and without pushing the main content text around.

The content is specifically left unfloated so that it holds open the height of the main containing div. Doing this keeps the footer at the bottom, but more importantly prevents the main div from collapsing to zero height.

Floats and Height

The drawback to floats is that they tend to auto-size their height. In some cases, floats will stick out of their parent elements. It's possible to force a parent element to wrap around floats, but getting floats to stretch taller is much harder. There isn't a reliable way to force a float to be as tall as its parent element (even though height: 100% *should* work . You can get a parent to wrap around a float by inserting at the end a clear: both element:

```
<div style="clear: both;"> </div>
```

Figure 7.23 shows the layout design using floats. You'll notice the left navigation bar stops short of the page length (7.23A), and that the footer doesn't match up with the table-based original (7.23B). These are unavoidable differences resulting from use of CSS divisions rather than table cells.

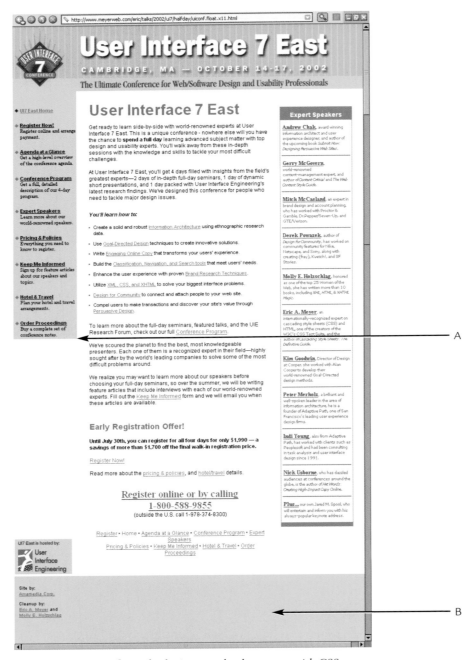

Figure 7.23: Using floats for laying out the document with CSS

Positioning to the Rescue

As mentioned, another method is to position elements rather than floating them. While this isn't as well supported as floating, it's more precise.

To position the elements in question, a containing block must be created to give some context to the position. The divisions will change as a result, as shown in Listing 7.10.

Listing 7.10: Establishing a Containing Block in Preparation for Positioning   **WWW.**

```
<body>
<div id="masthead">...</div>
<div id="main">
 <div id="nav">...</div>
 <div id="content">
  ...
  <div id="bottomlinks">...</div>
 </div>
 <div id="expertlist">...</div>
 <img id="hostedby">
</div>
<div id="credits">...</div>
</body>
```

With positioning, unlike with floating, placement is almost completely divorced from source order. The only constraint is the need for a containing block if you want elements to be placed in a common area. In fact, the navigation could appear after the main content and expert speaker list in the document source and still place it right where it's positioned.

 You'll notice that the source has already been rearranged compared to the float example earlier. The expertlist is now back *below* the content ID. It's always an advantage to be able to order sources as they make sense. This helps keep the content organized in cases where CSS positioning is unsupported by a browser, and it makes the document more logical to those reading it using a screen reader or Braille printout.

Examine how the bottom links have been placed within the document. Placing them in with the content makes sense because that's where they appear—inside the content box

With this reorganization, the navigation can be placed anywhere, and the styles for positioning can be applied, as shown in Listing 7.11.

Listing 7.11: Styling with Positioning   **WWW.**

```
<style type="text/css">
<!-
div#masthead, div#main  {
     width: 800px;
}

div#masthead img  {
     vertical-align: bottom;
}
```

```
div#main  {
     position: relative;
}

div#nav  {
     position: absolute;
     top: 0;
     left: 0;
     width: 140px;
}

div#expertlist  {
     position: absolute;
     top: 0;
                 right: 0;
     width: 160px;
}

div#expertlist  {
     border: 1px solid #467CC2;
     border-bottom-width: 10px;
     margin: 40px 40px 0 0;
         }

div#content  {
     margin: 0 200px 0 0;
     border-left: 142px solid #F4D532;
}

div#credits  {
     width: 788px;
}

img#hostedby  {
     position: absolute;
     left: 0;
     bottom: 0;
}
->
</style>
```

The main content is not positioned here, for the same reason it wasn't floated before. Figure 7.24 shows the results using positioning.

Compare and Contrast

Obviously, certain compromises were made to achieve the design using no tables whatsoever. And, while the page weight hasn't changed that much since the document was streamlined in the first place, there are a lot more options available for the designer when using CSS to lay out pages. Floating and positioning allow for a much more varied and flexible opportunity to create layouts, although, at this point, that comes with the price of using only style for layout.

Figure 7.24: Using CSS positioning for laying out the document

Lessons Learned

As noted at the beginning of the chapter, I wouldn't recommend using deconstruction/ reconstruction as a method by which to redesign websites to adhere to standards, but it's a great exercise through which to understand how structure and style work together to streamline documents. It makes documents render more quickly and makes them flexible and easy to update and alter; it also adds rich effects without your doing a bit of scripting. Ideally, you'll use CSS layouts as a starting point for your designs (Chapter 8, "CSS Design Gallery," shows off many CSS-based layouts).

You can see how an interim solution of using very clean, very simple tables along with CSS can address transitional needs for web designers and developers who can't address all layout with CSS due to specific browsers within the audience.

Even if you do decide to go all the way with pure CSS because you are willing to have certain audience members not see the layout, you can place the layout styles into one style sheet and import it and retain the presentation styles in another, linked style sheet. Netscape 4.*x* doesn't recognize the @import rule, so it will completely ignore the layout styles—the page layout won't be applied, but the content will still be readable and accessible.

Next Steps

In this chapter, you got a taste for the various stages of structure and style and how to make decisions regarding your layouts based on browser concerns and style limitations.

The next chapter will provide you with a tour and examination of a range of pure CSS layouts and techniques sure to inspire visually and provide insight into the technical means of creating interesting layouts using CSS design.

> *Hide not your talents, they for use were made. What's a sundial in the shade?*
>
> —Benjamin Franklin

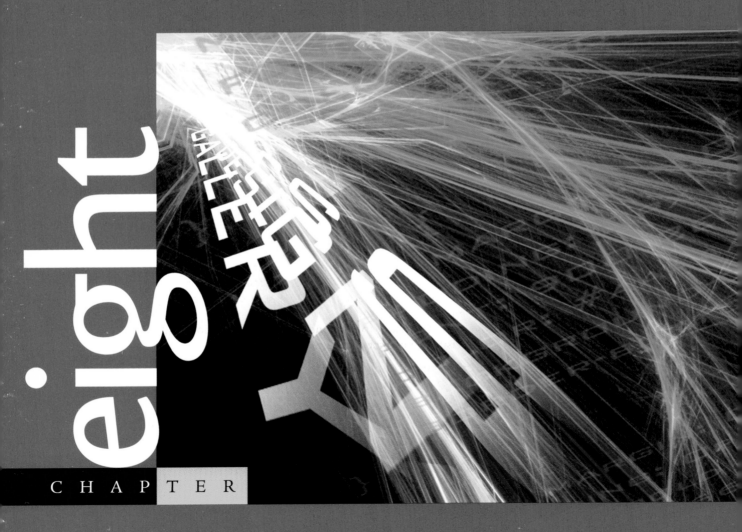

CHAPTER

CSS Design Gallery

One of the most important concerns at this point in the history of web design is figuring out how to use CSS in ways that produce the variety of sites we need.

This means that we must use CSS in practical as well as visionary ways. The true ability of designers working with CSS at this writing is largely yet to be revealed, but many interesting designs have come to fruition in the past several years.

To inspire and drive your design ideas, I've chosen what I feel are good CSS examples that address the range of visual design that you might need to accomplish your goals.

In this chapter you'll explore sites that show off:

- Information-rich design
- Visual design and promotions
- Tricks and effects using CSS

Designing for Information and Readability

One of the most difficult issues when managing websites—especially those that are content heavy—is ensuring the structure of that site, as well as ensuring readability.

Content has to do with how you organize your informational materials. Content-heavy sites tend to have a lot of, well, content! And content that is so vast tends to be deep in nature, meaning that it should be made as easy as possible to get to and to read.

If you're trying to ensure that your site is easy to read and that the information held within it is clearly organized for site visitors, keep these design concerns in mind:

Contrast Perhaps one of the most important aspects of readability, high contrast between the foreground and background is necessary when creating information-rich sites.

Chunking paragraphs The concept of "chunking" came about as web content creators began to realize that people want short sentences. There are several known reasons for this. First, reading onscreen is still not as easy as reading on the page, so keeping items short is more comfortable. Another issue is that shorter paragraphs help create more white space, which rests and guides the eye.

Width of text With the change in computer screen resolutions and the desire to keep websites fluid in design, sometimes you'll run across situations where body text runs very long. Using CSS to contain text and ensure that there are margins around it can go a long way to making your site visitors happy readers.

Page length Ever come across a page that scrolls and scrolls and scrolls, yet offers no means of going up or down the length of the page? Terribly inconvenient for site visitors, indeed. Try keeping page length to about 3–5 screens maximum, and if you do run long, use intra-page linking to allow for navigation along the length of the page.

Type size and font face Selecting the proper font face and size is a critical issue in web design. Type size has to be small enough to look good onscreen, yet large enough to be read by a person with average sight with ease. Font faces should be of normal weight for body text, and typically common sans-serif faces, such as Arial, are considered to be excellent for onscreen body text. (See Chapter 4, "CSS Typography," for more detail.)

 Information Architecture is the field of study that closely examines how information should be structured and presented. You might wish to get in touch with the Asilomar Institute for Information Architecture (AIfIA), a nonprofit organization with resources related to information architecture, especially as it relates to the Web: http://aifia.org/.

Case Study: World Organization of Webmasters Learning Center

The World Organization of Webmasters (WOW) is a nonprofit, member-driven organization that provides support to individuals and organizations that design and develop websites. This support ranges from the creation of local chapters for networking to the provision of high-end education and certification for a range of professional web topics.

Typically, WOW's members are from education, government, and industrial sectors worldwide. Their needs for information are broad, spanning a range of design and technology specialties. They tend to be busy people who need information fast, but do appreciate well-written, well-organized, and easily accessed resources.

In an effort to provide educational services to both WOW members and the public at large, an online Learning Center has been developed. WOW, as with many organizations looking to the future, has understood for some time that it must promote important professional and best-practice trends, including standards.

To that end, the Learning Center uses structured XHTML documents, CSS layouts, and CSS for all design. There is no presentation in any of the site's markup, and the pages are geared to comply with accessibility concerns.

Listing 8.1 shows the structured markup used to manage the site's general content. In this listing, look at how using the structural markup can help organize your information effectively.

Listing 8.1: XHTML Markup on WOW Website

```
<!DOCTYPE html PUBLIC "-//W3C//DTD XHTML 1.1//EN"
     "http://www.w3.org/TR/xhtml11/DTD/xhtml11.dtd">

<html xmlns="http://www.w3.org/1999/xhtml">

<head>
<title>World Organization of Webmasters: Learning Center</title>
<meta http-equiv="Content-Type" content="text/html; charset=iso-8859-1" />
<link rel="stylesheet" type="text/css" media="screen" href="core_style.css" />
<style type="text/css" media="screen">@import "global_layout.css";</style>

</head>

<body>

<div id="header">

<a href="index.html" class="topnav" title="go to the home page">home</a>
<a href="about.html" class="topnav" title="go to the about page">about us</a>
<a href="education.html" class="topnav" title="go to education">education</a>
<a href="certification.html" class="topnav" title="go to certification">
certification</a>
<a href="http://www.joinwow.org/" class="topnav" title="join WOW">join WOW</a>
<a href="sitemap.html" class="topnav" title="go to site map">site map</a>

</div>

<div id="content">

<h1>january 1, 2003</h1>

<h2>a new year, new directions</h2>

<p>These are formidable times facing our industry. With the economic
slowdown, buyer insecurity, news reports about IT Conference cancellations,
bankruptcies and consolidations, job opportunities in the Web profession is
unquestionably a hot topic.</p>

<p>There is no doubt that 2002 proved challenging for most people, and Web
professionals especially. There are few among us worldwide who can't say
that we, or someone we know, has either lost or changed jobs, or is
struggling with the economic challenges that the world events of the year
have left behind.</p>

<p>With the New Year, it's natural to take stock of the past year and make
plans for the new one to come. When things get difficult, it helps to start
```

counting blessings. In an effort to forge a much brighter and prosperous future for WOW members, we at WOW have done just that. And, one of our very first projects to help the optimism along is the WOW Learning Center.</p>

<h2>about the center</h2>

<p>The WOW Learning Center is a growing education resource provided through its parent organization, The World Organization of Webmasters (WOW). Our goal is to provide education in step with WOW's respected certification programs for both the interested public and well as current and prospective WOW members.</p>

</div>

<div id="menu">

<form method="get" action="http://search.atomz.com/search/">
<p><label for="search">search:
<input id="search" type="text" name="search" size="15" /></label></p>
</form>

<p>navigate:</p>

<p><a href="programming/index.html" title="go to programming">:: programming</a>
<a href="databases/index.html" title="go to databases">:: databases</a>
<a href="networking-security/index.html" title="go to networking and security">:: networking &
   web security</a>
<a href="ecommerce/index.html" title="go to ecommerce">:: e-commerce</a>
<a href="webservices/index.html" title="go to web services">:: web services</a>
<a href="markup/index.html" title="go to markup and css">:: markup &css</a>
<a href="design-usability/index.html" title="go to design and usability">:: design & usability</a>
<a href="accessibility/index.html" title="go to accessibility">:: accessibility</a>
<a href="internationalization/index.html" title="go to internationalization">:: internationalization</a>
<a href="business-law/index.html" title="go to business and law">:: business & law</a>
<a href="tools-products/index.html" title="go to tools and products">:: tools & products</a>
<a href="career-center/index.html" title="go to careers">:: career center</a>

```
<a href="clients/index.html" title="go to for the client">:: for the
client</a></p>

</div>

<div id="partners">

<p class="small">distinguished partners:<br />
<img src="images/partners.gif" width="148" height="38" alt="distinguished
partners logos" /></p>

</div>

</body>
</html>
```

Listing 8.2 is the global layout style sheet for the site. Here, you'll see layout styles primarily. Fonts, borders, colors and so forth are different for each site section, as you'll see in an example a bit later.

Listing 8.2: Global CSS Layout for WOW Learning Center Website   **WWW.**

```
body   {
     margin:0px;
     padding:0px;
     background: url(images/wow-education.gif) top left no
     repeat scroll;
}

h1  {
     margin:0px 0px 15px 0px;
     padding:0px;
     border: none;
}

h2  {
     margin:0px 0px 15px 0px;
     padding:0px;
}

p   {
     margin:0px 0px 16px 0px;
     padding:0px;
}

#header   {
     margin:50px 0px 10px 0px;
     voice-family: "\"}\"";
     voice-family:inherit;
```

```css
        height:14px;
}

body>#header  {
        height:14px;
}

#content  {
        margin:0px 210px 50px 10px;
        padding:25px;
}

#menu  {
        position:absolute;
        top:100px;
        right:20px;
        width: 190px;
        voice-family: "\"}\"";
        voice-family:inherit;
        width: 170px;
}

body>#Menu  {
        width:170px;
}

#partners  {
        position: absolute;
        text-align: center;
        top: 490px;
        right: 20px;
        width: 190px;
        margin: 10px;
        voice-family: "\"}\"";
        voice-family:inherit;
        width:170px;
}
```

NOTE You'll see that the box model workaround has been put to use in the layout of this site. For more information on that workaround, please see Chapter 6, "Working with CSS Layouts."

Managing Information within the Site

In addition to logistical and informational pages at the top level of the site, the Learning Center covers 14 specific topic areas, which is a significant amount of information.

Figure 8.1 shows the home page of WOW's Learning Center.

Figure 8.1: The home page of WOW's Learning Center

Several items are important to point out. First, notice the logo (8.1A). You'll see that this is consistently placed throughout the entire site. The same is true of the top navigation (8.1B) as well as the side navigation (8.1C), leading to the individual site sections.

Within the page itself, headers denote the topic of the page at hand (8.1D) as well as any subtopics (8.1E).

You'll also note a subtle background image that provides shape and movement without intruding on the visual design of the site.

Figure 8.2 shows an internal section page that is an excellent example of addressing readability concerns.

The font color for all body text throughout the site is black and it has a sans-serif face, Arial specifically (8.2A). Line length is variable depending upon browser sizing and resolution, but sufficient margins (8.2B) and white space make it appealing. Note also the use of small paragraphs (8.2C) and bullet points (8.2D) to keep information "chunky."

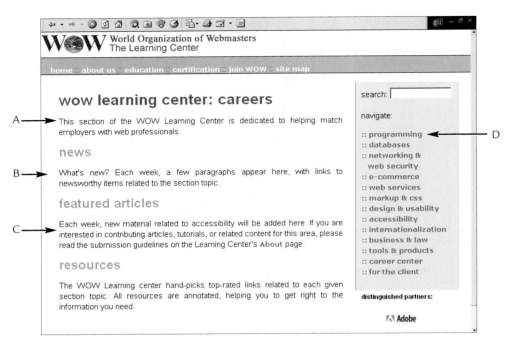

Figure 8.2: The Career Center at WOW's Learning Center

Finally, while navigation has been kept simple, each section is color-coded with global color design in mind. This has been achieved by using section-specific style sheets. Listing 8.3 shows the style sheet for the Business and Law section of the site.

WWW.

Listing 8.3: Business and Legal Section Style for WOW's Learning Center

```
body   {
       font-family: arial, helvetica, sans-serif;
       color:#000000;
}


h1   {
       font-size:28px;
       line-height:28px;
       font-weight:900;
       color:#884362;
       background: transparent;
}

h2   {
       font-size:24px;
       line-height:26px;
       font-weight:900;
       color:#B86389;
       background: transparent;
}
```

```
p  {
     font:15px/20px arial, helvetica, sans-serif;
     text-align: justify;
     background: transparent;
}

ul, li  {
     font:15px/20px arial, helvetica, sans-serif;
     text-align: justify;
     background: transparent;
}

a  {
     color: #666;
     font-size: 13px;
     text-decoration: none;
     font-weight:  bold;
     font-family:  Verdana, Arial, Helvetica, sans-serif;
}

a:link  {
     color:
#666;
}

a:visited  {
     color:#666;
}

a:hover  {
     color:#999;
}

a:active  {
     color:#cccccc;
}

a.topnav  {
     border: none;
}

a.topnav:link  {
     color: #FFF;
}

a.topnav:visited  {
     color: #FFF;
}
```

```css
a.topnav:hover  {
    color: #666;
}

a.topnav:active  {
    color: #999;
}

#header  {
    padding:17px 0px 0px 20px;
    height:33px;
    border-style:solid;
    border-color:black;
    border-width:1px 0px;
    line-height:11px;
    background-color:#BFC7B0;
}

#content  {
    background: transparent;
}

#menu  {
    padding:10px;
    background-color:#E6EBDE;
    border-left: 1px solid #656b78;
    border-right: none;
    border-top: none;
    border-bottom: none;
    line-height:17px;
}

#partners  {
    text-align: center;
}

.small  {
    font: bold 12px/13px Arial, Helvetica, sans-serif;
}
```

Figure 8.3 shows the Business and Law page, complete with layout and style.

You'll see that color coding sections in information-rich sites is a popular way to keep the site looking interesting without degrading the integrity of the design.

Figures 8.4 and 8.5 provide a look at two of the other internal pages.

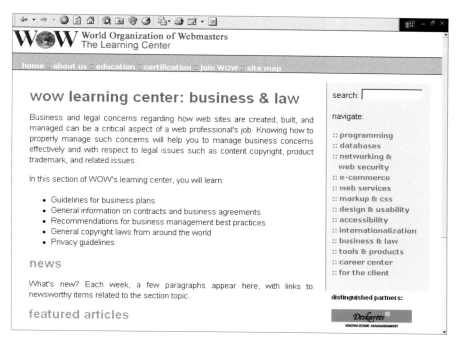

Figure 8.3: The Business and Law section, with an appropriately austere color scheme

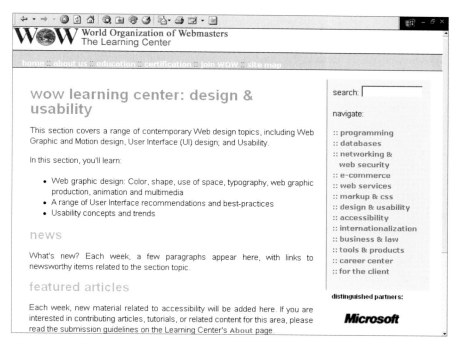

Figure 8.4: The Design and Usability page uses a bright, lively color scheme

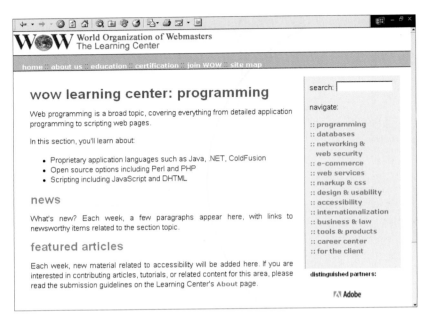

Figure 8.5:
The Programming
section, with
colors reflecting
technology (silver)
and progress (red)

CSS and Visual Design

The WOW Learning Center design makes the most of content and doesn't emphasize graphic presentation The colors are important to navigation and section identity, and the organization is overall quite clear. However, the design lacks a certain panache that a less information-oriented site, one that is geared to impress or promote, requires.

Real graphic design with CSS is still in its infancy. Typically, CSS-based designs appear clean and simple (Figure 8.6) even if the site designers make use of graphics.

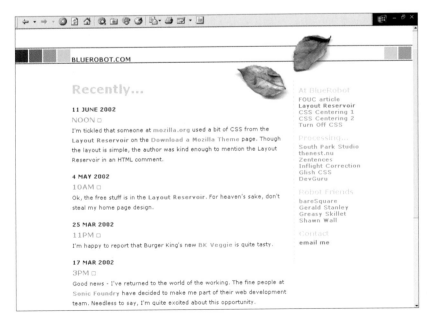

Figure 8.6:
The BlueRobot
home page is a
simple but attractive
CSS design.

Simplicity is a wonderful thing, but it's only one of many design options. There is no question that visual designers who take hold of CSS can do some impressive and sometimes surprising work when it comes to presenting more graphical or market-oriented sites. In this section, I showcase two visual designers who have used structured markup and CSS layout to make their sites work visually for their needs.

Douglas Bowman: stop|design

Artist and graphic designer Douglas Bowman shows off his interest in philosophy, design, and web standards on his site, stop|design, http://www.stopdesign.com/. What's impressive about Bowman's work is that he integrates not just the basic concepts of structured markup and CSS, but also more complex design that includes a variety of graphic images and type.

Figure 8.7 shows Bowman's home page. Note the use of a graphic background (8.7A) and the graphic images to emphasize navigation and separate it from the main content sections (8.7B). Bowman uses graphic type for headers (8.7C and 8.7D) but leaves links text-based (8.7E and 8.7F), which is a nice approach when you consider the diverse ways you can create link effects with CSS.

Figure 8.7: Bowman uses graphics effectively to produce a slick page appropriate for a visual designer

As with the color identifiers within sections in the WOW Learning Center site, Bowman uses color for each of his internal pages. He's a bit more experimental though, relying on the strength of his graphic headers and layout to carry the design as it goes from subtle to more dramatic colors.

Figures 8.8–8.10 show off Bowman's design.

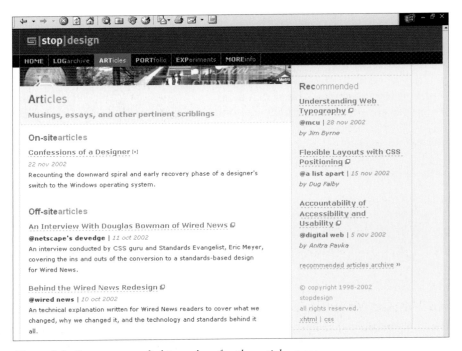

Figure 8.8: Bowman uses lighter colors for the articles page

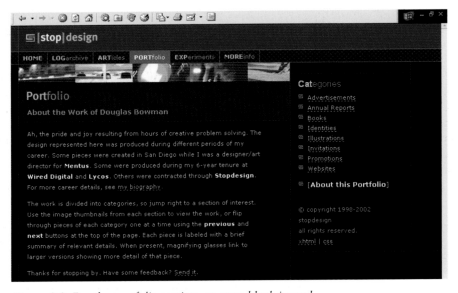

Figure 8.9: For the portfolio section, an artsy black is used

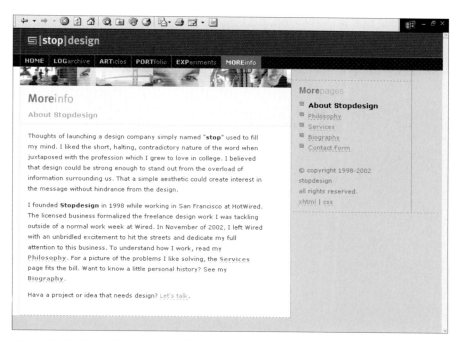

Figure 8.10: A combination of subtle grays and blues enhance the information page

Raymond Pirouz: Your Guide to Modern Living

Many times, a promotions-oriented site requires a sophisticated look. Designer Raymond Pirouz set out to make a site that promoted him, his design group, and his interests effectively. As with many progressive web designers, he was motivated to accomplish his design using web standards in the form of structured markup and CSS, and so he did.

As with all of the sites you've enjoyed in this chapter, consistency is a critical element of interface design and usability. Pirouz accomplishes this admirably yet proves himself flexible in terms of layout.

Figure 8.11 shows Pirouz's home page, which sets the look for the entire site.

In this case, the upper section (8.11A) of the Pirouz site maintains consistency across the entire site. The top navigation also remains consistent (8.11B). The lower navigation (8.11C) changes depending upon which section of the site you are in, as does the lower content area (8.11D).

Sometimes there are layouts, such as in Figure 8.11, making visible use of three columns, sometimes there are two columns (Figure 8.12), and sometimes only one (Figure 8.13).

Yet the constancy of Pirouz's figure and logo at the top left of the page keep you grounded, and there is never any question of where you are or how to get back from where you came.

 Offering a newsletter on a promotions-oriented site can be extremely helpful in getting your site out there. As Pirouz has, you can easily set one up using any number of free or low-cost newsletter management options.

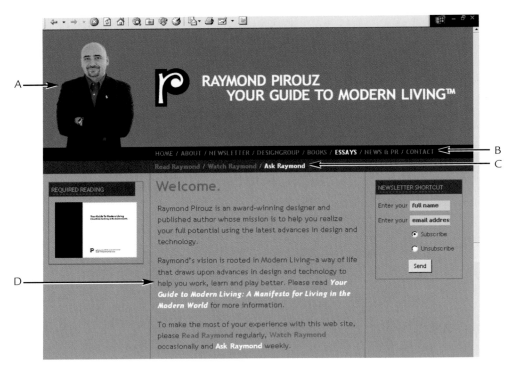

Figure 8.11: Pirouz opts for a sophisticated and consistent look.

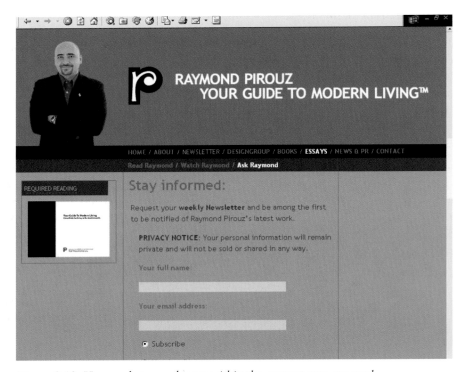

Figure 8.12: Here, only two columns within the content area are used.

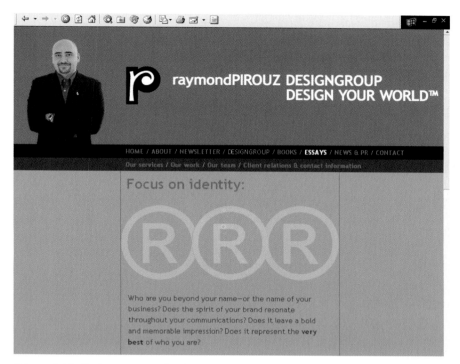

Figure 8.13: Only one central column in use

It's interesting to note that both Bowman's and Pirouz's sites *look* similar to sites that were developed using tables and graphics. Only an experienced web designer or developer could tell at first glance that they are not. This is the epitome of the possibilities of CSS design and suggests strongly how it can even be more effective in the future. By combining what you know of visual design with sensible use of technology, you can begin to approach a new and innovative means of achieving your website goals.

Visual Effects

In this section, I'm going to show you a number of my favorite visual effects created by Eric A. Meyer for CSS Edge, which is a portion of Meyer's website dedicated to using CSS to create unusual designs that use web standards, no scripting, and no proprietary extensions.

For that reason, not all the effects will be available on all browsers, but each of these effects are impressive in what they allow a designer to do.

 CSS Edge is available at www.meyerweb.com/eric/css/edge/. Since Meyer has complete details on how to achieve these various effects on his site, I won't step through that here. What I will do is point out the effects that I especially enjoy, as well as a bit of information regarding how to accomplish the effect.

The idea here is to inspire. As the CSS Edge site itself says: "Steal these ideas and use them yourself, or better yet, build on these ideas and do something better!"

Complex Spiral

The complex spiral page, www.meyerweb.com/eric/css/edge/complexspiral/demo.html, (see Figure 8.14) shows off several nice CSS effects, including an opaque look that creates a nicely enhanced navigation system (8.14A), as well as an attractive content area (8.14B).

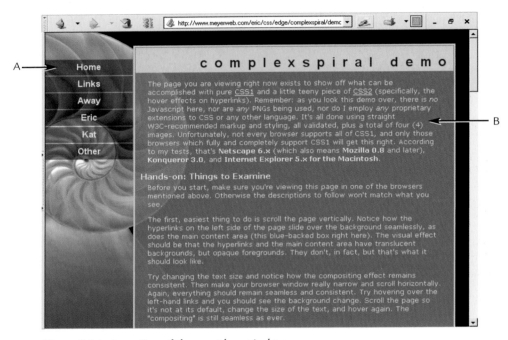

Figure 8.14: A portion of the complex spiral page

As the mouse passes over a navigation item (Figure 8.15), the background of the item changes, making the graphic background of the page appear as though it is coming to the forefront (Figure 8.16).

Figure 8.15: Kat's navigation link, normal state

Figure 8.16: Kat's navigation link, mouseover state

The effect is subtle, but the visual results create movement and clarity. What's more, the simple navigation and layout make the page an attractive and dynamic design.

CSS Pop-Ups

This is an effect that can be employed using text or images, and CSS Edge shows both in action. In the past, these types of pop-ups could only be achieved using technologies such as JavaScript or Java. But being able to create these effects with CSS makes the entire process not only easier to manage, but also to style in a variety of ways.

In the normal state, the navigation options appear as they do in Figure 8.17. Figure 8.18 shows what happens as the mouse passes over a navigation link (8.18A)—the associated text pops up at the bottom of the navigation (8.18B).

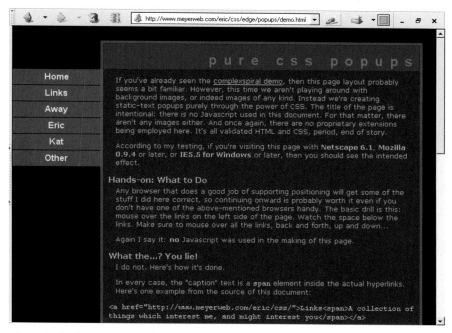

Figure 8.17: Navigation links, normal state

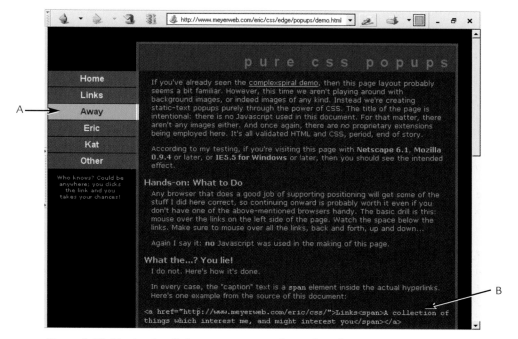

Figure 8.18: Navigation links, mouseover, with text based pop-ups

In Figure 8.19, the same navigation options are seen, but in this case, mousing over the option causes an image to pop-up at the bottom of the navigation.

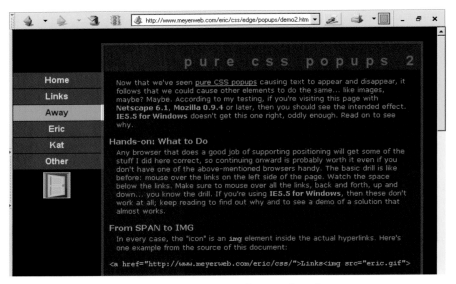

Figure 8.19: Navigation links, mouseover, with image-based pop-ups

CSS Menus

Another impressive effect that performs functions (as with all three of these samples from CSS Edge) *without* relying on scripting is the CSS drop-down menus that have been created by applying the :hover pseudo selector to an element rather than only the anchor element.

Figure 8.20 is the page without any of the menus activated.

Figure 8.20: The menus on this page look normal and innocent.

But, when you view the page in a supporting browser (in this case, Mozilla), the :hover selector is applied to the list item. That, with positioning, creates a hierarchical, linked navigation menu (Figure 8.21).

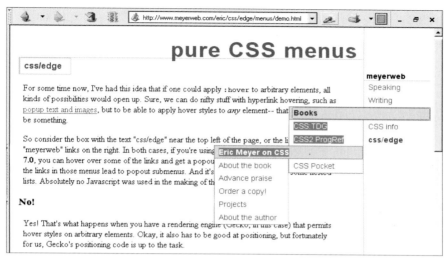

Figure 8.21: CSS-driven hierarchical menus

Next Steps

There's little doubt that there's a *lot* of room for the designer who learns to use CSS well. Skillfully applying the combination of structured markup and CSS for presentation offers the opportunity to create easily managed and beautiful websites.

The passion for CSS and web standards in general is an odd one. But it is part of a necessary movement if technology is to be firmly rooted in solid, reliable methods and still branch out to reach new horizons. That passion is what is revolutionizing the way people creating web pages work. In Chapter 9, "Wired News: A Visual Tour," you'll learn how a designer you met in this chapter, Douglas Bowman, helped make web history when he convinced Wired News to redesign its site using CSS layout exclusively.

> *The leader has to be practical and a realist, yet must talk the language of the visionary and the idealist.*
>
> —Eric Hoffer

CHAPTER

nine

Wired News: A Visual Tour

So, *what does it take to make structured markup and CSS work in the real world of web design? While there's very good support for modern web browsers these days, there are definitely legacy browser issues that many people designing websites must deal with, as well as a whole host of problems arising out of other technologists and designers still using old-school presentational markup without CSS. So, undertaking a large-scale, CSS-oriented site is a complex project indeed.*

What's more, there's also the fact that we've used CSS in a limited way, and now we're really just getting our big toes in the water—getting our skills wet a bit at a time. But each time we go deeper, we find new things to explore, and new ways to design using our growing collection of skills.

At this writing, there is perhaps no more daring a working website in terms of visual design, markup, and CSS than Wired News. The project was headed up by designer Douglas Bowman, whom you met in Chapter 8 while enjoying his personal website, and the site is a fascinating study in contemporary, cutting-edge design in the real world.

In this chapter, you'll explore the process that Bowman took to create the Wired News site, including:

- Motivation to move toward standards
- Accessibility initiatives
- CSS methodologies
- Color schemes and use of color

Wired News: Why Standards and CSS?

While I've made a strong case for standards-based design in this book, it certainly helps to take a look at how true change occurs. Wired News has consistently been ahead of the design game in both its print and web manifestations. Known for wild color schemes and interesting content for today's tech-culture savvy individual, Wired News has always stood out from the more conventional publishers by creating a persona that is edgy and contemporary (see Figure 9.1).

Figure 9.1: Wired News: Home Page

For that quality alone it stands to reason that Wired News would take the lead in the progressive choice of designing the Web the way web leaders believe the Web should be designed.

In Bowman's documentation of the process of redesigning Wired News to standards, he makes another important point: That other designers and developers should be "encouraged to follow as we help push the Web to a higher ground."

But make no mistake—Bowman's challenge was particularly difficult, despite the many advantages and impressive design that emerged as a result. Wired News isn't a home page, nor is it even a medium-sized business site. It is a large-scale, content-heavy, database-driven, highly trafficked, and ad-supported site. This means that it's the most complicated type of site to get up to speed with standards, because there are so many details to address.

What's more, anyone else working on the site, whether designer, markup and CSS person, programmer, or database designer, needs to have some modicum of standards education to make sure the end results are valid.

Bowman points out that despite these challenges, there are significant advantages to using XHTML and CSS. Some of the advantages Bowman describes include:

- Adherence to W3C recommendations "represents a broader participation in pushing the Web to a higher ground."
- The power of XML makes markup "cleaner, leaner, and more logical."
- Use of CSS for layout removes "complex nested tables."
- More support for more browsers.
- Portability and interoperability, because cleaner documents can easily be used for other platforms, such as wireless.
- Accessibility.

- Longer lasting documents and document structure—no need to create "hacks" for each new browser version.
- Error reduction due to valid documents.
- Speed of cleaner files is increased, file sizes are often decreased (see Chapter 7, "Reconstructing a Table-Based Site").
- Future redesigns can be managed efficiently.

While each of these points are conceivably entire topics of study, combined they make a powerful case for Wired News' redesign, and the use of XHTML and CSS in general.

Accessibility Initiatives

As mentioned throughout this book, making documents more accessible to people with disabilities as well as a range of user agents is a prime directive of the W3C. It's also mostly achieved via the way a designer approaches their design project, and the use of CSS can play an enormous role in addressing that concern.

To accommodate these concerns, a range of accessibility initiatives were developed for the Wired News site, as follows.

Use of style sheets CSS is used exclusively to control layout and presentation. This helps makes the site content accessible to a range of special devices and user agents.

Content is logical and useful *without* style Every page is organized and marked up so that it can be read logically even without the style sheets. Appearance of nonstyled content has been ordered so that the main column content (usually the most important) always comes first in the document (see Figure 9.2).

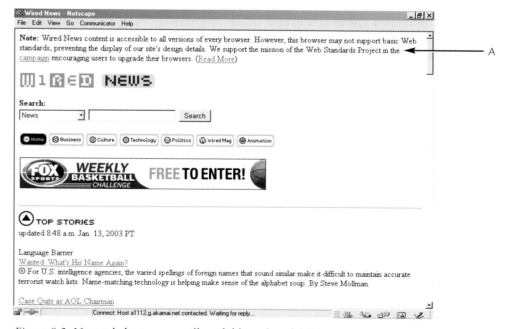

Figure 9.2: Nonstyled pages are still readable and useful (A).

Use of relative text sizing   Throughout the site, relative text sizes are used, so that the text can be resized using browser controls. A means of sizing the text up or down within the interface is also provided (9.2A), which is persistent from page to page through the use of browser cookies (see Figures 9.3, 9.4, and 9.5).

Figure 9.3: Text sizing option

Figure 9.4: Normal text size

Figure 9.5: Large text size

Removal of tables for page layout Bowman removed all layout tables from the site. This removes problems for screen readers, older browsers, specialized browsers, and other user agents, helping to facilitate accessibility. While Wired News still makes use of tables, they are only used for organizing columnar, tabular data, or contact forms.

Text equivalents for all images The alt attribute is used properly in all images:

```
<img src='http://a1112.g.akamai.net/7/1112/492/2002091422/
www.wired.com/news/v/20020914/images/cs1/nav_pol.gif' alt='[Politics]'
title='Politics Stories Index' width='63' height='25' />
```

 As you can see in this markup, only single quotes are in use. This is perfectly acceptable as long as the quoting style is consistent.

Skip links "Skip" links have been provided at the start of all documents, providing quick access to areas like search, navigation, and start of content. These links are invisible to sighted users, but can be used within text-to-speech readers as a way of skipping over redundant header elements straight to a portion of the page the user desires.

Color contrast and readability Wired News's site uses color extensively and makes use of changeable color schemes. Bowman carefully designed the schemes to ensure that contrast combinations of foreground and background were appropriately readable for anyone with color blindness or other vision issues. See the "Alive with Color" section later this chapter to learn more about the various color schemes used for Wired News.

Valid XHTML and CSS Pages within the new design are supposed to all validate to W3C XHTML and CSS standards. All deprecated, proprietary, or obsolete markup is avoided.

Logical structure in markup By using logical structure, such as the use of header elements, the structure of the document and hierarchy of content is defined.

While Wired News is continuing to implement these initiatives, Bowman does note that it will be an ongoing process to bring the site up to W3C WAI Initiatives.

 NOTE For more information on WAI, see www.w3.org/wai/.

CSS Methods

The Wired News site places all style information into CSS. Such information includes:

- Column structure
- Font faces, colors, and sizing
- Background colors
- Element colors
- Element width and height
- Margins, borders, and padding

Style information on Wired News has been broken up into multiple CSS files to accommodate a range of media types.

There are six external master CSS files in use, as follows:

Screen Media This is the master CSS file for use on screen for the specific color scheme.

Alternate Media This CSS file combines styles for other media including aural, Braille, and embossed media.

Print Media A separate set of styles for print is available.

Small Text Size This is an alternate style sheet that, when used with scripting, drives the text sizing feature, managing the small text size.

Large Text Size This sheet defines the large text size option.

Larger Text Size This style sheet defines the larger text size option.

Listing 9.1 shows the link scheme for the different CSS files in use.

WWW. **Listing 9.1: Linking to External CSS files on Wired News**

```
<link rel="stylesheet" type="text/css" media="screen"
href="/v/20020914/css/cs1/wnScreen.css" />
<link rel="stylesheet" type="text/css"
media="aural,braille,embossed" href="/v/20020914/css/wnOther.css" />
```

```
<link rel="stylesheet" type="text/css" media="print"
href="/v/20020914/css/wnPrint.css" />
<link rel="alternate stylesheet" type="text/css"
media="screen,print" href="/v/20020914/css/wnSm.css" title="Small Text" />
<link rel="alternate stylesheet" type="text/css" media="screen,print"
 href="/v/20020914/css/wnLg.css" title="Large Text" />
<link rel="alternate stylesheet" type="text/css"
media="screen,print" href="/v/20020914/css/wnLg2.css" title="Larger Text" />
```

Within the linked files, Bowman created multiple @import rules to bring in style sheets specific to color and other style features. This was largely done to remove specific style information from older or nonsupporting browsers.

Figure 9.6 shows Bowman's style schematic.

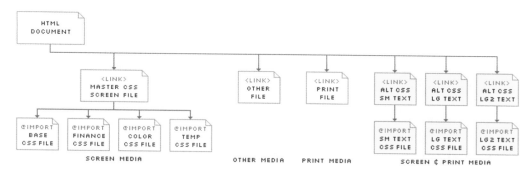

Figure 9.6: Examining the style schematic for Wired News

 An excellent article about working with alternate style sheets is available at www.alistapart.com/stories/alternate/.

Alive with Color

Early in Wired's online history, changing the color scheme every day was part of its appeal. Of course, this had to be achieved in a much more rudimentary way back then. With CSS, simply pointing to a different style sheet can change the scheme.

There are five preset color schemes available to use on a daily basis, as well as a sixth for weekend use. In addition, there is a base grayscale scheme, and two additional schemes for specialty use, such as holidays or special news events.

Here's a tour through Bowman's color work, with his original palettes and a working sample of each. The palettes show the RGB values of the individual colors for each style in use.

 The base scheme is not used within the design itself; rather, it's used as a default base should the color style somehow not be applied.

Grayscale base The grayscale base scheme is what the site colors will default to if no other style sheet is called. Figure 9.7 shows the palette, and Figure 9.8 shows the palette in use.

Monday scheme The Monday scheme uses blue, turquoise, black, and white as its main colors (see Figure 9.9). Figure 9.10 shows the Monday scheme in use.

Figure 9.7: Grayscale palette

Figure 9.8: Viewing the grayscale sample

Figure 9.9: Monday color palette

Figure 9.10: Monday color scheme

Tuesday Scheme Tuesday's scheme (see Figure 9.11) uses orange and hot pink. Figure 9.12 shows the results.

Wednesday Scheme Wired News' Wednesday scheme is a combination of bright and darker green (see Figure 9.13). Figure 9.14 demonstrates the complete look.

Thursday Scheme Orange and red color up Thursdays at Wired News. Figure 9.15 shows the palette, Figure 9.16 the results.

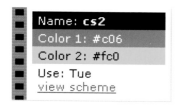

Figure 9.11: Tuesday color palette

Figure 9.12: Tuesday color scheme

Figure 9.13: Wednesday color palette

Figure 9.14: Wednesday color scheme

Figure 9.15: Thursday color palette

Figure 9.16: Thursday color scheme

Friday Scheme Blue and bright green are the TGIF colors at Wired News. Figure 9.17 shows the palette, Figure 9.18 the results.

Weekend Scheme Turquoise and orange are the colors of a Wired News weekend. The palette can be seen in Figure 9.19, and the full template in Figure 9.20.

Additional Schemes Two additional schemes for special purposes are available. Figure 9.21 shows the palette for the first of these, and Figure 9.22 shows the results.

The second additional scheme can be seen via the palette (see Figure 9.23) and the template with the scheme added (see Figure 9.24).

Figure 9.17 Friday color palette

Figure 9.18: Friday color scheme

Figure 9.19: Weekend color palette

Figure 9.20: Weekend color scheme

Figure 9.21: Alternate color palette #1

Figure 9.22: Alternate scheme #1:

Figure 9.23: Alternate color palette #2

Figure 9.24: Alternate scheme #2

Beyond the Browser

Another interesting aspect of the Wired News site is that it provides its news to PDAs. In the interest of standards adherence, the markup and styles used to deliver Wired News to PDAs uses HTML 3.2 and CSS. There are two CSS files, one for use with monochromatic PDA screens, and one for use with color screens.

Figures 9.25 and 9.26 show samples from the monochromatic PDA styles. Figures 9.27 and 9.28 show samples from the color styles.

Figure 9.25: PDA style, home page

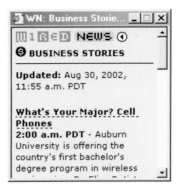

Figure 9.26: PDA style, business page

Figure 9.27: Color style, home page

Figure 9.28: Color style, business page

Pulling It All Together

Throughout this book, you've learned concepts critical to working with structured markup, CSS, and related concerns such as accessibility. You've learned theory and application, and have seen examples of working websites that use CSS as a means to push web design to new heights.

As the future unfolds and CSS becomes more familiar to you and other designers, there is no doubt that new and exciting ways of managing design will emerge. I hope you are as hopeful as I am that CSS will bring a new means of inspiring designers and make our responsibilities significantly more manageable and flexible.

Appendix: Value Types

The following table shows the value types, available values, samples, and some general comments regarding the use of property values within CSS.

 NOTE Not all value types are represented here, only the ones used in this book. There are additional types available for aural style sheets and counters. You can find information on these value types at www.w3.org/TR/REC-CSS2/syndata.html#values.

Value Types

Value Type	Available Values	Example(s)	Notes
Integers and Real Numbers	0-9	line-height: 1.3;	Line-height is the only property that accepts a real number; z-index is the only property to accept integers.
Lengths: Relative Units	Height of M (em) Height of X (ex) Pixels (px)	0.95em 1.0ex 14px	Relative unit lengths are scaled according to the size of the parent element.
Lengths: Absolute Units	Inches (in) Centimeters (cm) Millimeters (mm) Points (pt) Picas (pc)	1in 2cm 2mm 12pt 12pc	Absolute length units do not scale.
Lengths: Keywords	xx-small, x-small, small, smaller, medium, large, larger, x-large, xx-large	font-size: large	Keyword measurements do not necessarily scale. These keywords apply only to font-size.
Percentages	%	width: 100%	

Table continues on next page

Value Types *continued*

Value Type	Available Values	Example(s)	Notes
URL + URN =	URI url()	url(images/logo.gif)	Single or double quotes may be used inside the parentheses. You must escape commas, parentheses, whitespace characters, and single and double quotes which appear in a URI with a backslash.
Colors: Keywords	aqua, black, blue, fuchsia, gray, green, lime, maroon, navy, olive, orange, purple, red, silver, teal, white, yellow	color: orange;	Most named colors are not part of the web-safe palette.
Colors: Hexadecimal	#hexvalue	color: #FFFFFF	
Colors: Hexadecimal Shorthand	#hexvalue	color: #FFF	Only available for paired values. All web-safe colors can be written in shorthand.
Colors: RGB	#hexvalue	color: (255, 255, 255)	
Colors: RGB	%	color: (80%, 30%, 20%)	

Index